# FRESHWATER FISHING

BERNARD VENABLES

# Freshwater Fishing

*With illustrations by the author*

**BARRIE & JENKINS**

LONDON

ISBN 0·257·15919·3

Printed in Great Britain by
Butler & Tanner Ltd
Frome and London

# Contents

# Introduction

THIS is a book about fishing; its intention is to teach as well as it may all the ways of catching all the fish that live in freshwater in Britain. Were it about anything but fishing, that would be enough; but fishing is different from other things. It is concerned with so much more than just the physical facts; the centre of it is really a state of mind.

You will probably think now, as you start to fish, that to catch the greatest number of the biggest fish whenever you go fishing would be ultimate bliss. It is hardly possible that such a thing could happen, but if it could you would find that the real delight of fishing had evaded you; you would soon be bored. Fishing is a subtle compound and only a part of its pleasure is success. Success, some success, sometimes, is important, and the desire for it in the early days of fishing can be intense almost beyond bearing—and persistent failure can induce a desperation beyond the understanding of non-fishermen. The beginning fisherman is lured on by a vision of almost inconceivably big fish that, he feels, lurk within the weedy recesses of every swim he fishes. But there indeed is part of the joy of it, this involvement of the imagination, imagination pricked on by what, if anything, is most certainly at the heart of angling—the mystery and fascination of inhabited water. If you *had* to say what it is in a man that this touches, you could say that it is a sense of wonder. There are many men in whom a sense of wonder never entirely dies, and in any of them it could be said that there lies a potential angler.

Look back, look back to childhood to see the nature of this. When a man is a child all the world is wonderful; colours, textures, smells, captivate the senses. Morning sun, summer showers, drowsing insects, all the minor things of any day put a spell of wonder on a child, and nowhere has the wonder so much enchantment as in water. If it is no more than a lost small pond in the meadows the spell is there, the rapt pleasure in the flowers of the dank margin, the enraptured peering to prove the imagined creatures below the surface. That is the delight of childhood; but children grow, become men. The world takes them up, burdens them, gives them cares, and the pure sharp delights of childhood become lost within the tough skin that hardens over the senses.

But, in so many men, they do not utterly die; they glimmer on ready to respond if the call is made, and it is angling, and perhaps only angling, that can make the call. There, as much as anywhere, is the secret of the poignant grip that angling fastens upon its followers, and on none more than those who discover angling in their maturity. For them childhood and its sharp delights have become remote, forgotten, and then, suddenly, by angling, the hardened shell is dissolved away. Suddenly the senses are alive again, suddenly there is the touch of wonder that childhood knew.

That is the precious centre of angling; it is that, above all, which makes angling the refreshment and refuge that so many men have found it to be in these loud and clanging times of false values. In all times people have turned from cares to the forgetfulness of fishing, but never as much as now, when daily life has become so tense. Angling is a refuge from competitiveness, from rat-racing, from status-seeking. So let it remain.

But why it may be asked should it not so remain, and the answer to that question lies in the fact that fishing is as much as anything, a state of mind. It is a state of mind of placidity, of serenity, of a capacity for wonder, all indeed that makes it so much an opposite and antidote to what most of the rest of life has become. And, because life at large is as it is fishermen can too easily bring into their fishing those very evils from which they seek relief. In fishing there should be no vying, no seeking for pre-eminence; only the delights of fishing are its reward, its true success. To become involved in an urge for supremacy, competitive ascendancy, is to lose the essence of fishing.

CHAPTER ONE

# The Quarry

MOST anglers probably began to fish in much the same way; they had fallen under the spell and, quite blindly, they began to fish. They did not think of themselves as fishing for a particular species of fish, nor did they relate their fishing to a reading of the natural history of the water. It was entirely mechanical; they hung a bait on a hook suspended from a float at a random depth, and awaited results. So waiting they saw more experienced fishermen and, by copying their methods, came by degrees to some sort of success. Thus, by copying, they learnt a set of rule-of-thumb methods; these did bring some success at times, though less than more thoughtful fishing would have brought. And, intense though their pleasure was, it could have been greater. They learnt the mechanical motions of fishing, without an awareness of what is really the greater part of fishing—the observation, the reasoning, that led originally to the devising of the methods.

All angling methods were originally solutions to problems of natural history. Anglers watching the fish that were their quarry learnt enough of their lives to formulate basic means of offering baits to them in a way natural enough to deceive them. Succeeding anglers progressively modified the original means, building by degrees a range of standard techniques; but the use of these techniques should not be allowed to obscure the real nature of angling—the study of the mood and situation of the fish at the time of fishing so as to decide how to offer a bait so that it will appear entirely natural. Then standard techniques may be used, or some personal modification of a standard method; or, possibly, a new one devised for this situation. It is thus that the techniques of fishing grow. The objective must be to make the approach seem to the fish to be a part of Nature and, therefore, safe.

A fish, like any other wild animal, lives in a remorseless jungle; two things enable it to survive the menace of every moment of life. They are fear and suspicion, and it is these that the angler has to overcome. The more he knows of fish, the greater his chance of doing so.

The basis of all-in angling then is knowledge of the fish, the watery world in which it lives, and the factors that affect it. The lore that has grown up in angling over the centuries, its conventions, fetishes if you

1

like, tend to obscure some truths about fish. Anglers recognize three broad divisions of fishing—game fishing, sea fishing, coarse fishing—and the general acceptance of this has tended to give the impression that there are fundamental differences between the fish that are the quarry in each case. This is entirely untrue. Fish of all kinds, in fresh water and salt, are subject to certain universal factors of life, have broadly the same physical nature, live by the same general rules. They are all fish, and recognition of that induces in the angler a flexibility which gives him a good start towards success.

## Game fishing, coarse fishing, sea fishing

Look at these three divisions of fishing, so strongly, so artificially upheld by many anglers. Game fishing is fishing (in Britain) for members of the salmon family—the salmon itself, the sea trout, the trout. In America certain other species are apt to be included in the term, such fish as the black bass and some sorts of sea fish. Coarse fishing is fishing for all those other species of freshwater fish that are not members of the salmon family—roach, rudd, chub, dace, bream, tench, barbel, eels, carp, perch, pike. The grayling occupies a not very clearly defined position between the game fish and the coarse fish. It is a member of the salmon family, but does not spawn in the winter as its cousins do, but in the spring as the coarse fish do. It is rather despised by some game fishermen in Britain—though greatly appreciated by others. The inference has been that the fish of the salmon family are separate and superior, that the coarse fish are lower, and that the fishing for them is also lower.

To enjoy his fishing to the maximum the angler should fish for any of these fish, by any appropriate method as the chance comes to him. Later, with more experience, he may find that he has preferences for certain species. There is rather more reality in the separation of sea fishing because it is done in the sea. But there too the broad truths of fish natural history apply just as certainly as in freshwater.

## Primary factors

That fear and suspicion are primary factors in the lives of fish has been said; two other factors are equally important. They are comfort and food. Much of an angler's success (or non-success) depends upon how well he divines how these last two are affecting the fish's behaviour at the time of fishing. He has to learn early that fish are not evenly distributed, at random, throughout the water. Their whereabouts at any time are decided by where they will be comfortable, where they will find food that currently interests them. In the case of shoaling fish, such as the roach, this will decide the position of the shoal; in the case of fish of a more solitary tendency, such as the pike, it will decide the position of the individual.

## Water temperature

The comfort of fish is dominated by the fact that they are what is called, loosely, cold-blooded animals. Their blood, unlike that of a warm-blooded animal, such as ourselves, has not a constant temperature, but one which varies with that of its environment. Fish, consequently, are sensitive to changes of temperature; they easily become distressed by an uncongenial one, moving to deeper water, to shallower water, to more activated water, or to quieter water, as they seek the temperature that best suits their nature—and that is something which varies from species to species. The grayling, a legacy of the Ice Age, likes cold water; the tench likes relatively warm water. Most fish become torpid when water temperature drops below what is congenial for their species, and do so too when it becomes too warm. As water becomes warm beyond a certain point its oxygen content falls, and this has a profound effect upon fish; they will not feed.*

Temperature and oxygen content control the lives of fish both in still water and in running water, but the effect is more easily to be seen in rivers. In times of prolonged drought and heat, when rivers run low and stale (that is, low in oxygen), fish tend to lie in shallow broken water because it is cooler and has a higher saturation of oxygen; the deeper channels of water tend to become depopulated. The effect in still water is similar; shallow water absorbs more oxygen than deep water, and it is in the shallow water that fish are to be found in hot weather. It may be said, broadly, that in the heat of summer fish will seek cooler water, and in the cold of winter they will seek warmer water. So, in winter, fish are more likely to be in deeper water, which is warmer, than in shallow water, which is colder. That anyway is the case with shallow lakes.

Deep lakes, such as those of the English Lake District, the large deep Scottish lochs, and the great deep loughs of Ireland, are different. When the rising temperatures of summer fall upon the surface, the water

* How profound an effect the level of oxygen in the water has on fish behaviour is analysed in that revolutionary book, *Salmon Taking Times* by R. V. Righyni. Although it is salmon which are discussed, the findings apply as sharply to other fish.

temperature is, naturally enough, raised. *But* it is only the surface layers, down to, perhaps, twenty or thirty feet, that are so warmed. Below lies the great abyss of water which remains cold. On that there lies, quite sharply separated, the warm surface water, and it is this which is hospitable to fish. Anywhere in that layer should provide places where the angler may expect to find fish if the other considerations are appropriate.

But windy days are frequent, and windy days change the situation. A wind of any strength rolls the warm top layer from the windward side of the lake to the leeward side, and, because it cannot pile up on the lee shore, it turns under and rolls along the bottom of the warm zone, on top of the deeper cold zone. It behaves indeed like a very elongated, very flattened wheel, revolving at the push of the wind. If the wind is strong and continues to blow for some time, it will tend to concentrate the warm water near the lee shore. The wheel of water changes shape; it becomes deeper against the lee shore and progressively shallower against the windward shore. So far may this go that the cold water from the lower depths is brought right to the surface by the windward shore.

Now this windward shore is inhospitable to fish; they will leave it, seeking the warm water concentrated against the leeward shore. This is important to the angler—to fish with the wind behind him is more comfortable; casting is easier. To fish from the leeward shore into the strong wind is not comfortable; casting is difficult and there is a tendency to wind-induced tangles. *But* the more comfortable fishing from the windward shore is into water that holds no fish; the fishing from the leeward shore, uncomfortable as it is, is into water where there are fish.

## Current

In rivers the comfort of fish, and therefore the positions in which they lie, has much to do with current. In slowly flowing rivers in summer it matters much less, so slack may current become; but in the more quickly flowing rivers it is important. It is a basic rule of life for a fish (as it is for any other animal) that the less energy it uses for a given intake of food the more benefit it gets from the food. Every expenditure of energy demands fuel for its replacement, and the fuel is food. A fish will not wantonly fight strong currents; it will prefer a position where it can be supported by the current rather than fighting it. The effect of this fundamental rule varies greatly from one species of fish to another— what *is* a strong current obviously has different meanings for the superbly streamlined trout and the rather unwieldily deep-bodied

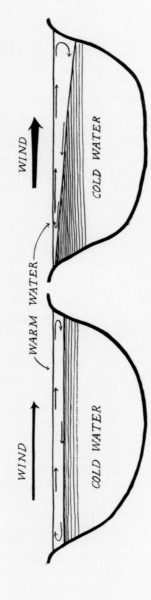

Fig. 1. The shallow layer of warm water lies over the deep cold water, and is rolled by strong wind

bream. And, further, there is great variation within one species according to the nature of the river in which it has spent its life. Different
rivers condition their fish differently. The River Avon of Hampshire
has a fast heavy current from which there is little easement anywhere;
its roach, for example, must obviously be very differently conditioned
from those of the gentle River Great Ouse. All this, at this stage, may
sound alarmingly complicated, too much to remember and apply; but
as the fish are described later in this book species by species, it will be
found that everything drops into place.

The appearance of a fish is a good guide to the water it naturally
frequents. Look at the exquisitely precisioned streamlining of the
trout, the sea trout, the salmon—it is obvious that they are likely to be
found in the more quickly flowing parts of a river; and, generally, so
they are. Then look at the bream, like a lazy tarnished old metal dish
set on edge. Where would you expect to find it but in gentle easy water?
And in such water, again generally, you do find it. Then the barbel, that
strong hump-backed slab of fish; it is flattened below, easily arched
from snout to tail above—a perfect shape for those parts of the river
in which it lives. Its home, mostly, is in fast heavy runs of water over
gravel bottoms. The current flows over its back, holding it comfortably
against the bottom; the fish need use no energy to maintain position.

There is the key to a fish's relationship to current. A fish that by
nature lives in faster water has no need for a lifelong struggle against it.
Fast water turns, forms eddies and easements between currents; it is
these that the fast-water fish use, letting these easy pockets hold them in
position, a position from which they can, as need arises, make quick
sallies, sallies aided by their beautifully adapted shape. You may catch
a trout from what appears, superficially, to be a uniformly rapid run of
water; but there is indeed some sort of easement which holds the trout.
It is the business of the angler to learn so to read the water that he will
recognize such places and expect to find a trout there. Observant
experience on the water is a quick teacher of water reading.

The situation must of course change with the seasons. A roach or a
chub that lies in the quite quick shallow runs of summer will find them
too tempestuously heavy, too cold, through much of the winter. Then
it will have retired to gentler, deeper places that, though they were
almost dead water in summer, now have just that quiet flow which is
hospitable. This is again a matter of variation from species to species,
and that will be brought out later. It is the object here to show the
meaning of the principle, that a fish's chosen place is decided by its
need for comfort and food. It will choose the most comfortable place in
the water which is advantageously close to what, at that time, is its
food. That is what the angler has to learn to deduce; the first part of

his problem is so to judge that the place in which he seeks to catch fish is a place where fish are.

## The food of fish

The food of fish then; what of that? Again there are some broad fundamentals that are universal, that govern the feeding of fish everywhere, in freshwater and saltwater. If it can be established what sort of fish, in terms of food, the quarry is, there at once is a signpost to it, whatever the difference of scale—whether in a small brook or in the ocean. The real difference is scale, only scale. The main difference between a bottom-feeding fish in a pond and in the sea is that the bottom in the sea is hugely bigger, vastly deeper—and of course it has tide, roughly comparable to current in a river.

As kinds of feeders fish fall broadly into three categories—bottom-feeders, middle-water feeders, and those that find their food at or close to the surface. How they find their food at these levels cannot be fully understood without some knowledge of the working of their senses, a knowledge indeed that affects so much of what the fisherman does.

## The senses of fish

A fish has the five senses we know in ourselves, and has one other. Sight, though apparently variable between the species, is fairly good. Its variations are related to the mode of living of the species. Thus the pike, an entirely predatory fish, has keen sight which is binocular, both eyes focusing on an object together, with vision trained forward and upward—sight which is efficient for the detection of prey. A majority of fish have monocular vision—each eye sees separately, with a wide field of vision at either side—an efficient mode of sight for fish that go always in the fear of becoming prey. It has often been debated, and no doubt will continue to be debated, whether or not fish have colour vision. But there is no reason for debate; fish have colour vision, quite good colour vision it seems. Observation suggests this to be the case; experiment has proved it—common sense could scarcely have allowed denial of the fact indeed. Why, otherwise, should male fish of species that come into shallow water for spawning assume brilliant coloration at spawning time, while those that spawn in deep water make no such change? In deep water the colour change would not be visible; in shallow water it is visible. Nature does nothing without a purpose, and it seems hardly possible that this is not a form of sexual display for the beguilement of

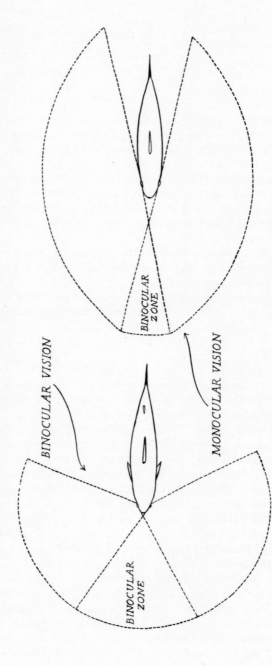

Fig. 2. Binocular vision of predatory fish and monocular vision of preyed-upon fish

the female. Then consider a fish's adaptation in pattern and colour to changes of background. A trout that lies on a bottom of yellow stone is most beautifully suffused with glowing yellow. One, perhaps a few yards away, that lies in the shadow of heavy green growth will be mostly dark and greenish in colour. But if the positions of those fish are transposed, their colours will soon change similarly, the dark fish becoming yellow on the yellow stone, and so on. The flounder, a fish of salt and brackish water which runs up into freshwater, changes its colour and pattern within minutes to match precisely the bottom on which it lies.

Are we to suppose then that these colour changes are invisible to fish? If they are, at what creatures are they directed? What is their purpose? The eye is the agent for colour change; the environmental colour is assessed through the eye of the fish, and this activates the colour change, regrouping the colour cells in the skin of the fish so that they form a pattern to match what the eye has seen. If a fish loses its sight it becomes uniformly dark.

Smell, though variable between the species, is important in the feeding of fish. Broadly it has less importance in the highly predatory fish than in the more omnivorous ones, because the predators rely so greatly upon sight and that other additional sense still to be described. But for the omnivorous fish, those feeding on a wide variety of foods, smell is a cardinal sense. For them indeed smell and taste are the primary means in the finding of food, whether in fresh water or salt. The two senses are not, as in us, directly connected; usually the nostrils of a fish are on the upper side of the snout, and form a U-shaped channel with openings at the upper end of the two uprights. Between the two openings is a flap which, receiving against it the current of scent, deflects it into one opening so that it passes down through the U and out at the second and rear opening.

Taste, which we know as something experienced only within the mouth, is adapted in fish to the difference of environment, to the difference of living in water, not air. Taste is borne on water as smell is borne on air, and fish have taste buds not only within the mouth, but on exterior surfaces too, often on surfaces of the head, even in some species on the body. There too is the explanation of those odd appendages borne about the snouts of some fish, particularly about the mouth, curious pendulous beard-like members called barbules. Barbules are organs of taste; they bear taste buds. It is bottom-feeding species that have them, and as their wearers go browsing about the bottom, the barbules are sensing between the stones or weeds, or what it may be, picking up tastes that will lead their owners to food.

It is particularly the bottom-feeding species that have such reliance on the senses of smell and taste, and if they live in relatively shallow water (as is the case with our freshwater fish) they have a comparatively poor development of the eye. The eye of a tench, that bottom-browser, is small compared with that of the pike. For saltwater bottom-feeders there is another consideration; their eyes are usually large because of the greater depths in which they live. The eyes have to be bigger to have vision in the dim light of the depths.

As to the sense of touch, there is no need to say more than that fish have it, as any sentient creature must. But hearing? Here we are on more curious ground. Hearing in fish is so much modified to their different medium, and hearing is crossed with the working of the fish's sixth sense. What may be said is that fish hear, and probably hear well, sounds beneath the water's surface, but that the surface is a fair

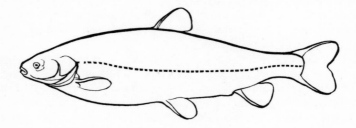

Fig. 3. The lateral line running from gills
to tail

insulator of sounds from above the surface. Many sounds, it appears, do not penetrate the surface film, though sounds of a high thin nature do so more effectively than lower sounds. A high thin whistle could be expected to penetrate better than a shout.

And now the sixth sense, so vital for fish, the lateral line sense, the fish's orientator, its preserver from peril, its locator of prey. On a majority of species of fish there is to be seen along either side a line. It runs from the rear edge of the gills to the tail; it is the lateral line. It appears as a line but is really a series of openings, pores, in the series of scales that runs the body's length. The pores communicate with a canal beneath the scales, a canal filled with mucous that, in turn, communicates with the fish's auditory system in the head. The functioning of the lateral line may be compared to that of radar, or echo-sounders; it is a pressure organ, a receiver of vibrations.

As such it is of extraordinary sensitivity, accuracy, bringing precise information about the proximity of objects and animals. If a shoal of fish is watched it will be seen that as the shoal moves, wheeling this

way and that, the members of the shoal maintain position, not collid-
ing. The means for this is the lateral line, sending its messages second
by second, reporting proximity experienced as pressure. And thus, in
total darkness, objects are avoided (as a bat avoids objects in its
nocturnal flight). Now think of the crucial value of this lateral line
sense in the finding of food and the avoidance of becoming food. For
the hunted fish, those apt to become the prey of the predators, it is a
messenger of the approach of danger. Sometimes of course the warning
is insufficient—how otherwise would the predatory fish survive? But
without the warning the preyed-upon fish would be decimated.

For the predatory fish the lateral line has a function no less essential
than sight. Notice of the approach of potential prey is conveyed as
much by it as by the eyes. In some predatory fish, our main example of
which is the pike, there is an extension of the lateral line sense into the
head. Forward branches of the canal extend over the top of the head,
round the opercula (gill covers), and evidence of this is to be seen in the
pores opening to the head surface in these places. The effect of this is
that the pike, lying in its typical way, low in the water, waits; its eyes
and its lateral line sense, so forwardly adapted, are aligned to receive
notice of the approach of small fish. Then, with deadly accuracy in
most cases, the pike's lethal pounce is made; the fish is seized. The
pike indeed is doubly armed, almost redundantly it might seem, for it
has been found experimentally that a pike deprived of its sight can still
locate and seize its prey. The lateral line sense is the agent.


## Feeding patterns of fish

Now, in the light of the knowledge of the senses of fish, their feeding
patterns can be looked at more intelligibly. The bottom-feeders then;
they are mostly omnivorous—or so at least it is in freshwater. Among
the saltwater bottom-feeders there is a much higher incidence of fish
preying one upon the other—one bottom-feeding fish has always
another bottom-feeder nearby whose object it is to engulf the first. But
in freshwater the typical bottom-feeder is a quietly living creature that
feeds on a wide range of foods, mostly not other fish. But it must be
recognized that the terms predatory and non-predatory are only relative. No fish is entirely non-predatory; all fish will at times eat other
fish, if only the very young of their own kind. Generally though the
food of freshwater bottom-feeders consists of insects, worms, snails,
tiny creatures of the ooze, freshwater shrimps, algae such as that one
known to anglers as silkweed—most small animals found in the environment, in fact, and some forms of weed. What is eaten in a particular

case is dependent on the species of the fish and its typical environment; a bream for example is typically a lover of a muddy bottom, and a roach will go for preference to a gravelly bottom if there is one within reach. The most typical bottom-feeders, those whose feeding is almost or entirely confined to the bottom, may be recognized as such by the shape, and, in some cases, by the possession of barbules—something which will be explained when the fish are described individually later in this book. The midwater feeders are largely those which are wholly or partly predatory, though there is overlapping here. A pike will lie low in the water to wait for prey, but will shoot up to grab that which swims above it; but it will also, on occasions, take its food from the bottom—in particular being ready to pick up from the bottom a dead fish. The perch, though omnivorous in youth, becomes very largely a predator as it becomes bigger, chasing the small fry in the middle waters. The chub again is an overlapper, sometimes a bottom-feeder, more often a middle-water feeder—and this is because the chub is the most truly omnivorous freshwater fish of all, eating anything that may be eaten, and lustily chasing the smaller fish to make of them prey. Its shape is typically that of the middle water rather than the bottom, more streamlined.

So far, all this is paralleled in the sea, only the scale differing. There are the fish that lie upon and quarter and feed upon the sandy bottom, those that live in rocky bottoms and feed upon their rather different diet there; and there are the midwater fish, those that range freely, restlessly searching for food, such fish as the pollack. This is emphasized to show that an understanding of the broad aspects of fish life can be applied in widely different circumstances. The basis of all successful angling is understanding the way of life of the fish; that must be the basis of fishing methods.

Some fish are preponderantly rangers and feeders in the upper waters, at or near the surface, and in all of them there is the absence of the typical bottom-feeder's shape; there is a general tendency to a streamlined shape, as in the trout. In the rudd, that rather solidly yeomanlike fish, there is nothing so elegant as trout-like streamlining; but its mouth should be noted. It is upturned, the lower jaw projecting beyond the upper; this should be contrasted with the mouth of the roach, a fish rather similar in look to the rudd. The roach's mouth is the reverse— the lower jaw almost recedes from the upper one. Thus are shown the two habits of the fish. The rudd, in summer anyway, feeds mostly near or at the surface, taking flies from the surface, and to that its mouth is adapted. The roach is preponderantly a feeder off the bottom; and for that *its* mouth is adapted. Absolutes are rare in fish though, and these surface-feeders are not inevitably so engaged—something to be remembered in angling for them. The trout, as the fly fisher's quarry, is thought of as taking flies on or near the surface, and so it does for all to see; but, less obviously, it spends much time searching in the weeds, even grubbing on the bottom for such animals as caddis larvae and shrimps. So with the dace, well known as a slim sporter near the sun. Winter finds it more often seeking food on the bottom than elsewhere— and so indeed with the rudd too. But, of course, the movements of fish are most strictly related to the movements of those organisms on which they feed.

## Seasonal movement related to food

In the spring, when the sun first finds its warmth, it brings a burst of life suddenly in the upper waters. It warms into being teeming myriads of the tiny creatures known collectively as plankton, minute freely float-ing swimming animals such as the daphnia. On them feed the rather larger animals, and on them larger still till the pyramid of life reaches the fishes, the giants of the water—though some of the fishes do feed directly on the plankton. An example is the basking shark, a vast sea fish of the surface, the biggest of all our fishes, twenty-five and more feet long. *Its* consistent diet is the plankton.

From the spring awakening on through the summer the shallow waters teem with life; and there too of course are the fishes. It is funda-mental that fish will be only where their food is. In the autumn the tide of life recedes; the upper waters cool, life sinks back. Those areas near the light that have seethed with tiny life all through the warmer months now become largely depopulated. And so with the fish; they too forsake the higher levels. Those species that do remain active through the winter tend to seek their living on the bottom or close to it rather than in the former places.

Something of the same pattern is to be seen just in the diurnal span. Consider for example the typical pattern of the carp's round of twenty-four summer hours, and let us start at sunrise. The sun rises, slants across the water, then rises high enough to begin its warming. The carp, following the temperature's effect, following the rest of the life in the water, move into the sunny shallows, feeding on the plankton, feed-ing on the weed, on the creatures in the weed, and those in the bottom.

Then as early hours wax to middle-morning ones, the sun's heat grows and the water temperature goes beyond that in which the carp still have appetite. It rises to seventy degrees, and higher; the carp now are torpid. They drowse in the sun, near the surface, and as the hot hours pass over them they sleep their fishy summer sleep. Then evening comes; the sun declines, the water cools. For a time the shallows stand within that optimum band of temperature, between, say, fifty-eight degrees and sixty-eight degrees, and in this water down to five or six feet of depth the whole quiver of life is active. From the plankton up to the great ambling amber carp themselves, all is active, all feeding.

But twilight deepens, temperature sinks, and soon the marginal shallow water has fallen below the feeding optimum. As the temperature declines so does the level of activity of the plankton, and so, all else. The carp that have been in water three and four feet deep move down, into water five feet to perhaps eight feet deep, and there find still the impulse to feed. There the temperature is such as still to encourage them. Midnight comes, then one o'clock, and air temperature, with that of water following, sinks further, sinks below the level at which carp will feed. The plankton has become inactive. Now the carp are torpid again, and, as is so often so in summer nights, it remains cold till dawn and the sun calls life into being again.

That is a frequent pattern; but as so much in Nature may, it may vary widely. The day may not become so warm as to raise the water temperature greatly, and then carp may feed all day. The night may not become so cold, and may indeed drop the water temperature to just the optimum level. Then carp will feed, and may be caught, in the hours of total darkness. So they may sometimes be for the first two or three hours of darkness, with, following, an interval till dawn during which the temperature *is* too low.

This pattern of the carp has been so fully traced because it is more clearly to be seen than is that of some other fish whose band of feeding temperature is wider, less closely circumscribed. But it does demonstrate what is the general pattern. In the sea the same pattern is broadly valid, but reversed. There the plankton rises and sinks with the times of day, high in the water during the dark hours, sinking by day, taking with it the general trend of the whole activity of the fauna of the water.

## The angler's first lesson

This discussion of fish as animals would be better not left till all that it has revealed is related to what is really the first lesson for one who sets himself to become an angler. It is a lesson which needs to be so well learnt, so assimilated, that it becomes a part of instinct. For the rest of this book it will be assumed as a constant background to all else. It has been pointed out that fear and suspicion are basic keys to a fish's retention of life, that a fish has six senses that arm it well against danger. It is the angler's business so to form his tactics that, having interpreted the phase of life at which he finds his fish, he interpolates himself into it undetected. He must seek to suggest that his activities are part of the activity of Nature. The angler must not be detected by the fish.

First he must not be seen by the fish. To this it is relevant that a fish in water, looking upwards, sees a mirror. That mirror is the underside of the water's surface. In it, immediately over the fish, is a circular opening through which the fish sees to the world of air above the surface. If the fish is near the surface the opening is a small one. The deeper the fish lies the bigger is the opening. So, so far, it emerges that a fish lying deep has a wider chance to see the angler than one lying near the

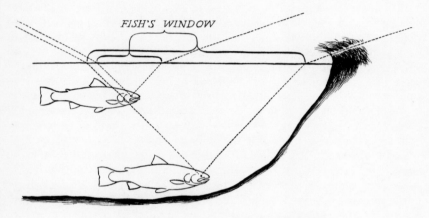

*FISH'S WINDOW*

Fig. 4. The fish's window, showing how
fish's line of vision is bent on passing
through the surface

surface. A fish just under the surface may, on that basis, be approached more closely than one that lies deep. An example is the trout that lies 'in position' (as anglers say) just under the surface to intercept surface flies floating down on the current.

But another consideration enters. Water refracts the rays of light, and the line of vision of a fish, looking upwards through its window, is bent, so that it sees not in a straight line but a bent one, the angle of bend coming as the line of vision passes through the surface. The effect is that the angler, low down on the bank, is seen as if he were in fact high above the bank, in a straight line from where the fish looks. It is necessary then for the angler to remember this, to take all the means he can to overcome it. If the bank is an open one, free of background growth, he will be a silhouette against the light of the sky. His only hope if he must fish from near the edge of the bank, is to crouch low, even lie, certainly kneel or sit low.

Fortunately other considerations also have their effect. If there is a background, of trees or bushes perhaps, the angler may be absorbed into the fish's view of the background provided his clothes do not contrast strongly with the general tone of the background. In such a situation it is often possible to stand at full height and watch fish under the feet. On days of strong wind a sparse background may become an effective concealment. The bushes, plants, whatever the background is, are so agitated, make so broken a pattern, that they conceal the angler and, what may be so important, his movements.

It is often movement that betrays the angler when otherwise he might be undetected. Suppose an angler wades from a low open bank into shallow trout-inhabited water—all the fish in that vicinity will bolt. But, if he remain absolutely still, like a post, like a heron, presently the fish will return. Suppose an angler finds a low-growing bush overlooking water he proposes to fish. If he hides *behind* the bush and only very slowly raises himself behind it to look over it, he is unlikely to alarm the fish. *But,* at his first movement he will be realized as meaning danger and the fish will bolt. He would do better to go in front of the bush, to sit down in front of it, so melting into it.

So much for the fish's sight. Its other main means of detection is the lateral line sense. It has been pointed out that sounds from the angler, speech for example, are unlikely to be perceived by fish. Vibrations set up by the angler's movements are another matter. Impacts by movement, seeming trivial on the bank, are magnified in the water, are inevitably picked up by the fish's lateral line. Footfalls too heavily planted, the too heavy putting down of articles, the knocking out of pipes—all these are betrayers. Anglers on the bank should go as a cat goes; anglers in boats should remember that the lightest object dropped on bottom boards may be thunderous below the surface. One scraped boot may alarm a shoal.

There is one more odd fact of fish of which fishermen should have note, the fear substance. Its existence was only quite recently discovered, but it may explain much. A fish when frightened secretes a substance at once discernible to other fish in its vicinity and which passes on the contagion of its fear. Another sharp admonishment to the angler, this is, for the stringent need for caution on his part. One fish frightened may mean many fish frightened. That fish that goes arrow-like in panic at a careless approach takes its fear with it, spreading it.

# CHAPTER TWO

# Out of natural history, by observation, come fishing methods

WHO the first men were who fished, in what misty recession of time, we cannot know. But we can divine that these primitive foregoers of ourselves pored long over the water, watching life in it, making clumsy attempts at means for the deception of the fish, coming by long experimental degrees to the first rough forms of what are now basic assumptions of method. They, we must suppose, thought first of offering a bait on a hook matched to the fish's natural food, and then sought to devise tackle on which to offer it. The facts of natural history which they saw before them evolved the methods, the methods evolved the tackle. So, no doubt, the idea of a fishing rod was arrived at; so all else gradually followed.

To the beginner in angling today this may seem obvious and not very relevant to what he has to do; but his good fortune in having so much of the experience of the past to draw upon should not obscure for him that this is still and must remain the only logical approach to fishing. It is too easy for him to accept, off the peg, so to speak, the established methods, and apply them without thought as to their significance. He should try (though this is difficult) to look at the water and its fish as if he were the first man to do so, while using the advantage of the experience of all who have done so before him. That has been, and still is, the attitude of the great innovators in angling methods.

Such a thing has happened in our own time. Until after the Second World War, big carp were regarded as virtually uncatchable. A few possessed, patient, and perhaps not very thoughtful men attended interminably upon carp they saw wallowing unattainably. Only rarely did they catch carp, and then the biggest eluded them; most anglers accepted as a fact the impossibility of catching big carp. Those who did fish for them used methods, with only minor adaptations, that worked with other fish. Then one man, Richard Walker, looked at carp, pored over carp, as if he were the first man ever to have done so, and evolved methods, and from the methods tackle, that were based solely upon what he saw of carp. *He* did catch big carp, caught carp bigger than had been supposed to exist. Other anglers applied his methods and caught carp too. Now you may often hear anglers say that the difficulty of carp fishing is grossly exaggerated, that if you wait long enough carp are not specially difficult to catch. On many carp waters (though *not* all) this is true; but those same carp were virtually impossible to catch until Richard Walker had looked with his fresh uncommitted eye and thought with his uncomitted mind.

Fortunately for the majority of us we do not have to start so far back each time we go fishing. We have the results of Richard Walker's observation and thought, and we have the results of the observation and thought of many other remembered and forgotten anglers of the past. We can have the best benefit from it if we relate it all the time to its origins; what those origins are we can recall from the previous chapter —the most immediately important are that fish of different species, and fish of most species on different occasions, feed in three main ways. They feed by grubbing on the bottom, by pursuing prey in the middle waters, by taking food (for example flies) at or close to the surface. This is of course a very arbitrary classification; it has all kinds of variations and overlappings. But at least the feeding of fish does fall sufficiently closely into this pattern to form a basis for methods of fishing. Fishing methods then are broadly to be described by the same classification. Here it is necessary only to identify them in principle; they will be described fully, for practical purposes, later. They are called bottom fishing, spinning, fly fishing.

## Bottom fishing

Bottom fishing is a general term which covers all the methods that seek to catch fish that find their food actually in the silt of the bottom, that take it as it is brought to them by the current on or near the bottom, that seek it in the weeds. It is applied particularly in fishing for what are known as the coarse fish—roach, rudd, tench, bream, carp, barbel, perch, dace, chub, eels, crucian carp. It is sometimes used for pike, and it is one method of fishing for grayling. Though it may be a very simple form of fishing, it can demand very high levels of skill and experience —even, some say, higher than in any other form of fishing. There are two broad divisions of bottom fishing—float fishing and leger fishing. In float fishing, one of the most deeply fascinating forms of angling, the key to the sub-surface world is the float. It suspends the baited hook at what is judged to be the appropriate depth, it signals the taking of the bait by the fish, and it is a means of carrying the amount of lead that is necessary to take the bait down to the proper depth against the push of the current.

In leger fishing, in one way or another, the tackle is laid on the bottom, and is used when it is judged that the quarry is a fish that is interested in food that lies actually on or in the bottom or rolls along the bottom. To meet all contingencies leger tackle may be stationary on the bottom or may roll along it. It may have a lead threaded on the line and free to slide on it; it may have no lead at all, or it may be weighted with lead shot. A leger may be used in conjunction with a float, or without a float.

## Spinning

There are many forms of spinning arising from the differing natures of the fish sought, from the differing natures of the water being fished, and from differences of weather and water. But the broad intention is the same in all cases—to imitate the appearance and behaviour of the prey pursued by the predatory fish; more often than otherwise that prey is a small fish. The angler's bait may be a small dead fish or it may be an artificial bait that simulates the look and movement of a fish—or it may sometimes be some other creature that the quarry is prepared to eat.

The method of fishing is also broadly the same in all cases. The bait is cast across the water, often for long distances, and then brought back to the angler in such a way that it appears to be swimming as the natural fish or other animal swims. The name of the method, spinning, arises from the fact that in a majority of cases the bait is caused to spin on its own axis. Why this should be so needs a reference back to fish themselves.

Fish. as we see them out of water are shining, colourful, sometimes gorgeously decorative; in the water, as other fish must try to see them, they are so inconspicuous as often to be nearly invisible. That silvery shine of a fish's flanks reflects what is about it—the green of weeds, the yellow stone of the bottom, so it becomes not flashing and brilliant, but a means of concealment, of camouflage. The dark back of a fish melts it into the background when seen from above; the pale belly melts it into the light above when seen from below. So it is too with the markings, often so lovely out of the water, the spots of the trout, the black stripes of the perch; they are means of camouflage. A perch is often to be found among the vertically growing stems of weeds and reeds; its stripes imitate the pattern of the stems. A trout is often to be found over gravel, in the dapple of light in the weeds; its spots imitate that.

So a fish, ordinarily, is hardly visible to other fish. Though you would think it to be like a shining light in that liquid shadowy world, it is a shadow among the shadows. But sometimes a fish turns suddenly, going a little off vertical balance as it does so; in so doing it emits a flash. That a predatory fish can see; that is a signal for attack. There is another signal for attack—the proximity and vibration signals picked up by the predatory fish's lateral line sense. These signals the spinning bait must imitate. By spinning it emits at each turn a flash, and the spinning movement emits vibrations. In not all methods coming under the main heading of spinning does the bait spin, but there is always the same attempt to suggest the flash and vibration of fish.

## Fly fishing

Fly fishing is a method that, in most cases, seeks to imitate with artificial flies the natural flies that fish take either on the surface or below it. It has a broad division into dry fly fishing and wet fly fishing. Dry fly fishing is concerned with the imitation of actual flies that float upon the surface of the water. Wet fly fishing may suggest, according to circumstances, the larval stage of life of those flies, flies drowned by turbulent currents, beetles, various other animals that have fallen into the water, such as caterpillars, or it may suggest such animals as freshwater shrimps. There comes under the heading of fly fishing one fishing method that has indeed no connexion at all with anything like natural flies; it is fly fishing for salmon. It is only known as such because the tackle and casting techniques used are those of fly fishing, and the lure itself, though representing quite other things, has, out of the water, some similarity of look to true artificial flies.

Though this broad survey of the principal fishing methods has been mainly concerned with freshwater fishing, it must be emphasized that they arise so logically from the fundamental facts of fish life, that they are, inevitably, the broad basis of sea fishing techniques. To point this out may seem irrelevant here; but it does emphasize the fact from which all fishing must start and to which return must always be made—that angling is the interpretation of and the interpolation into the natural history of fish.

# CHAPTER THREE

# Out of method, tackle

IT is typical of fishing that its instruments are as deeply fascinating as the pursuit itself; the beginner may be forgiven if he becomes so drunk with the gleaming pleasures of them that his choice in buying is sometimes less practical than bewitched. But fishing tackle is indeed (or should be) a set of very precisely devised answers to the mechanical problems of fishing. This must not be taken as implying that all tackle that may be bought, all tackle that is in use, is as fitly suited to the problem as it should be. Prejudice and misconception are as riotously indulged in fishing tackle as in anything else.

Nothing that may be said here will prevent the beginner following all sorts of brief enthusiasms, buying rather wildly tackle which he later discards—that is part of the pleasure of passing from angling innocence to experience. Out of that, as well as the delight that any new rod, any new reel, brings, will come gradually a firm grasp of what the true functions of them are. But at least let this book set forth the functions, and how tackle should interpret them. The object for so doing is not to lead the angler to a set of tackle that will be the be-all and end-all, so that, for evermore, his pleasure in tackle buying is ended, but to guide him to things that *are* of practical value. Tackle buying continues over a lifetime, and collections grow vastly; but it helps greatly at early stages to be able to buy tackle that will meet the widest possible range of uses—tackle is, after all, expensive.

Because tackle is the follower and servant of method, it falls into those same broad divisions as were described in the last chapter. There are rods and reels, and all the rest, for bottom fishing, for spinning, and for fly fishing; and those are quite sharp differences. It may be said in the broadest possible way that the job of a rod is to cast the tackle and to play and land the fish, and that the reel has to hold the line; but from that point the divergence of use is wide. Let us look first at bottom fishing.

## Bottom fishing tackle—rods

Rods for bottom fishing are, generally, on the long side by the standard of rods for other purposes. The greater part of bottom fishing is done

from a fixed position, often over marginal growth, and to the deeper
levels of the water being fished; these factors dictate at least fairly long
rods. Apart from exceptional and specialized rods, those for bottom
fishing vary from ten feet to fourteen feet. Suppose, for example, you
are bream fishing in the River Great Ouse. Many bream swims (note
that word 'swim'—it is what the bottom fisherman calls the section of
water in which he fishes) on the Great Ouse are deep, ten feet deep, as
much as fourteen feet deep. If float fishing is the method used in fourteen feet of water, the rod cannot conveniently be less than that length.
If it were the float would jamb against the top of the rod to complicate
casting and the landing of fish. In varying degree these are factors that
affect the length of all bottom fishing rods.

Because bottom fishing may be done in so wide a range of waters,
from deep slow rivers such as the Great Ouse to still mill ponds, the
techniques of fishing vary equally widely; these differing techniques
demand a parallel difference in what is called the 'action' of the rod—
that, in simple terms, is the way it bends. A rod may have its action all
the way down, or it may have it concentrated in certain sections of the
rod—we speak of a tip-actioned rod, or a butt-actioned rod. A rod may
have a lot of action, or it may be stiff, with little action. Rod action has
a profound effect on the fishing of its owner; an action very unsuited to
the fishing being done and to the rest of the tackle used with it can
produce miserable frustration in the angler. It is important to know as
early as possible what the effects and purposes of action are.

Rod action is that which, properly, provides the energy for the casting of the tackle. Sometimes the swim being fished is almost under the
feet of the angler, and then no problem of casting arises. But, often,
the swim is a varying distance removed from the angler's position. It
may be some distance out from the bank of a lake; it may be near the
farther bank of the river. Then a cast has to be made. That which has
to be cast is a line of only negligible weight, and on it a float and shot
and bait, or such weight as there is in a leger lead and bait. The whole
does not, usually, weigh much. If you will imagine trying to cast that,
say, ten yards, with a pole that is completely stiff, you will see that a
great effort of strength of arm would have to be used, and, even so, the
result would be poor. But imagine that, instead of the pole, you use a
long steel spring. The bending back followed by the consequent springing forward of the spring would cast the tackle. *That* is the significance
of rod action in relation to casting. The more the nature of the rod
action is adjusted to the weight that has to be cast, the more effortlessly
and efficiently the angler can cast. Well-designed rods are given an
action suited to a certain range of weight which the rod is likely to be
called upon to cast in the type of fishing the rod is designed for.

That is one aspect of the rod's duty. It also has to play fish after they are hooked. In far more cases than not the line used is a fine one—a fine one in the sense that its breaking strain is less than could withstand a direct pull of the whole weight and strength of the specimen fish the angler hopes to catch. So here the rod has the function of acting as a buffer between the fish's weight and strength and the weakness of the line. Again the important factor is the rod's action. If the spring of the rod is too heavy and powerful it is likely to break the line under stress; if the action is very stiff it will give less relief to a fine line than it would if it were more lissome.

There is yet one more aspect of the effect of rod action. When the float dips to signal the bite of a fish, or a pull on the leger tackle does the same, the angler must respond by striking so that the point of the hook may be sent home over the barb. Under differing fishing conditions, for different fish, a quick sharp strike may be needed, or a slow strike, or perhaps, if the fish is a long way from the angler, downstream of him in a river, a sweeping strike may be needed. A stiff rod with a tip action— that is, an action in which just the last part of the tip has mobility—will give a quick strike. The more action a rod has all the way down its length, the slower the strike will be. If a long sweeping strike is needed, an easy lissome action right down the rod is necessary so that the strike shall not break the line, but will absorb and cushion surplus shock.

Now it can be seen why there are so many differing types of rod for bottom fishing, and how easily reasons can be found for adding and adding to a store of rods—the impression may be given that it is essential to have such a store. That it is delightful and greatly adding to the pleasure of angling to have so many rods is not to be denied, but so many are not essential. One well-chosen rod will take the beginner a very long way.

To help him, he should know that there are many rods, widely used, that are based upon fallacies. Look at the odd case of what are some-times known as match rods, sometimes as roach rods. They are more to be seen in the Midlands and North than elsewhere. In those places there is a particular practice of match fishing, and in many of the waters in which matches are fished, in or near industrial areas, the standard of their fish populations is low. Big fish are scarce, little fish abound; so there is an enforced concentration on little fish. It has been found that to have the best chance of winning it is better to catch little fish as quickly as possible rather than to try for fewer bigger fish. This is of course a generalization, with numbers of exceptions, but it is broadly true. It is true enough to have fixed like a law of Nature the type of rod used, the match rod.

Because the fish are little, they, in the way of little fish, bite very quickly. The response to the bite must be instantaneous if it is to be hooked; so the match rod is stiff throughout its length until the tip—that has an instantaneously rapid strike. And because the fish are so little there is no need for a strong rod or a rod with action to absorb shock. But the rod must be long to reach out over whatever may line the bank—the match angler cannot choose his swim, judging from his knowledge of fish where they are most likely to be. He draws a number, and then fishes from a peg holding that number. From that place he may not stir. So, because his rod is long but should not be heavy, it is often made, for much of its length, of what is called Spanish reed, which is a light but very fragile cane, dangerously light for the playing of strong fish. Nowadays, it is true, the much stronger fibreglass is tending to supplant Spanish reed.

These match rods, for almost any purpose of true angling, are very inefficient; but they are highly efficient for their purpose—the quickest possible catching of little fish. Even for this they have one serious fault. Because big matches are attended by many contestants, as well as stewards, spectators and bookmakers, fish tend to avoid proximity to the bank from which the fishing is being done. To reach them long casting is needed, and for this what is called the 'punch cast' has been developed—punching with the rod to force it to a casting capacity for which it is not built. The result is often the snapping of the light but tender Spanish reed.

So much for that, you would think; that is the match rod, devised for match fishing. But, because so much match fishing is done in the Midlands and North, and because that rod is used for it with success, it has come to be believed that it is the best sort of rod for all fishing, and that there is a virtue in its use—a virtue in catching fish on it in spite of its inadequacy for fish of more worthy size. To use it for fish of whatever size has become almost a matter of morality; it is not 'sporting' to use tackle of more suitable strength and design. It is as if you were to take a moral stand on using a table fork for digging the garden rather than a garden fork. Yet the strength of the match rod in relation to the power of those little fish is much greater than, say, the strength of a carp rod is to the power and weight of a thirty-pound carp.

There is another odd quirk deriving from match catching of little fish. The majority of them are roach, dwarfed roach, and because they, in the way of midgets, bite quickly, the legend has become established that roach always bite quickly and need a fast-striking rod. Big roach do not usually bite quickly (though they may do so on very hard-fished waters); there is no need for the angler for good roach to be so handicapped.

Let us assume then that whatever temporary fancies the learning fisherman may have for this rod and that, he will at least be protected by what has foregone against attempting to fish for fine fish with a match rod. Later in this book there will emerge some description of rods for specialized bottom fishing purposes; at this stage it is enough to describe what is the nearest approach to a universal bottom fishing rod, that one which was referred to earlier. There is a school of fishing, known as the Nottingham school of bottom fishing, which arose from the problems of the River Trent, originally a quick clear stream of urgent currents and splendid fishing (now, alas, pollution has reduced it to a contaminated shadow of its old glory). Out of the methods of the school, which often needed long casting, and nearly always fishing at long distances from the fisherman, there came a particular combination of a very easily running reel and a lissome rod. Later the style of fishing was taken to and adapted to the River Avon which runs down from Wiltshire and across Hampshire to the sea—the Hampshire Avon, as it is known, almost a holy name to anglers, so fine is the fishing. There the rod was developed to a standardized type which is known as the Avon rod. It is a rod which, so far as any one rod may, will meet all the angler's needs for some time.

It is an easy-actioned rod, bending throughout its length, eleven feet usually, and in its original form having three joints. The bottom or butt joint was of whole cane—which means that it is a piece in unaltered form of the tonkin cane which is the basis from which most fishing rod cane comes. The middle and top joints were of split cane (also called built cane). Nowadays rods of this type are more often of split cane throughout, and with two joints, not three. One of these rods has a reversed taper going down to the bottom of the butt, and this has produced a rod very like perfection.

Split cane is a material of such importance in rod making that it must be described. Lengths of tonkin cane are split longitudinally, and the sections split off are planed into a triangular section, the outer faces of the cane forming one face of the triangle. Six pieces so formed are brought together and bonded, forming a hexagonal whole. The result concentrates all the tough resilient qualities of the outer part of the tonkin cane, with the outer surface of the six pieces forming the outside of the rod section made. This built material, built cane, is light, has tremendous tensile strength, and by manipulation of the taper from top to bottom can give a wide variety of actions. Split cane is, till now, the best of all materials for freshwater fishing rods.

## Bottom fishing—reels

Reels for bottom fishing fall into two main types—centre-pin reels and fixed-spool reels. The centre-pin is that type which revolves, wheel

fashion, on its own axis, the simplest sort of reel. The highest development of it is that which arose from first the Nottingham school and then
the Avon school, a reel so finely balanced and free-running that the
least flick on its rim will set it spinning for a long time. It is often called
the Nottingham reel. Really of this type, but designed originally for
spinning (but now much used for bottom fishing), is the Aerial reel, a
beautiful reel. The Nottingham reel is narrow from side to side—compressed, as it is called; the Aerial reel is less compressed, and is
designed on an open-cage style.

The fixed-spool reel would scarcely have been recognized by our fore-
fathers as a reel at all—and perhaps not by our contemporaries who are
not anglers—so different is its principle. Imagine a cotton reel; then,

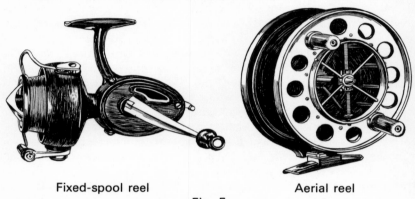

Fixed-spool reel                          Aerial reel

Fig. 5

instead of drawing cotton from it by rotating the reel, do so by drawing it off over the end of the reel, coil by coil. It is on that principle
that the fixed-spool reel works. The spool (which is the cotton reel, so to
speak) has its end facing up the rod, and when the cast is made and the
weight of the terminal tackle pulls on the line, the coils of it fly off over
the end of the spool. By this means the frictional inertia which acts as a
drag on the spinning of a revolving reel is avoided. The result is a reel
that can make long casts with the greatest ease, and can cast baits far
lighter than can be cast by other reels. It, like the Aerial, was first
designed as a spinning reel, one for the casting of very small, very light
baits in spinning for trout in times of low clear water; but that first
purpose has long been left. The reel is now more used for bottom fishing than is the centre-pin, for several reasons, and one is that its use is
far more easily learnt than are the not-at-all-easy skills of the Nottingham reel. A novice may have the freedom of the fixed-spool reel in a
short time of starting to fish. Another is that it provides an answer to

certain bottom fishing problems that are not fully met by any other means—what they are will emerge in a later chapter. A third reason is that it is a universal reel; with that one reel an angler can do all sorts of fishing except fly fishing. Many do so use it.

But it has its disadvantages. One (often cited as an advantage) is the slipping clutch. In the reel is this slipping clutch, which can be varied in its tension by an adjustment device on the face of the spool, and which, so it is said, can be used as a buffer against the strength of a fish. So, it is declared, a line may be used which is disproportionately lower in its breaking strain than would otherwise be appropriate to the strength and weight of the fish which is the quarry. Providing the tension of the spool is adjusted suitably any pull from a fish which is heavier than the breaking strain of the line, will cause the slipping clutch to slip, thus allowing the angler to be as ham-handed as he may. That is the story, and it has led to much bad fishing—fishing for strong fish with very light lines, resulting in many fish escaping with hooks in their jaws and lengths of line trailing from them. If fish lived in bath tubs the slipping clutch would no doubt work thus; but fish live in natural waters in which there are weeds, sunken logs, rocks, all sorts of snags. That is not the true purpose of the slipping clutch. Choice of line for the fixed-spool reel should ignore the slipping clutch; the breaking strain of lines should be judged by the same standards as they are for any other reel.

The slipping clutch is a necessity for another reason. If the pull of a fish demands the release of line from a centre-pin reel, the reel revolves and yields line. That cannot be with the fixed-spool reel; it does not revolve. So it has a slipping clutch; that provides the means for the yielding of line in response to a pull.

It is the practice of some anglers to vary the tension of the clutch during the playing of a fish, a cumbersome means of controlling the pressure on it. It is better to set the tension of the clutch lightly, and use finger pressure on the edge of the drum—a sensitive means of varying pressure. But this really is a matter for later discussion. It does however lead to another disadvantage of the reel. The sensations of the fish's fight, all its plunges, all its heart-stirring runs, reach the angler obscurely through the complications of the reel, its gears and clutch, so that all is, as it were, muffled, as if, as someone said, the fish were being played through treacle. The reel's protagonists, and they are formidable in their fervour, claim that this is cancelled by playing the fish by finger pressure on the drum with a light setting of the tension of the clutch. There is much truth in what they say, though still there is *some* loss of sensation; the thrilled sense of delight in the fish's fight is not *quite* what it is with the centre-pin reel.

## Bottom fishing—lines and other tackle

In lines for bottom fishing recent developments have left little room for choice—and little need for it. The use of one kind of line is now nearly universal. Nylon monofilament has so many advantages; it has some real disadvantages.

It is translucent, therefore inconspicuous in the water; it is fine for its strength, thus enhancing its inconspicuousness; it is cheap, it is very tough, it is waterproof. An imposing array of virtues. One of its faults is that it stretches, stretches extraordinarily. To the beginner it may not be obvious why stretch should be thought to be a fault; but this stretch muffles the effect of striking, particularly at long distances, and, to some extent, lessens the absolutely firm sense of contact with a hooked fish. This latter effect, though, is a slight one. It should be said too that occasionally a spool of monofilament will be found to be weak, breaking at the least pull—and a line kept too long in use, or in store, may rot suddenly, losing almost all of its strength. Another of its faults is that it is difficult to see on the water and has less sense of feel in the hand when the hand must be used to complement the reel in some long-trotting—it is indeed inclined to be rather unmanageable in some circumstances.

The alternative to monofilament is braided nylon or braided Terylene. Like monofilament it is waterproof, very strong for diameter; but it is not translucent and it is not cheap. It lacks the slight springiness of monofilament which may sometimes be troublesome in the higher breaking strains, but instead lies snugly on the spool of the reel. In such forms of fishing in which it is an advantage to be able to see the line clearly on the water, braided line is greatly better. It is, then, a line for special purposes in bottom fishing; though for most purposes it has advantages over monofilament. A final word on monofilament should be that, owing to its extreme smoothness—indeed slipperiness—knots used for it must be particularly secure. A later chapter will give guidance on that.

Floats might be supposed to be the simplest part of the angler's tackle, and a beginner is usually happy to sit enslaved before the fascination of any kind; but on no part of the bottom fisherman's tackle has more scholarship, more wisdom and experience, been lavished than on floats. The beginner will think of the float as nothing more than a means of suspending his tackle in the water, and that is one of its functions. But it must also be the means of revealing all kinds of bites, subtle and bold, and in all kinds of water from fast heavy currents to still water; and it must be of such a size that it will carry just the weight

of split shot that the fishing conditions dictate. Floats then are infinitely
varied, from mere two-inch slips of bird quill to great bulbous things of
great buoyancy to carry the heavy weight of lead often necessary to
take the bait down to fishing depth in the Hampshire Avon. This variation will be developed and explained in later chapters. Now it is sufficient to say that many floats are made of quill, sometimes with cork
or balsa wood bodies on them, and that they may also be made of such
things as Norfolk reed stems, porcupine quills, and elderberry pith. It

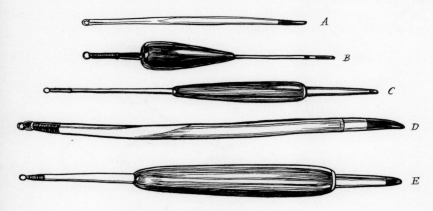

### Fig. 6. Representative floats

A  is a small bird quill float for light fishing.
B  is an antenna float; it is used in windy conditions. The
   body of the float is submerged, and the antenna stands
   above the surface—and, thus, the movement of the
   surface is not passed down to the bait.
C  is a medium float to carry a few shot.
D  is a swan's quill float to carry a larger number of shot in
   a strong current.
E  is a heavy-fishing float to carry a lot of shot on the
   Hampshire Avon.

is better that that part of them that goes below the water's surface
should be of inconspicuous watery or reed-like colours, and that part, a
mere tip, an inch or often less, which shows above water, should be of
a colour to show as clearly as possible. Orange is the best colour for
most lights, though white may sometimes be better in a failing light. A
white ring below the colour, immediately at the water's surface, may be
a help in visibility.

The most usual way of weighting the line below the float is by the use
of split shot. The split in the shot is made to go rather more than halfway through, and into the split the line is put and the shot pinched tight.
A very good means of thus pinching the shot is by surgeon's artery

forceps—or one of the pliers sold by tackle dealers that are very like artery forceps. There is a second use for such pliers.

When a fish has been hooked and landed, the hook must be removed, and it should be done with as much neatness and absence of mauling as possible. It is the admirable and humane custom of coarse fishermen to return their fish alive to the water, and to maul, squeeze, or in any way injure the fish would leave it with a poor chance of survival. Many forms of hook remover, known as disgorgers, are to be had; but the only truly satisfactory means is this same artery forceps or pliers.

The bend of the hook can be engaged and the hook neatly pushed down and then lifted out. This makes virtually no injury to the fish.

Fig. 7. Artery forceps

It may sometimes be that the current of the river being fished—and this applies specially to the Hampshire Avon—is so strong, so heavy, that a great deal of weight needs to be concentrated at one part of the line, often near the hook, so that the bait may be taken quickly down to the fishing depth. In such a case, rather than using a large number of split shot, one may be pinched on at a selected distance from the hook and a barrel lead threaded on the line above the shot, to be stopped by the shot. A barrel lead is shaped like a very elongated barrel perforated through the centre.

This lead is, really, a lead for leger fishing, one of the many that can be used. All those leads known as leger leads are made in some way to be threaded on the line. In most of them this is achieved by a perforation through the centre, but they are becoming increasingly displaced by leads having in the top of them a small swivel; the line is threaded through the eye of the swivel. The parent of all such leads is the Arlesey bomb, invented by Richard Walker for a specific angling purpose, but since found to have innumerable other applications. This Arlesey bomb is bomb-shaped, a sort of streamlined pear shape, and the swivel

Fig. 8. The Arlesey bomb, and simple
method of using it as leger lead

is set in the top of it; its streamlining leads to ease in long casting. More about it will emerge in later descriptions of methods.

There is another lead the bottom fisherman must use, an indispensable one, the plummet. In its commonest form it is conical, with a ring at the top and cork let into the bottom. It is the means by which the angler discovers the depth of his swim—vital information for successful bottom fishing. Its use too will be described at the appropriate time.

Fig. 9. Plummet

## Hooks

And now hooks, something to be taken very seriously. It is the final factor that decides whether, having hooked your fish, you land it. If the hook is too small, inferior, or in other way less in virtue than it should be, it may, and probably will, lose for you a fish that might be the best you ever hooked. The better the fish indeed, the more likely it is to escape by the failure of the hook.

The bottom fisherman uses four main sorts of hooks—eyed hooks, hooks-to-nylon, spade-end hooks, and (less often) treble hooks. Hooks-to-nylon are probably more used than the others, but for no good reason.

All but treble hooks tend to fall into two main shapes, crystal hooks and round-bend hooks. There are certain proprietary hooks which are not entirely in the one category or the other—for example Allcock's Model Perfect hooks are almost round-bend, but not quite. They are, incidentally, very good hooks indeed, forged at the bend and reliable.

Hooks-to-nylon, which may be crystal or round-bend, are whipped to a short length of nylon monofilament which has at its upper end a loop for attachment to the line or what is called the cast. Many anglers do still use a cast between the line and the hook length, but they do so unnecessarily if the line is monofilament. Before the invention of mono-filament lines were made of plaited silk, and were, of course, opaque and thicker than nylon. Therefore it was necessary to have between the

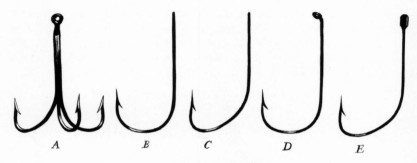

Fig. 10. Types of hook: A—treble,
B—round bend, C—crystal, D—eyed,
E—spade-end

line and the hook length a yard of gut (the predecessor of nylon mono-filament) to make the tackle less obvious in the water. This yard of gut was the cast, with a loop for attachment to the line at one end, and another for attachment to the hook length at the other. Nylon mono-filament lines have cancelled the necessity for a cast (unless a braided line is used).

Hooks-to-nylon are almost equally out of date, their necessity nearly as much cancelled by nylon lines as that of casts. A basic law of angling is that the simpler tackle can be for a given purpose, the fewer points of weakness there will be. Knots and other such junctions *are* points of weakness.

The proper companions to monofilament lies (proper in terms of reliability and ease) are eyed hooks or spade-end hooks. To either the line may be tied directly, 'Eyed hook' explains itself, but a spade-end hook needs description. The shank, which in an eyed hook ends in an eye, is flattened to a spade-shaped end—thus, when the nylon is knotted round the shank, the knot can be drawn up tight against the spade-end. Eyed hooks though are a little to be preferred because if there should be the slightest roughness on the spade-end, it will chafe the monofilament and so be a source of weakness. Both eyed hooks and spade-ends have the advantage that they are cheaper than hooks-to-nylon. Knots for the tying of line to hook will be found in the chapter on knots.

Treble hooks have occasional uses in bottom fishing. They, and the other hooks described, are sold in a range of sizes from one upwards;

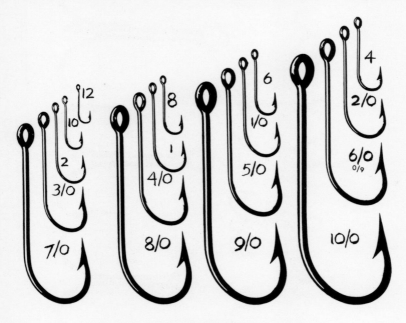

Fig. 11. Hook sizes

the higher the number the smaller the hook—and the matter of hook sizes must take us back to the relationship of match fishing to real fishing.

Just as the tiny immaturity of the fish which are so often the match fisher's quarry dictates the use of the match rod, equally it dictates the use of very fine lines (often of one pound breaking strain) and tiny hooks. The sizes of hook most used in match fishing are eighteen and twenty—and they are very small indeed. For the hooking and holding of tiny fish they are suitable. But suppose the fish to be fished for are roach of one pound, chub of three pounds or more, barbel of any size

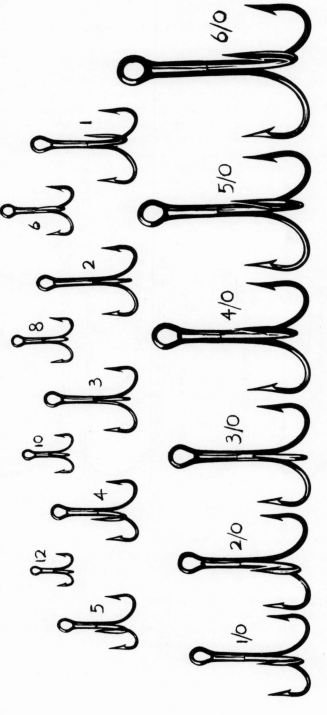

Fig. 11A. Hook sizes—these are same size

up to twelve pounds? Are these powerful fish to be hooked and held through what may be a prolonged fight on such little hooks? The use of bigger hooks (within reason) will not lessen the chance of deceiving much more worthwhile fish, and they will greatly increase the chance of hooking and holding them.

Here though it must be pointed out that there are waters in the North, usually clear-water canals, in which the fish are so consistently, and persistently, fished for that they do become very nervously sensitive to tackle. For them only the finest tackle has a possibility of acceptance, so there match fishing and true fishing must share the same tackle.

## Landing nets, keepnets

When a fish has been hooked, played, and brought to the bank, it must be landed. The means for this is a landing net; and for the choice of it there is a good general principle. Many a good fish has been lost because the landing net was too small; it is very doubtful if any fish have been lost because the landing net was too big. A landing net should be chosen in the belief that sooner or later it will be needed for the landing of a very big fish indeed. It is the hope of such a fish that sustains the whole lifetime of most anglers—a too small landing net is likely to lose it when it comes.

A landing net should be deep; it should receive, engulf, entirely enmesh the biggest fish. A great many landing nets are too small in the frame, too mean in the net; often the frame is far less strong than it should be. The handle should be long, not less than five feet, and preferably longer; it must often reach over marginal growth, over weed beds in the shallows, down high banks. Triangular or circular metal frames for landing nets are nearly universal, and if strongly made serve well. But the best of all landing nets has become rare—even if still made at all; it is the old-fashioned pear-shaped wooden frame with a deep oil-impregnated net. In time the net will rot, but it can be replaced. Many nets of today are of nylon thread which water does not rot and which is very strong; its only disadvantage is a disinclination to sink.

Though it is the custom of bottom fishermen to return their fish alive to the water, they mostly do it not at the time of capture but at the end of the fishing time. To return the fish at once could, in some cases, alarm those left in the swim—by the 'fear substance' perhaps, or by the agitated behaviour of the returned fish. So they are retained alive, and the means for doing it is the keepnet.

It is a cylindrical or square-sectioned net, with metal rings along its length to keep its shape open. The topmost ring has a screw which engages into a screw socket in what is called a bank stick. This is about four feet long, metal shod, and is pushed into the bank to secure the net while all but its top is in the water. Thus the keepnet holds the catch alive until the fishing is finished. So, theoretically, it holds them in safety and freedom from injury; and so it would be if keepnets were of a sensible size. The majority, unhappily, are not of a sensible size. They are so small in diameter that, if the catch should be big, the fish are crowded and may well be crushed or suffocated. Fortunately bigger keepnets are to be had if searched for—my own, specially made, is two feet in diameter.

## Spinning—rods

The significance of action in rods has already been pointed out in discussing bottom fishing rods; in those one of the functions of the rod's action was casting. In spinning the capacity for casting overshadows all other qualities; the whole fishing is a sequence of casting and retrieving. The more effortless casting can be, the more accurate it can be, the better the tackle will be performing its function.

A stiff rod, a rod, that is, lacking in action, is a poor caster. To cast well a rod needs a spring-like action that goes right down the rod, an action that makes the whole length of the rod contribute its share to the work that the rod must do. Think again of what is the mechanical process of casting—the rod is flexed backwards, and that sets the spring; then it is flexed forward and that releases the spring. The spring projects the tackle to the place it should go.

Spinning rods, therefore, are lively rods; they have a tense spring-like action running right down into the butt. Most of those in use fall into two types—long ones, short ones. Long ones are invariably about ten feet long (though they may be nine feet); short ones are usually about seven feet long. The length and the lightness or heaviness depend upon the kind of fish to be fished for and the kind of reel which is to be used with the rod. Light spinning, with the fixed-spool reel, and for such fish as perch, pike, trout, chub, sea trout, and in some cases salmon, is more often done with a rod of seven feet than with a longer one (though the fixed-spool reel is sometimes used with a longer rod, particularly in salmon fishing). Heavier spinning, most often with the multiplying reel, is more often done with a rod of nine or ten feet than shorter ones (though sometimes the multiplier is used with a seven-foot rod, particularly for pike). Medium heavy to heavy spinning may, in some circumstances (or according to the taste of the angler *and* his skill), be done with a centre-pin reel such as the Aerial. Spinning rods, whether of ten feet or seven feet, are more often of split cane than any other material— and beautiful to see and use a really good split cane rod is. Good spinning rods are also made in tubular steel, and those of hollow fibreglass may now be as good.

There is a third category of spinning rods, ones that came here first from America, devised for use with the multiplying reel and, primarily, for fishing from the cramped quarters of boats. They are a mere five feet of length, with a cranked handle so that the reel seating is set within the cranked part. The most commonly used material is fibreglass. Though such rods did for a time have some sort of popularity, it has declined. A short rod, so short a rod, is an inconvenient and awkward means of playing a heavy fish, far less efficient and comfortable than a longer one, and its lack of length can be a severe handicap in playing a fish from a shaggy bank which has all sorts of twigs and brambles to reach out and clutch the line.

## Spinning—reels

There are three main types of spinning reel; they are the centre-pin reel, the multiplying reel, the fixed-spool reel—and of the last there are two forms, the normal, and the closed-faced reel which stems from the

Fig. 12. A—multiplier, B—closed-face reel

normal. The original spinning reel (in this country), with which all spinning was done, is the centre-pin reel. Now it is partially obsolescent, for several reasons.

Be it as beautifully made, as smoothly efficient as it may be, there is in the centre-pin a certain inertia to be overcome on the spool to set it revolving; once it *is* revolving, it does so with sweet and silky freedom. But the need to overcome the inertia prescribes an amount of weight in the terminal tackle which narrows its usefulness. As much as an ounce or more of lead must be used in addition to the weight of the bait. And, except in very skilful hands, it cannot cast a bait with absolute accuracy into small spaces—often a necessity in spinning. Some, those with the skill to use it, still prefer it to any other kind of spinning reel because the angler is in direct touch with a hooked fish, not communicating through a system of gears as in the other reels. It is, also, still the best reel for spinning with a very big bait, such as quite big dead fish, for big pike.

The best all-round reel for spinning is the multiplying reel. It is less difficult to acquire the skills needed to use it well than is so with the centre-pin, it will cast lighter baits (down to a third of an ounce) and cast them as far as any reel will in normal fishing (as apart from tournament casting). And, most importantly, it is a great deal more accurate than any other reel. In skilled hands it will drop a bait with great neatness in the smallest spaces at all distances.

It and the centre-pin are very different in appearance. The centre-pin is, so to speak, the typical reel shape, a simple straightforward drum revolving on its centre pin or spindle. Some proprietary versions have braking and tension adjusting devices for use with baits of different weights; but fundamentally centre-pin reels are this simple type, varying usually from three and a half to four and a half inches in diameter and compressed at least to some extent from side to side. Pressure against the running of a hooked fish is done with the finger on the smooth rim of the reel.

The multiplier is smaller, not compressed from side to side, but with an elongated spool of small diameter. This, with the feather-light weight of the spool, makes its inertia very much less than that of the centre-pin. Each turn of the handles passes through gears to give up to four turns of the spool, thus overcoming the fact that one turn of so small a diameter of spool takes up little line. On most multipliers a line guide, called a level-wind, travels transversely back and forth across the spool laying the line evenly. It is important, incidentally, that at all times, whether on the rod or off, the line should be coming straight off the spool and through the level-wind. If the line leaves the spool at an angle to pass through the level-wind, it will snarl up, shorten casts, cause tangles and overruns. So, when the reel is out of service, tie the line or loop it securely round the foot of the reel so that it shall not slip back through the level-wind on to the spool. The multiplier is used on top of the rod, with the rod rings upward; not, as is the case with the centre-pin (usually), the reel being *under* the rod with the rod rings downward. All control of the speed of running of the spool of the multiplier, as in the playing of a fish, is done by thumb pressure on the line-loaded spool.

The fixed-spool reel, that maid-of-all-work, has already been described in its association with bottom fishing; but it was to spinning that it owes its origin. Its inventor (his name was Illingworth) was, in the early part of this century, seeking a means of casting very light baits, natural minnows of no more than an inch in length. This he wanted to do because often, about July, trout rivers run low and thin, deficient in oxygen, and trout become unwilling to take an artificial fly. Then a small minnow, cast upstream and wound back at rather more than the speed of the current, will induce trout lying in the clear shallow water to take it. But how to cast that bait, so small, so light? That was Illingworth's problem, and his answer, that so efficient answer, was the fixed-spool reel. Now, in its highly developed and various forms, it is more used than any other sort of reel. It is also more abused than any other sort of reel.

Its best use in spinning is still for the lightest baits—little spinning baits, artificial or natural, for trout, for perch, for chub. There are, also, certain conditions of salmon fishing in which it is invaluable—those times when a very small and light spinning bait must be cast upstream to the fish, little baits too small to be cast by any other means. For these purposes the fixed-spool reel is very useful indeed. It is not, though, as efficient an instrument for medium spinning—that which is usually done for pike and salmon with baits that vary in weight from about a third of an ounce to an ounce. It *can* be used for such fishing, with lines with the same breaking strain as would be used for any other reel for the same purpose, say twelve pounds breaking strain; and its use (in the more elementary stages at least) is easier to learn than is that of the multiplier and still more than the centre-pin. But it is less accurate than the multiplier, and it lacks that sense of direct contact with the fish. There is *one* form of medium spinning, however, for salmon and for pike, which only the fixed-spool reel can cope with.

There are rivers, small wild overgrown ones, in for example Wales, where the twiggy tangle of alder and willow and bramble is so continuous along the bank, so little broken with gaps, that spinning by conventional means is impossible; to this problem the fixed-spool reel gives an answer. The angler works himself through the tangle with the rod held out over the river, and then with a vertical see-saw of the rod sets the bait swinging back and forth. At the outward swing of this pendulum he releases the bait, and it flies out neatly to the desired place—that anyway is what happens in reasonably skilled hands. Should a fish be hooked, a fresh-run salmon perhaps, then other and desperate problems arise until the fish is landed or lost.

What bedevils the use of the fixed-spool reel for big fish, pike and salmon, is the slipping clutch, and the belief that its real purpose is to allow the use of very fine lines. The slipping clutch, so believers say, is a sure buffer between the worst the fish will do and a breakage of the line. A dangerous belief. Just keep on winding, they say, and all will be well. So many salmon and pike are hooked on lines from three to six pounds breaking strain and are lost, going off with a spinning bait in their jaws and trailing yards of nylon. With whatever sort of reel, the line should be suited to the size and strength of the fish.

That is not the only unhappy result of misunderstanding of the slipping clutch. Many anglers, too many, having hooked a fish, start to wind and continue to wind, whether the fish is coming in or whether it is running and taking line. The handle of the reel *should not* be wound against the running of the fish. Every turn of the handle puts a kink into the line, so weakening it that it must soon break—and so snarling it that hideous tangles will spring suddenly into awful life.

## Spinning—lines

For spinning today only two lines are practical, two we have already met—nylon monofilament and braided nylon or Terylene. For fixed-spool reels monofilament is nearly universal, though a few people prefer braided line for its lack of stretch and the snug way it beds down on the spool of the reel. But monofilament has better casting properties for the reel, slipping off the spool more freely. Monofilament is also sometimes used on multiplying reels, and for those it is far less suitable than braided line. Its tendency to slight springiness (less than it used to be) is against it, and the multiplier gives no reason, as the fixed-spool reel does, for putting up with its excessive stretch. It does not sit so well on the spool, and is less suited to the thumbing technique used on the multiplier. It has another disadvantage—not only does it stretch, but, subsequently, it retracts, and the squeezing that sets up may crush the spool of a multiplier. For centre-pin reels too, braided line is greatly better than monofilament.

## Spinning—traces

In spinning, between the line and the bait a trace must be used. A spinning bait, as we know, spins; at least it wobbles and weaves even if it is one which does not truly spin. If these movements connect directly with the line, every revolution of the bait, every roll, passes a twist up the line, a kink, and kink is the bane of spinning. Kink causes tangles on the reel, makes it sieze up in what anglers call a 'bird's nest'; a bad bird's nest may be the tortured work of hours to undo. Additionally kink weakens lines so severely that they may, after a time, break at the least twitch. So a trace is used, and its function is to cancel out the spinning of the bait.

It is short, a foot to two or three feet, and at its top, where it is joined to the line, there is a swivel. At the bottom, where it attaches to the bait, there is a swivel with a means of fastening to the bait—it may be a link swivel, a snap swivel, some sort of swivel with a fastening device, a spring link or something like a safety pin. Whatever this means of attachment is, it is better that it shall be small and neat so that the body of a Devon minnow may slide over it. The duty of the swivels is to absorb the spinning of the bait. By far the most efficient

Fig. 13. Swivels: A—ordinary swivel,
B—link swivel, C—ball bearing swivel

swivel is the ball-bearing one, but because of its inescapable minimum of size it is not suited to very light spinning—for lines of two pounds breaking strain and tiny baits it is too big. The whole of an assembly of tackle must be proportionate, one part to another. Because the ball-bearing swivel is so efficient the lower end of the trace may be tied to the bait, instead of using a link swivel.

In spinning for pike the trace must be of wire because the pike is formidably armed with teeth that would cut nylon. But for other spinning, from perch to salmon, the trace can be of an appropriate strength of nylon monofilament.

In spite of its swivels, the trace alone will not guard against kink; the swivels must be aided, made to work. An anti-kink device must go on the line above the upper swivel—or so it is in a majority of spinning cases. The most usual means is an anti-kink lead, and the principle of it is that the main weight of the lead hangs below the line, thus, as it were, anchoring the swivel, compelling it into working.

In light spinning, with the fixed-spool reel and light lines and small baits, the same end is more often achieved by an anti-kink vane of perspex or celluloid.

Jardine spiral anti-kink lead

Anti-kink lead with link swivel attachment

Fig. 14

## Spinning—baits

Spinning baits are of two main kinds—natural baits, artificial baits. Natural baits are more often small dead fish than anything else; minnows, gudgeon, small dace, small roach, loaches, the tail of an eel, all serve as spinning baits and catch many fish; and in salmon fishing prawns are used. They must be mounted on a suitable tackle, or, as it is called, spinning flight. Flights fall into a few main types.

One, of which there are many variants, has a pair of vanes at the head of the bait, turned opposite ways so that they induce a spinning

Fig. 15. Straight-spin dead-bait flight

action when the bait is drawn through the water. Usually it has some sort of spear which is pushed into the mouth of the bait and down the inside of the body. On either side short lengths of wire or nylon carry treble hooks. One treble is hooked into one side of the bait, and one into the other side; then the whole is bound with fine wire for security.

That flight gives a straight spin to the bait. Another main type gives a slow rolling spin, a wobble, and is known as a wobbling flight. Its action is achieved by putting a bend into the body of the bait—how it is done the illustration shows.

A third type of flight is very simple indeed, and none the worse for that; its principle use is in pike fishing. A treble hook is fastened to a length of nylon or wire (wire in the case of pike). Eight inches or thereabouts is a suitable length, and if it is nylon a loop is made at the top; if wire, a swivel is attached. Now what is called a baiting needle must be used—a needle about five or more inches long with a divided eye. The nylon loop, or the swivel, is slipped into this divided eye, and

Fig. 16. Dead-bait wobbling flight

the needle inserted in the vent of the bait fish, from whence it is passed up the body of the bait and out of the mouth, drawing after it the nylon or the wire so that the treble hook is drawn against the vent. It is an advantage to thread a rather large bead above the hook to prevent it pulling into the vent with continual casting and retrieving.

A fishmonger's sprat so mounted, and drawn through the water, is possibly as deadly a spinning bait for pike as there is. Small roach or dace can be used, but they have not quite as attractive a flash as a

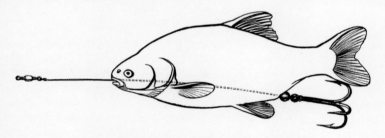

Fig. 17. Single treble dead-bait mount

sprat has—and in spinning it is flash in a bait which is very important. But roach and dace do withstand better the wear of continual casting. Of artificial baits there is a glittering and fascinating choice; but for all their diversity they fall into three main types—the Devon minnow, the spoon, the plug.

The Devon minnow is a simple streamlined rather cigar-like shape with a pair of spinning vanes at its head. It has a treble hook at its tail, and when a fish is hooked the body of the minnow (the 'shell') slides up the trace so that it shall not give the fish leverage by which to work out the hold of the hook. It may be as small as half an inch or as much as three inches; it may be all sorts of colours. Usually it is one colour on the back and another lighter colour on the belly—as a fish is, but the purpose of this division of colour is to create flash when the bait is spinning. Common colours for the back are blue, brown, green; commonest colours for the belly are gold, white, yellow. Devons are also made in plain gold and plain silver.

Devon minnows vary in weight as well as colour, weight variations for various purposes. They may be heavy so as to sink well and work deeply in heavy currents; and they may be of varying lightness up to what are called buoyant Devons. Such light Devons are useful for the fishing of shallow water; and they have another use. A heavy Devon will work deeply, as desired; but it will do so without much response to the play of the water, except in very strong currents, and so lack life.

Fig. 18. Devon minnow

They are also very liable to becoming snagged on the bottom. But if a more buoyant Devon is used, and the necessary weight put instead into the anti-kink lead above the swivel of the trace, the lead can bump along the bottom while the minnow rides a little higher in the water, relatively free from snagging and behaving in a far more lively and attractive way. Buoyant Devons are also useful in salmon fishing at that time in late spring when the water is becoming warmer and it is good tactics for the Devon to work about mid-water instead of near the bottom.

Spoons are widely, almost wildly, varied in design, though the principle of all is the same. It is that a spoon-shaped piece of metal responds to being drawn through the water (or being held against the current) by spinning. In spinning it sets up vibrations, and it flashes. So far all spoons go together; beyond that they diverge extravagantly. They do however still adhere enough to be of two main kinds—the simple spoon and the bar spoon. The simple spoon has a treble hook at one end and swivel at the other for attachment to the trace; its action is usually a rather slow rolling wobbling spin rather than a straight fast one. Such spoons, in large sizes (sometimes very large), may be very attractive to pike, and are then sometimes copper one side and silver the other, red one side and silver the other, gold and silver, all silver, all gold, all copper. The treble hook is sometimes garnished with a red tassle.

Fig. 19. Bar spoon

The bar spoon is so mounted that it spins independently round a bar which does not spin. An eye, or a swivel, at the top of the bar is attached to the trace, and at the other end the treble hook is mounted. In a majority of cases the bar is leaded—to give casting weight and so to anchor the bar that the spin of the spoon is not taken up by the bar. Theoretically at least, a leaded bar spoon does not transmit spin from the spoon to the line; in practice it is usually found that this is only partially so—at least with the more strongly spinning spoons—and an anti-kink device is still needed on the line above the swivel of the trace.

Fig. 20. Light spoon for use with
fixed-spool reel

It is more particularly in leaded spoons that there is such wide variety—and particularly in those small ones designed for use with the fixed-spool reel. Some of them, Continental ones especially, are deadly —deadly for salmon, deadly for the smaller fish that may be taken by spinning.

All spinning baits tend to be brightly attractive, but no others are so with quite the luscious abandon of plugs. Plugs, in fact, are not truly spinning baits, though their use comes within the general technique of spinning. They do not spin; they rely upon other means for the simulation of life. There are jointed plugs and unjointed plugs; there are sinking plugs and floating-diving plugs; there are shallow-working plugs and deep-working plugs; there are surface plugs. Plugs came to this country from America, and all of them have one characteristic in common: when drawn through the water or worked against the current they wriggle and flutter and weave with a very accurate imitation indeed

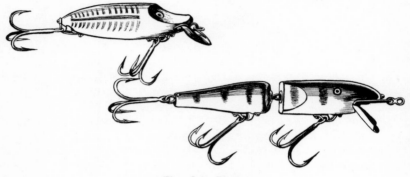

Fig. 21. Plugs

of the movements of real fish. Not only fish indeed—some imitate frogs, some swimming mice.

Their action is achieved by having facets on which the water can work, and in some cases metal diving planes at the head which induce diving as the bait is retrieved. A different action, a different wriggle, is had by the bait's being jointed or unjointed. The finish of the baits, their colour and pattern, is beguiling and inspiring. On their occasions they can be deadly, sometimes working when nothing else will work. There are various British and Continental baits which broadly can be described as plugs, and which sometimes work very well.

# CHAPTER FOUR

# Tackle for fly fishing

## Rods

IT is impossible to consider fly rods in, so to speak, a vacuum. It might be said that a fly rod has no significant being until it is partnered by the line with which it is to be used. Rod and line together are the casting engine. The reel has no more importance than as something to hold the line.

In spinning the weight of the bait and the anti-kink lead are the means of calling into action the power of the rod, setting and releasing the spring of the rod. In fly fishing it is the weight of the line which does so. Fly rods for trout, today, are shorter than those of even quite a few years ago; for the general run of trout fly fishing a rod is seldom more than eight and a half feet, often only eight feet. It may often be shorter for small streams. Its action, relatively, is an easy, lively one, and that may often be deceptive in these small contemporary rods. Frail as they often look, they have more power, more capacity for casting and for mastering strong fish, than far stronger-looking and longer rods of yesterday. Split cane is much superior to any other material for fly rods.

What is true of trout fly rods is true of salmon fly rods, with a difference only in scale and the fact that a trout rod is used single-handed and a salmon rod double-handed. Most salmon fly rods of today are from twelve to thirteen and a half feet. They used to be longer—and more tiring to use with no more effective power. Between the typical trout rod and the typical salmon rod there comes a longer more powerful single-handed fly rod, nine to ten feet, used for sea trout or, in some circumstances, salmon.

## Fly fishing—lines

Fly lines were, at one time, all made of oil-impregnated silk; and many exceedingly good lines are still so made; but many more are now made of nylon or Terylene. Lines for dry fly fishing are also made of synthetic

material which, by means of a low specific gravity, are self-floating,
without greasing; others, also synthetic, are made to sink with equal
certainty for wet fly fishing. However made, a good fly line has a
smooth and lovely finish, nice in the hands. Except for some forms of
wet fly fishing, fly lines are tapered, and they may be so in one of two
ways—double-tapered or forward-tapered. The necessity for tapering
arises from the necessity for weight in the line. The line must be thick
in diameter so that it may have the weight to work the rod, but it may
not be thick at the end near the fly because to be so would crash the
fly heavily on the water, not feather-light as it must if the fly is to
appear natural. So the line is tapered.

If it is double-tapered, the fat, or weight portion, is in the middle of
the line, and from there it is tapered to either end. Thus it may be used
either way round; and when one end becomes worn with use, the line
may be reversed. A disadvantage of the double-tapered line is that the

Fig. 22. Greatly exaggerated diagram of
the difference between forward-taper
and double-taper fly lines

benefit of the weight portion is not felt until quite a lot of line is out,
thus reducing the capacity for short casts.

In a forward-tapered line the weight portion is put well forward,
towards the front end of the line, and tapered down from there to the
end, or point. Behind the weight portion, back along the whole length
of line towards the reel, the line is, as it is called, level, which means
that it has an even diameter. The result is that in quite short casts the
weight portion is out and able to do its duty in working the rod. So it
may be said that the forward-tapered line is better for short casts,
though in middle to long casts there is little to choose between forward-
tapered and double-tapered. In long casting there tends to be a slight
advantage in the double-tapered. However, in most river fishing for
trout there is far more short casting than long casting; and it is invariably better to be at pains to approach nearer to a fish with a short
line than to remain far off with a long line, if there is a choice.

Most trout fly lines are about thirty yards long; most salmon fly lines
are about forty yards long. So, in both cases, there is a need for backing
—that is as long a length of finer but strong line as will go on the reel, to

come into use in the playing of a fish that makes long runs. It also helps to fill the reel so that each turn of the reel takes up more line—gives a faster recovery in fact. Braided nylon or Terylene makes good backing.

No doubt it is already apparent that the weight of a fly line is exceedingly important—that its weight should suit the power of the rod. Too light a line will fail to draw out the power of the rod; too heavy a line will swamp the power of the rod, make it seem weak, and casts will fall heavily on the water. Fly lines are graded in sizes, and manufacturers have, till now, designated the sizes by combinations of letters, each letter denoting a diameter in thousandths of an inch—thus A represents $\frac{65}{1000}$ inch, I represents $\frac{22}{1000}$ inch. So a line designated as HBG is precisely described as long as all lines are made of the same material. But fly fishermen more often use a rather loose method of description by which lines are known by number—No. 1 being the lightest line, and so on upwards. This has worked reasonably well. For the majority of trout rods a No. 2 or No. 3 line is suitable.

From January 1962, however, an entirely new system has come into use. The old system of letters that denoted diameters was accurate as a guide only as long as all fly lines were made of silk; and now many are not so made. Nylon, Terylene, and other synthetic materials are used. These materials have different specific gravities from silk and from each other, so diameter ceases to be significant as an indication of the weight of the line—and it is the weight of the line which determines its suitability for a rod. The new system is entirely a definition of the weight of the line.

This statement of weight is based on the working part of the line, the part that provides the weight which works the rod. This is standardized as the first thirty feet (from the front of the line), but does not include any level section of the line in front of the taper. The weight is stated in grains. Lines are numbered from one to twelve, and each number indicates a particular weight in grains, though this means in practice a range of weight on either side of the weight indicated by the number. Thus number six indicates 160 grains, but this covers a range of 152–168 grains. So, if a rod is declared as being balanced by a number six line, it means that a line weight within that range suits the rod.

Some other symbols are used to complete the identification of a line. They are as follows: L—level, DT—double taper, WF—weight forward, ST—single taper, F—floating line, S—sinking line, I—intermediate. So DT9F means double-taper 240-grain floating line, and if a rod is bought which is marked thus it is known that any number nine line preceded by that symbol will fit the rod precisely. A silk fly line known under the old system as a number two is likely to be either a number four or a number five under the new system.

Silk lines, oil dressed, should be stripped from the reel and dried after use; failure to do so may hasten what is the ultimate end of a majority

$$FT \; \# \, 9$$

Fig. 23. AFTM line weight symbol—
signifies forward-taper, size 9

of silk lines—an oncoming of tackiness which makes them unusable. There is no adequate cure. Nylon and Terylene and other synthetic lines need no drying and are free of the fate of tackiness.

## Fly fishing—reels

It has already been pointed out that the main function of a fly reel is to hold the line. Beyond that the less it obtrudes the better. Traditionally it was believed that a fly reel is suited to the rod if, when the reel is on the rod, the rod and reel together will balance across a finger an inch or two above the top of the cork butt. This suggests that there should be an optimum weight in the reel to balance the rod; it is now thought that the less a fly reel weighs the better. It is the line that should balance the rod, not the reel. But, none the less, there should be a harmony between the weights of rod and reel; too heavy a reel will kill the action of the rod. The modern tendency is to make fly reels as small as line capacity will allow, and to make them as light as possible by perforations of the face of the reel and by using light aluminium alloy. A trout fly reel is put at the bottom of the cork butt, secured by a permanently fixed mounting. A salmon fly reel, used as it is on a double-handed rod, is put near the bottom of the butt, just above where the left hand grips the rubber button on the end of the butt. Bottom fishing reels and spinning reels have what is called an optional check mechanism—that is a ratchet device which can be engaged optionally instead of the completely free running of the reel. It is so used against the running of a hooked fish, or at any time other than in actual fishing so that the reel shall not overrun and cause a tangle. In fly reels, in most cases, the check mechanism is not optional, but is permanently engaged.

## Fly fishing—casts

The nature of the cast in fly fishing is important; it must continue the tapering which runs from the weight part of the line down to the fly.

So, anyway, it is in most trout fly fishing. In salmon fishing it is less important, and many salmon fishermen use a level length of nylon monofilament cut from a spool as need arises.

For a great deal of trout fishing the cast (in America called 'leader') is three yards long; but on a windy day, particularly when much of the casting must be made into the wind, it may be better for it to be two yards. Formerly, the material universally used was silkworm gut, and it is still preferred by a decreasing minority of anglers. It had its advantages, but imposed some disadvantages. While dry it was brittle, treacherously brittle, and before fishing it was essential that it should be soaked for at least half an hour in a cast damper. Failure to soak it sufficiently meant the certain loss of a fish hooked as soon as fishing began. But gut, once soaked, had a good and resilient feel; it had backbone, and turned over nicely in a cast.

Then came nylon monofilament, and at first it made a poor showing. It did so because the first nylon casts were made to the same design as gut casts—with an even taper from thick at the top to fine at the fly. The result was floppy, lacking in backbone, useless for casting into a wind. A radical and very happily successful departure in design was made by Charles Ritz.* He designed a series of casts for all possible fishing occasions, but which had one principle in common. In his casts, instead of the even taper made by the tying of even lengths of descending diameters, the taper was made much steeper and was varied throughout the length. Thus a typical cast has first, at the top, a length of three feet seven inches of stout nylon, and this is followed by two feet eleven inches less stout, and that by two six-inch lengths of further decreased taper, followed at the bottom by twenty inches of the finest diameter. Such a cast is both precise and delicate in use. Latterly it has been found that a cast of even lengths of nylon, but much more steeply tapered than gut casts were, also works well.

Gut casts were designated in thickness as being $1\times$, $2\times$, $3\times$, and so on, $1\times$ being the thickest. $3\times$ or $4\times$ were the strengths most typically used at the point of the cast in trout fishing, and they were about three pounds and two pounds breaking strain respectively. This was a roughly convenient but not very accurate system. With nylon, diameters in thousandths of millimetres or inches are used, and the appended table will be helpful. It should be noted that the tendency is to progressive lessening of diameter for a given breaking strain.

The overcoming of the original disadvantages of nylon by Monsieur Ritz and others has left freedom to enjoy its great advantages. It does not have to be soaked, but may be tied while dry. A selection of spools of all diameters needed can be carried, and new casts tied at any time

---

* See *A Flyfisher's Life* by Charles Ritz, published by Max Reinhardt.

| Diameter | | Breaking strain |
| --- | --- | --- |
| mm. | inch | lb. |
| 0·08 | 0·003 | $\frac{1}{2}$ |
| 0·10 | 0·004 | $1\frac{1}{2}$ |
| 0·15 | 0·006 | $2\frac{1}{4}$ |
| 0·175 | 0·007 | 3 |
| 0·20 | 0·008 | 4 |
| 0·225 | 0·009 | 5 |
| 0·25 | 0·010 | 6 |
| 0·275 | 0·011 | 7 |
| 0·30 | 0·012 | 9 |
| 0·35 | 0·014 | 11 |
| 0·40 | 0·016 | 14 |
| 0·45 | 0·018 | 18 |
| 0·50 | 0·020 | 23 |

needed—or such is the case once the not very difficult tying of blood knots is learnt (see chapter on knots). Gut casts were expensive, and all lengths had to be soaked before tying if the angler tied his own from the still expensive raw material. But nylon is cheap. Gut easily rotted, and as easily kinked and split; nylon is waterproof, is much more resistant to rot, and does not kink and split.

To summarize: trout casts are commonly three yards long, but may be two yards long for casting into a wind—and it is then a further help if they are more steeply tapered. Salmon casts are commonly four yards long, and work well enough without being tapered. At the top of a cast there should be a loop for attachment to the line (see Chapter Five for the 'blood loop').

## Fly fishing—flies

Here indeed is a large subject, of which only a working outline may be given here. It is one to which, over the centuries, devoted anglers have given their meticulous attention. A trout fly is small, often tiny, but it is the final decisive factor, to be accepted or rejected by the fish. It will accept it if it has been properly presented, and therefore behaves naturally, and if its structure, colour, texture suggest that it is the natural insect upon which the fish feeds. So fascinating, so absorbing can this simulating with artificial materials become, that for many anglers who tie their own flies it becomes another passion contiguous to the main passion of fishing itself.

Trout flies, like fly fishing methods for trout, fall into two main kinds —dry flies and wet flies. A dry fly must float as well as possible; a wet fly must sink as easily as possible. This is reflected in their shape and in the materials with which they are tied. In wet fly fishing a further modification arises according to whether the fly is for downstream fishing or upstream fishing. The illustration shows typical flies of each sort.

The materials for fly dressing are silk, feather, tinsel, fur, wool, horsehair, such animal hair as that from squirrel tail and deer's tail, artificial silk, some synthetic materials such as nylon. Raffia may be used for big flies, such as mayflies. Many of the natural materials are used either dyed or undyed.

DRY FLY

DOWNSTREAM WET FLY    UPSTREAM WET FLY

Fig. 24. Typical flies

Let us look first at dry flies. The most important agent for its capacity to float well is the hackle. For a majority of flies, wet or dry, the hackle is made from a neck hackle feather of domestic poultry; those from hen birds are soft and yielding, those from cock birds (if they are not less than two years old) are glassy, springy, resilient. Dry flies, therefore, are hackled with feathers from cock birds—ones as old as possible. The illustration shows how this hackle is put on to splay out, forward as well as backward, to give the maximum floating platform for the fly. A further floating aid is given by the whisks (or tails)—though not *all* dry flies have them, because not all natural insects upon which trout feed have them.

Though floatability is not the only factor affecting the choice of materials for the bodies of dry flies, it is an important one, and if the material can be water-repelling, so much the better.

For the wet fly all is different, opposite. The hackle must be that from a hen bird, and for some flies feathers from other birds are used, soft feathers from such birds as snipe, partridge, grouse, starling, and so on. If the fly is for downstream fishing the hackle, which must be sparse, is tied to slope backwards, thus helping what is called a 'good entry'. That means a sort of streamlining which will offer the least resistance to the current. But in upstream wet fly fishing the fly will swim down with the current, and it is desirable that the hackle shall work with an appearance of life. So, though a soft sparse hackle is still used, it is so tied in that it stands out from the hook, well forward, so braced that the fibres shall not cling to the hook.

Another quality greatly to be desired in both dry flies and wet flies is at least some degree of translucency in the body—because most insect bodies seen from below, as the trout sees them, have translucency. Many furs are translucent, particularly hare's fur and seal's fur. Floss silk when wet has some translucency, so does artificial silk when wet or oiled—wet for wet flies, oiled for dry flies. Ribbing is often given to the body, with tinsel or silk or horsehair or something else, because that suggests the segmentation of the natural insect and also helps to protect the body against the very sharp teeth of trout.

So far all that has been said has assumed that artificial flies imitate natural flies; and so a great many of them do, but not all. Artificial flies may be roughly divided into those which do imitate a specific insect, into general flies and fancy flies. General flies are those which suggest living insects in a general way rather than a particular species. Typical of those (and *very* good in use) are Partridge and Orange, Gold Ribbed Hare's Ear, Tup's Indispensable.

Fancy flies, of which there is a very large (and enchanting) number, tend to be just attractive and suggestive of life in a general way. Some suggest insects, though no particular insect; some, when working in the current, suggest little fish. There are fancy dry flies and fancy wet flies; but in wet flies there is a greater range of fancy flies than in dry flies.

Many fancy wet flies are used particularly for fishing for lake trout and for sea trout; they are mostly of the sort that tends to the use of bright materials—red bodies ribbed with silver, red tags, hackles dyed in bright colours. Good ones are Mallard and Claret, Zulu, Peter Ross, Butcher, Bloody Butcher, Invicta, Teal and Silver, Teal and Orange.

Some fancy wet flies (and dry) are used a good deal on trout rivers of the fast rocky sort in which trout see something that is, in a general way, living and insectivorous and is sweeping by them and must be seized while the chance is there. Flies of this kind are those of the bumble family—Yellow Bumble, Mulberry Bumble, Orange Bumble, etc, and the palmers, Red Palmer, Soldier Palmer, etc. Both the bumbles and the palmers have a hackle which goes right down the body. The spiders

SPIDER          RED TAG

BUMBLE          PALMER

Fig. 25. Fancy flies

also come into this class—very light sparsely dressed flies with only a whisp of body and a thin straggling hackle, rather spider-like.

Before trout flies are left, wings should be mentioned. It was originally the practice to give a majority of trout flies wings made from the web of feathers from birds such as starling, coot, blackbird, and these wings were dull, opaque, reducing rather than enhancing the simulation of the translucency and fragile delicacy of the natural insect. Now the tendency is either to leave out the wings altogether, or to suggest them with bunches of hackle fibre, tufts of hair, or some such means. Wings so made *may* help the imitative purpose (they certainly do not go against it), but they also help the fly to fall softly and lightly by their parachute action, and in dry fly fishing it makes easier the seeing of the fly at long distances.

One other rather specialized kind of trout fly should be described; that is the artificial nymph, as it is known on the chalk streams. Life for trout is easy on chalk streams, those gently flowing streams, so clear, so rich in all that makes life opulent for trout. There they feed upon ever abundant flies (as well as other foods), and they can afford to scrutinize and select from what comes to them. Of the flies they take, the most important are the ephemerid or upwinged flies (to be described later), and they take them in the underwater stage of their lives as well as that

Fig. 26. Artificial nymph

later stage when they are free-flying flies. In this underwater stage they are called nymphs, and artificial nymphs are often a fairly precise attempt to imitate them. The shoulder hump that conceals the wings of the future fly is suggested, so are the rather short and stumpy tails, and the flies are tied with water-absorbent materials so that, when the fly is cast upstream above a fish seen to be taking natural nymphs, it will sink at once and come down to the fish naturally. The bodies are sometimes tied of wire for the same purpose, weight being used instead of water-absorbency.

## Salmon flies

To call them salmon 'flies' is something of a courtesy title; they are more properly what the fisherman calls 'lures'. Their relationship to trout flies is that they are tied by much the same methods and of much the same materials; and that is all. A trout, after all, is a fish to which you can offer something similar to what you judge it to be eating; but salmon do not eat in freshwater. All their eating, all their growing, is done in that part of their lives which is spent in the sea. In freshwater they fast; opinions vary as to what impels them to take a fly or a bait in freshwater at all. The theory that has the most probability—though it cannot be proved—is that memory of sea feeding induces a salmon to take something which by its appearance and action stirs that memory.

Salmon flies are divided into two main kinds—sunk flies and flies for fishing very close to the surface, sometimes called greased-line flies, sometimes low-water flies. Sunk flies, traditionally, are heavily, often gaudily dressed, bedecked with all sorts of fine and exotic feathers and tinsels and silks. Nowadays the tendency is to dress much more lightly and with an increasing use of animal hair, dyed and undyed, instead of feathers. They work the better for this change, which induces much more life and movement in them. Sunk flies, generally, are used in

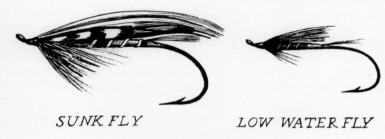

SUNK FLY          LOW WATER FLY

Fig. 27. Salmon flies

bigger sizes than greased line flies, and are intended to be worked deeply in the water when it is at its lower temperatures—though they may, up to a point, be used in smaller sizes when the water has warmed up.

Greased-line flies are light, light and sparse and spare; their bodies are short upon the shank of the hook, their wings often a wisp of hair or feather. The hooks are fine and light in the wire. Thus they must be because, fished on a floating line, they should work only just under the surface.

## Fly fishing—accessories

In dry fly fishing for trout and grayling the line must float; so it must in greased-line fishing for salmon. The normal method of achieving that is by rubbing the line with grease, and for this there are many proprietary greases, mostly based nowadays on silicones. Latterly, however, lines have been introduced with a sort of cellular construction so that they will float without the aid of grease. It is reasonable indeed to regard as obsolescent lines which are not self-floating.

In dry fly fishing the fly also must float, and again the traditional means is grease. It used to be paraffin, the medicinal kind; but proprietary fly floatants of today are based on silicones. These now are even to be had in spray cans that, at the press of a button, cover the fly with an atomized spray. But no fly floatant will withstand interminable use or the chewing of trout without losing potency. Then the fly must be washed in the river and re-greased after having been dried. The old method of drying was with a slip of a fungus called amadou; and this is not now always to be had. Fortunately it has been supplanted by toilet tissues, such as Kleenex tissues, which are indeed more efficient than amadou ever was. The damp fly is squeezed in the tissue, persuaded back to shape, and then re-greased.

In trout fishing a landing net is an essential, and it may be of various kinds. The author's favourite is that kind which has a pear-shaped wooden rim and slides on its handle from the carrying position to the active service position. Its disadvantage is that it is often impossible to fit into a suitcase, and then the kind that has a collapsible frame and a telescopic handle is better. A landing net should always be amply big.

Salmon, in most cases, are landed with a gaff, that sharp-pointed hook on a handle that is also used for the landing of pike. Those that screw into the handle are best avoided because there is a risk of the thread turning at the moment of use. A gaff that has its head strongly whipped to the shaft is better. Telescopic gaffs are also to be had, and are efficient if their reach is adequate.

On some rivers it is the rule that in spring, when kelts are still in the river, and in autumn when many salmon are ripe for spawning, a gaff may not be used because of the injury it does to a fish that may have to be returned to the water. A tailer is then the tool to use. It is a steel cable noose which is passed over the tail of the fish and snapped tight round the wrist of the tail.

Salmon and trout, when landed, have to be killed mercifully and quickly, and for this a priest is used—and that is a euphemistic name for a small handy cosh, usually lead loaded.

# CHAPTER FIVE

# Knots

To the fisherman knots are important; the best tactics, the most skilled approach, the most consummate casting, are made meaningless by a knot that slips. A slipping knot is more likely to slip against a big fish than a small fish. It is essential to master a range of knots that meet all the angler's contingencies.

There are innumerable ones that might be learnt; the devising of curious and ingeniously neat knots appeals to some minds. But there are a basic few that will cover all the needs of the angler.

The most useful of all knots is the Blood Knot—that and those other

Fig. 28. Blood knot—method of tying and
finished knot drawn tight

knots which derive from it. Nylon monofilament is extremely suscep-tible to slipping, and many knots that could be reliable enough for other materials are not so for nylon. For joining two lengths of nylon, as in the tying up of fly casts from lengths of differing diameters, or indeed for the joining of two lengths of anything else, the blood knot is unrivalled. The end of link A is taken three times* round link B, then doubled back and through the centre of the knot. The end of link B is taken three times round link A in the opposite direction, then doubled back and passed through the centre of the knot, also in the opposite direction. Now, holding down the standing lengths between little fingers and palms, draw on the two ends with forefingers and

* Three turns are enough for most materials, but with nylon monofilament it is safer to make five turns.

thumbs to draw the knot tight. Finish by tightening on the two standing lengths. The waste ends can be cut off close to the knot, though with nylon it is safer to leave ends about a sixteenth of an inch long.

Deriving from the blood knot is the Half Blood Knot, and an abundantly useful knot it is. There are various knots recommended for

Fig. 29. Half blood knot

the tying of fly cast to fly, and they have in common a gripping of the knot round the neck of the fly—something which has been held to be essential. More recent practice has shown however that the half blood knot, while being absolutely secure, loses little by not gripping the neck of the fly. For tying spinning lines to the eye of the swivel at the top of the spinning trace, for tying nylon to the swivel of a spinning bait, for many purposes, the half blood knot is admirable. Pass the nylon

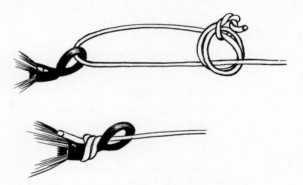

Fig. 30. Double turle knot. This is an improved version of the knot as used by R. V. Righyni

through the eye to which attachment is to be made, then bending it back take it five times round the standing length of the nylon. Now bend it back towards the eye again and pass it between the eye and the first turn round the standing length. Bend it back again, this time away from the eye, and tuck it through between the standing length and the length which has been turned back to the eye. Hold the end and draw

tight on the standing length. The knot will bed down nicely against
the eye. This method of tying the knot is the improved half blood knot,
or the tucked half blood knot. The original half blood knot lacked the
final turning back and tucking through, and was sometimes found to
be less than fully secure against slipping. The tucked version is completely secure.

Many fishermen still prefer to tie on flies with a knot which *does* grip
round the neck of the fly, and there is no doubt that such a connexion
is more firmly neat and secure. The best method is the Double Turle
Knot. Pass the nylon through the eye of the fly and make two turns
round the standing length. Then bend the standing length back and out
of the way, tucked into the palm, and pass the free end through the
double turn to make a circlet round them, and tuck the free end twice

Fig. 31. Knot for tying on eyed or
spade-end hook

through the circlet and draw tight. Now pass the double turn over the
eye of the fly and draw tight on the free end and the standing length.
Finally draw on the free end with artery forceps or something similar,
and trim off the free end fairly close to the knot. For tying a salmon fly
to the cast the double turle knot is admirable. For tying on eyed hooks
or spade-end hooks for coarse fishing a very secure and snug knot is the
one shown in Fig. 31.

In coarse fishing it is sometimes necessary to tie in something on the
line, perhaps a slip of monofilament to act as a stop for a sliding float.

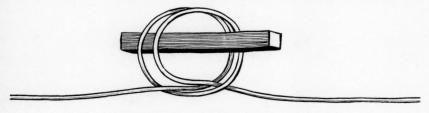

Fig. 32. Clove hitch

For such a purpose the Clove Hitch is simple to make, is reliable, and is
easy to take out without leaving a knot or kink in the line. Make two

Fig. 33. Attachment of trout fly line to cast

Fig. 34. Figure-of-eight knot for attachment
of salmon fly line to cast

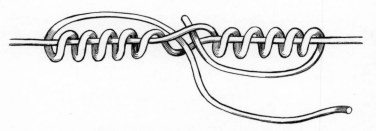

Fig. 35. Blood knot dropper link

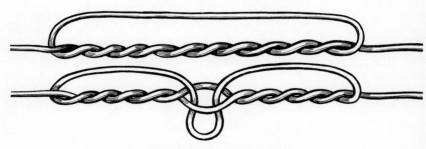

Fig. 36. Blood loop dropper knot

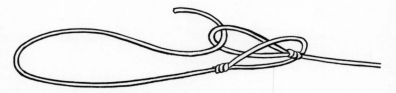

Fig. 37. Joining two loops

circles in the nylon (or line), and put them against each other in the manner shown; then put the slip through the circles and draw tight while holding the slip and holding the circles together.

The attachment of a fly line to the loop of the fly cast can be done simply but very securely. An overhand knot, which may be permanent, is put into the tip of the fly line. Then this knotted end is passed through the loop, then under the loop, then round and up and tucked through as shown. This, drawn tight, will never slip. But, to attach a salmon fly line to the loop of the cast needs something more solid for peace of mind, and the Figure of Eight Knot is reliable; some fishermen prefer it for trout fishing too. Pass the line through the cast loop from underneath, take it over the side of the loop, under the loop, over to the upper side of the loop again, pass it under itself on the upper side of the loop and then over itself, and then tuck it through as shown so that the point is pointing down the cast. In wet fly fishing dropper links may be needed on the cast—short links about three inches long at yard intervals from the point. Two is a common number. There are two good ways of making dropper links.

This way is nothing but the blood knot with one length left long, so as to give a three-inch link standing at right angles to the cast. It is, of course, necessary either to make the link while tying the cast in the first place, or to cut the cast at a knot and retie it in this way.

This is the Blood Loop Dropper Knot. Form a circle so that there is a long overlap in the side of it. Now twist this overlap till ten twists have been formed. Enlarge the centre twist so that it makes an opening, and double the opposite side of the circle through it so that a small loop is made through the opened twist. Put a pencil through the loop and draw tight on the main lengths. This will leave you with a small loop to which you can tie a dropper link with a half blood knot.

It may sometimes be necessary to join two loops. It may be done thus. Pass one loop through the other and then pass the standing length of the first loop through the second loop, and draw tight. This has a useful adaptation. In very light spinning, with the fixed-spool reel and fine nylon, it is desirable not to have a swivel attachment of the trace to the bait. One swivel at the top of the trace is all that is needed. At the bottom of the trace have a long loop, three inches long perhaps. Pass this through the eye of the swivel of the bait, then pass the bait through the loop. Then draw tight.

This short list of knots should meet virtually all the normal contingencies of fishing.

# CHAPTER SIX

# Bottom fishing

A MAJORITY of those who fish in freshwater, for whatever sort of fish, started as bottom fishermen. There could be no better start. To become a good bottom fisherman needs so close a study of the fish and its environment, so observant an understanding of the natural history of fish, that a subsequent turning to, for example, fly fishing for trout, is done with a great initial advantage. For this majority the start was, in many cases, the spellbound watching of someone else's float. To watch a float is the best of all ways of starting to fish.

It is indeed more universal than that; if the angler who has started as a bottom fisherman should turn to saltwater fishing he will find that there is no intrinsic difference; there is a difference of scale, but there, as in freshwater, consistent success comes from reading the natural history of the fish and their environment and translating that into tactics.

## Simple float fishing in still water

Let the start be in the simplest possible way, by using float tackle in still or very slowly flowing water. This is the sort of fishing that might be done in a pond, a lake, a gravel pit, a canal, or in a very slowly flowing river such as, for instance, the River Great Ouse is in summer in its broad and placid middle reaches.

## Setting up the tackle

The rod is probably eleven or twelve feet long, and it is to be hoped that it is not stiff and lifeless through all its length but the tip. For the best efficiency and pleasure it is probably the Avon rod already described. Before fitting the joints together it is as well to take some precaution against the ferrules sticking so that it becomes difficult to take the rod apart afterwards. For those who use a hair dressing containing grease, a light rub of the ferrule over the hair is enough; failing that the very lightest smear of grease should be used. Grease though should not be allowed to accumulate and become dirty. Ferrules should be thoroughly cleaned after every use of the rod. Be sure to see that the line rings of each joint are in alignment.

Now put on the reel—which may be a centre-pin or a fixed-spool reel. The most convenient place for a centre-pin is rather more than halfway down the butt, so that the right hand which holds the rod will be just above the reel and will be able to control its spinning by pressure of the little finger on the rim. A fixed-spool reel can be put where the hand grips the rod, so that the pillar is between the first and second fingers. This is convenient for control of the reel.

Thread the line through the rings now, and, though this may seem obvious, be very careful to see that no rings are missed. The rings have been so spaced on the rod as to lessen as far as may be the friction of line against ring. To miss one ring sharply increases the friction. While doing this, incidentally, have the check of the centre-pin reel engaged— if you don't the reel will overrun and give you a tangle on the drum of the reel.

Now the terminal tackle must be put on, and first put on the float. A function of the float (not its only function) is to carry the amount of split shot that is needed to take the baited hook down to the appropriate fishing depth; that is what controls the size, and therefore buoyancy, of the float. Because it is still or very slow water that is going to be fished it is likely that very little shot will be needed—perhaps one or two BB shot—there being no strong current to interfere with the sinking of the baited hook. So quite a small float can be used, probably a simple quill float. The amount of shot, and the float, are properly balanced when the float cocks into an upright position in the water with not more than an inch of the top showing above the surface—the less there is showing the greater the sensitivity of the float as an indicator of what is happening below. Sometimes, for example, with very shyly biting fish, only an eighth of an inch may be allowed to show above the surface.

The usual means of attachment of the float is by what is called a float cap and the bottom ring. The cap is a band, usually of rubber, which is slid on to the top of the float; the ring is at the bottom of the float. Cycle valve rubber, cut into pieces a sixteenth or an eighth of an inch deep, makes excellent float caps. Thread the line through the cap and then through the ring; then slide the cap down on to the top of the float, down to the point where the water's surface will be. The float is now mounted on the line, and can be slid up or down as need be. For the next stage there is a traditional way and a modern way. Formerly bottom fishing lines were of plaited silk, so a cast had to be used between the line and the hook, a cast, as it was then, of gut, or as it is now, of nylon monofilament. The cast had a loop at each end of its yard length. The line was tied to one loop, and to the other was attached a hook-to-gut—or as it would be now, a hook-to-nylon. A hook-to-nylon is a hook with a short length of nylon with a loop at its top. This was a

CAP

Fig. 38. Putting on a float

rather complicated set-up dictated by the nature of the line, and it is a sound principle that tackle should always be as simple as circumstances allow it to be. The simpler it is the less there is to go wrong with it, and the less conspicuous it is in the water.

Silk lines have gone. Almost universally they have been replaced by nylon monofilament, and that removes the need for separate cast and hook-to-nylon. The one length of the nylon of the line can serve the purpose of the former three parts. So, instead of using a hook-to-nylon, an eyed hook can be tied directly to the end of the line with a knot shown in the previous chapter (Fig. 31). Let it be, for this beginning, a size twelve hook; that is a useful all-round size. Now the two **BB** split shot must be pinched on. The lower one can be, say, twelve inches from the hook, and the other three inches higher. The arranging of shot on

Fig. 39. Mounted bottom fishing tackle

the nylon can be of very great importance in various specialized kinds of fishing, but this will do now. To pinch on the shot use the artery forceps already described. Now this first simple form of bottom fishing tackle is set up ready for use. The illustration shows it.

As we know, fish are not distributed evenly everywhere in the water; we use our judgement and knowledge to decide where they will be. Similarly they are not evenly distributed at all depths. We have to decide not only where in the water we will fish, but also at what depth. We are hoping to catch roach in this still or very slow water, and roach are more often to be caught on the bottom than higher in the water, so we decide to fish on the bottom. We must, therefore, find the depth of the water. Our means to this is the plummet. The hook is passed through the ring of the plummet, and just nicked into the cork inset in the bottom. It is guessed that the depth of the water is five feet, so the float is pushed up the nylon until the bottom end of it is five feet from the hook. Now the tackle is lowered into the swim with the line tight from plummet to rod top, and it is found that the tip of the float is underwater, about four inches. So the float is pushed up another five inches in the expectancy that this will leave an inch showing above the surface when the hook is against the bottom. It is found that this is not quite accurate; rather more than two inches of float stand above the surface. Now, then, the float is pushed down rather more than an inch, with the result that just an inch stands above the surface—what was aimed at. All is ready for fishing.

Now these fish, these roach, that it is hoped will be caught, are in this swim which is to be fished, if judgement has not been at fault; but they will be preoccupied with their own business. They will be finding such food, down there below, as they ordinarily do in the course of nature. We are going to offer them something different, and if they see just that one example of it, attached to the hook, they are not very likely to take it—or the bigger fish are not. It will be strange, and therefore suspicious; there will be only this one piece of it and therefore not likely to engage their already preoccupied attention—preoccupied with other normal food. We have to attract their attention from what they are eating, persuade them that what we offer is not unnatural and suspicious, and arouse in them an appetite for it. The means for this is groundbait.

The bait we are going to use on the hook is maggots, or as they are also known, gentles—the larval form of the bluebottle. We have to bring the fish to a stage of acceptance of maggots. To do this we must put into the water a quantity of maggots that will be enough to induce the roach to look for and eat maggots, but not to overfeed them so that they are unwilling to take any more. Additionally experience shows that for many fish the creation in the water of a murkiness is suggestive of food. Our groundbaiting for this still or very slow water is done by two means—the use of cloud groundbait and the use of maggots. Cloud groundbait may be of various materials; poultry meal (that known as layer's mash is particularly good), sausage rusk, bran, which is fair; and, too, proprietary bags of cloud bait may be bought—though this is an unnecessarily expensive way of doing it.

The cloud bait, of whatever sort, is made wet (not sloppy) and some is taken in the hand and squeezed to about the size of a pullet's egg. Into this ball a few maggots are put, put into a hole made with the thumb and then closed. The whole is tossed into the swim, and, as it sinks, it will dissolve into a milky cloud; but it will not disintegrate entirely till it reaches the bottom and there sheds the maggots—those *few* maggots. The baited tackle is introduced where the cloud has been formed. Now, as the fishing continues, this little allowance of cloud and maggots is put in often so that the water in the swim is hardly allowed to become entirely free of cloud and this scant sprinkling of maggots. Little and often is the principle of this sort of groundbaiting. It may be said, in passing, that this sort of fishing may be highly productive of the average run of roach, but it is not the most probable way of taking very big roach. But of that, more later.

We must suppose that this is a case in which the tactics work; it is a good fishing day, the fish are prepared to feed (which they are not on all days), and, presently, the tip of the float dips. It may not go right under; it may do little more than flicker, or it may stab quickly down and under. Whichever way it is the response of the angler must be to strike, so that the point of the hook may be sent home over the barb. Consider this strike. The fish that has taken the bait may weigh half a pound, it may weigh a pound; it is, anyway, quite a solid resistance. The line with which you are fishing may be two pounds breaking strain or thereabouts. If your strike is violent the nylon will break and you will lose fish and hook. Let the strike be gentle, just a quick lifting of the rod point—the force of which will be augmented by the spring of the rod. Your fish is hooked; now you have to play and land it. The principle of playing any fish, big or small, is the same. You induce the fish to tire itself, use its own strength to tire it.

Often, if not in this case, the strength of your tackle is not enough to bring the fish straight in just by hauling on it, matching it strength for strength. One ally you must use is the resilience of the rod, the action of it. That acts as a shock absorber between you and the inadequate strength of the line. To have the best benefit of the rod's action there is a particular angle at which to hold the rod. Every beginner, sooner or later, will be told by well-meaning anglers of greater experience to 'keep the rod up, keep the rod up', and this is usually meant as bringing it up more or less to the vertical. That does not use the play of the rod well, *and* in the case of a strong and heavy fish, it may do permanent damage to the rod top. Equally, to point the rod at the fish prevents the rod's spring playing its part. If the rod is held at an angle of about forty-five degrees, *that* will bring out the best aid it has to offer.

So now there is the rod bending and pulsing to the pull of the fish, and for the sake of experience we will pretend that it is a really big and heavy fish. When it pulls we do not resist the pull, refusing to let it go; we let it run against no more pressure than that provided by the check of the reel, reinforced a little by sensitive finger pressure on the rim of the drum of the reel. If the reel is a centre-pin we do it with the little finger on the reel behind the hand. If it is a fixed-spool reel we do it with the forefinger on the reel in front of the hand. Soon this first run of the fish slackens and stops, and, carefully, with readiness to give line again, we wind it back towards us. And soon, the fish does dash off again, though not as far and not as hard this time; again we let it go against carefully felt pressure. This continues for a time, and then the fish

RIGHT        WRONG              WRONG

Fig. 40. Right and wrong angles of rod for
playing a fish

becomes too tired to resist further. It rolls half over on to its side. It is ready to land. We take the landing net in the free hand. It is at this point that many a good fish has been lost. A sweep or snatch with the net will almost certainly lose the fish. The net is lowered into the water and held still; then the fish is drawn over the net, and the net is lifted. The fish is landed.

That then is float fishing in its simplest form, and, necessarily, there are variants on it. One is to present a slowly sinking bait because this may appear more natural to the fish. If maggots are still the bait, some may be thrown in loose so that they sink by their own weight. The shot used to cock the float are put only a little distance below the float, and then the maggot or maggots on the hook will also sink slowly, by their own weight.

## Float fishing by tight line

Now, we will suppose, we are going to fish a swim needing different tactics. It is in a river with a perceptible though not strong flow; it is the sort of swim that is often to be found on the Thames. There is, perhaps, a rather long declivity in the bed of the river, a sort of gravel-bottomed trench, banking up at either end. So much may be visible (though you must not show yourself in looking), use of the plummet may have revealed it, or the action of the water may show it. The swim is against the bank, and, just upstream, some crinkling of the water's surface shows that the water is relatively shallow; the same is shown downstream. But, for the length of the swim the surface is smooth, showing that there is sufficient depth of water for unevennesses of the bottom not to disturb the surface. The length of the swim is, perhaps, ten yards. Your station for fishing it is opposite the middle of it; you sit there, but are careful not to be a high and obvious silhouette against the light. You find the depth with the plummet, and, by the same means, trying with the plummet down the swim, any unevennesses of the bottom. For the fishing of this swim a rod on the long side, say twelve feet, is better than a shorter one—this is tight-line fishing, and reach is needed.

But first you must groundbait, and the groundbait needs to have a little more substance than served in still water; at least that may be so. Your bait may be bread in some form (bread baits will be discussed later), and in that case the groundbait needs to have a basis of meal, as before, but made just a little more solid by having mixed in with it stale bread which has been well soaked and then mashed down small. Such a groundbait will prepare the fish for acceptance of a bait which is bread in some form. The slightly firmer and more substantial consistency will prevent the current carrying it away without any settlement in the swim.

It is important that this groundbait shall go into the water at the right place. If it is put in within the limits of the swim the action of the current will carry it while sinking so that it comes to rest halfway down the swim or even further. That will mean that much of the upstream part of the swim will not have the effect of it. The groundbait then is tossed to enter the water upstream of the head of the swim. How far upstream is a matter for judgement—judgement of the pace of the current and the density of the groundbait. In this not-very-fast current a few feet upstream of the head of the swim is likely to be right, particularly as the swim is not deep, five feet or so, and the groundbait is squeezed into firm balls each about the size of a hen's egg. These balls of groundbait will now come to rest on the bottom just about the head of the swim, and will there disintegrate by degrees, sending down a constant trickle of fragments to engage the interest of the fish. Now the hook must be baited, and it can be done with what is often a very good bait indeed— flake. This is a pinch taken from the crumb inside a new loaf; the hook is passed through it, and it is pinched quite firmly where the shank of the hook lies inside it. Where it is pinched it will take on a paste-like consistency which will retain it on the hook; the rest will be filmy and lacy round the hook. Now we must refer to the illustration to see how the swim is fished.

This is tight-line fishing, and you will see that the angler, settled opposite the middle of the swim, uses a constant length of line—as if, in fact, all the line he has is that from the top ring of the rod to the hook; that is why it is called tight-line fishing. With an underhand lob,

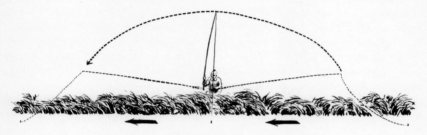

Fig. 41. Tight-line fishing

giving the rod an upward swing then down again, the baited tackle is swung out so that it enters the water at the head of the swim. The rod is now nearly level, nearly parallel with the water's surface. But, now, float and tackle have started to come down, carried by the current. The angler progressively lifts his rod and moves it round so that it maintains contact with the float, keeping a nearly tight line but not so tight as to drag on the float. The float must move only at the bidding of the current so that, as far as possible, the bait appears to be trundling down quite naturally as natural fish food does. The float has been set, after plumbing of the depth, so that the bait is just about bumping the bottom; that is exactly how much of the natural food comes, and that is where bottom feeding fish will be expecting it—and the angler's groundbait, trickling through the swim in the same way, is stimulating the fish to look for breadlike fragments coming along the bottom, bouncing and wandering among the stones of the gravel.

The angler has discovered by plumbing that there is a bit of a hump on the bed of the swim in one place, so when the tackle reaches that point he checks the float a little with his finger on the reel so that the bait rides up a little from the bottom, just enough to clear the hump. The hump being passed, the extra pressure is relaxed and the bait drops back to the bottom. It is possible that bites may come anywhere down the bait's passage of the swim; but one place does look more probable than the rest. The swim, you will see, is terminated by a banking up of the gravel, and this is likely to act as a trap for food borne on the current. Till that point the food fragments will be carried along, floated and rolled and trundled; but when the rise is reached, many of the food fragments will be caught by the gravel there. The current will shed much of what it carries. Obviously then this is a good place for fish to wait—is it not a firm principle of fish to allow the current to bring the food to them rather than to chase it?

So, when the tackle reaches the end of the swim, even if the float shows no indication of a bite, the angler strikes gently before retrieving the tackle to cast again to the top of the swim. Now he repeats all as before, lifting the rod smoothly and progressively as the float comes down until it is opposite him; then, as it goes downstream away from him towards the bottom of the swim, he lowers it again and brings it round, giving this close attendance of the rod upon the float, keeping direct contact but not pulling the float.

Perhaps, at the end of one swim down of the tackle, the precautionary strike does find a fish mouthing the bait without moving the float, and the fish is hooked. If nothing happens there though, at this promising-looking tail of the swim, a different tactic is tried. By bringing down a finger on the reel the float is held stationary there; the result is that current action induces the baited hook to ride up, wavering over the gravel slope. If there are indeed feeding fish waiting there, this may very well make one of them take the bait.

When a fish is hooked, raise the rod and turn it away from that bottom end of the swim, so as to draw the fish away from the taking place. Play it out as quietly as possible against the bank upstream, net it gently and without splash. The fish in the swim must not be alarmed. When one has been caught others may be caught steadily if nothing is done to frighten them. Put them into the keepnet that has been put into the water against the bank, with the bank stick pushed into the soil of the bank.

## Boat fishing on a river of medium pace

In this sort of river, like the Thames, with a fair flow but not a fast heavy one, a quite broad river, there are often swims out from the bank. Sometimes they are long ones, and, obviously, not fishable by the method that has just been described. They are boat swims.

One angler, alone, may fish from a boat in such a swim, but two anglers can fish as easily; and two in a boat make easier the deft and quiet handling of the boat into position. What must be done is to come quietly down to the swim from upstream, drifting down, just guiding and manipulating the boat with a paddled oar. In the boat are two long poles (on the Thames they are called ryepecks, and are iron-tipped). When the bows of the boat reach that point, just upstream of the swim, from which the fishing is to be done, one of the anglers, in the bows, pushes the pole into the river bed and ties the bows securely to it. The other angler, in the stern, coaxes the boat to swing round with the current to come broadside across the current. There he pushes the other pole into the river bed and secures the stern to it. So now there is the boat, tied to the two poles, moored broadside-on across the

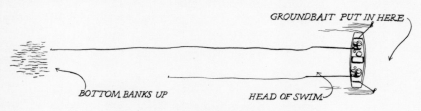

Fig. 42. Long-trotting from a boat

current. At first attempt it may be a little difficult to carry out this manœuvre without fuss and noise; but the trick is soon acquired.

The depth is plumbed and the floats set so that the hook barely clears bottom. Then trial swimmings down of the tackle are made to find, by trial and error, if the depth is even right down the swim. At one point the float may stop and then drag under with its tip pointing down-stream; that means that there is a rise in the bottom of the swim there, and that must be remembered so that the tackle may be ridden over it by holding back the float there. Probably the end of the swim will again come with a banking up of the gravel bottom.

Now the groundbait has to be put in. As the illustration shows, the boat is three yards or so above the head of the swim, so, if the ground-bait is dropped in over the upstream side of the boat, it will reach the bottom just about the head of the swim. Now the baited tackle is dropped in on the downstream side of the boat and allowed to go down with the current, just very gently and sensitively kept under control of the finger on the reel. This is called trotting the stream, or long-trotting. The tackle is trotted right down the swim until it reaches that part where the bottom banks up—and this length of trot may vary from only ten yards or so up to as much as thirty or forty yards.

At any point during its passage of the swim there may be a bite which must be responded to by a strike. Again, as in bank fishing, it is as well to strike when the tackle reaches the end of the swim just in case a fish is mouthing the bait; and the tactic of allowing the baited hook to wander over the banking up of the bottom there should also be tried.

It may be that all this produces no results, or much less result than might be expected; now is the time then to try stret-pegging. This means doing at intervals all down the swim what has been done so far only at the end of the swim. The tackle is allowed to trot a short way down the swim, then is held stationary for a few moments by finger pressure on the reel. The bait rides up from the bottom, wavers in the current, and then, as the float is allowed to continue down the swim, goes to the bottom again. So the whole length of the swim is treated—every few feet the float is stopped and the bait induced into this attractive wavering up from the bottom. That is stret-pegging, and it will often bring bites when ordinary trotting has failed.

## A variation on trotting

It is usually recommended in trotting, whether from the bank or from a boat (it may be done from either), that throughout the swim down of the tackle the reel should be just slightly retarded so that the float shall not go in advance of the bait. Instead, by this slight holding back of the float, the baited hook is made to go a little in advance of the float. Thus, it is said, the angler is more directly in touch with the hook and the fish that may take it, that he may have instant notice of a bite, and may be able to make a direct contact with the fish, and so hook it securely. So it may often be; but the criticism may be made that the bait, fished thus, goes down the swim in a rather tight unnatural way, not wavering down into hollows in the bottom or reacting in any way to all the minor undulations of the bottom as natural food does. Additionally, a fish that does take the bait, nevertheless, may in the instant feel the restraint of the line and be scared into ejecting the bait. The angler therefore has an all-too-brief time in which to strike and hook the fish. Larger fish are more likely to be made suspicious by the behaviour of the bait than smaller fish are. There is a method of overcoming this difficulty which is rather flying in the face of what is nearly universally accepted.

First look at the way float and split shot are chosen and arranged for the normal method. For long trotting in a river of moderate current the float is a rather bigger one than that used for still water because more shot have to be used to take the bait down to the bottom against the push of the current. Where one or two shot were used in still water, three or four perhaps will be used in this moderate flow. The float is correspondingly a little bigger to have the added buoyancy to carry the greater weight of shot. The most common way to use the shot is grouped quite low down the nylon, a foot to eighteen inches, it may be, from the hook. By this means the baited hook is taken to the bottom at once so that no part of the swim is unfished. That part of the nylon which is below the shot streams out along the bottom.

For this other method the float may be a little bigger, a little more

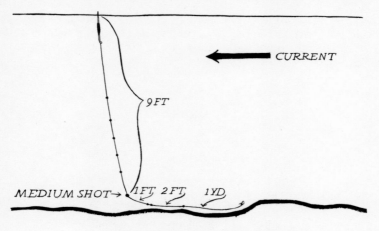

Fig. 43. The trail method

buoyant, because more shot will be needed, and the shot will be of different sizes. Let us suppose the swim is ten feet deep. A yard above the hook a very small shot is pinched on, then, two feet higher, two more of the same size are put on. A foot higher a medium-sized shot goes on, and nine feet above that is the float, with small shot spaced out between to give enough weight to cock the float with half an inch showing above the surface. So there are fifteen feet below the float for ten feet of water; but the medium shot will clear bottom, and the little shot below have very little weight. When the tackle goes down the swim the cast will drag only slightly between float and medium shot; but the rest of the cast, and the baited hook, will trail behind going just a little faster than the current, rising over snags, undulating into hollows. This will appear natural to the fish and, thus, be as attractive to bigger ones as to smaller ones. There will be no taking and rejecting of the bait because no restraint will be felt; bites will be firm and leisurely. There will be no lightning dips of the float; however gentle the bite the float will slide under quite positively.

## Long-trotting—further points

Before going on there are certain other points on long-trotting which should be gathered up. As was suggested earlier, trotting is not confined to boat fishing; it is also done from the bank. Sometimes the swim to be trotted may be close to the bank, and then the angler has no more to do than drop his tackle in and let the current take it. Sometimes too a projection or shoulder of bank may give him a point of vantage for trotting the tackle down the swim. But, quite often, the swim is out from the bank, further out than the rod will cover. In such cases the tackle must be cast.

Fig. 44. Casting with float tackle and
fixed-spool reel

If the reel used is a fixed-spool reel, casting has no difficulties. The right hand holds the rod just over the reel, which is near the top of the butt, and the left hand holds the butt near the bottom. The forefinger of the right hand goes round the line and holds it against the butt, and the pick-up of the reel is turned over to the off position. Now the rod is brought up to the vertical and taken in a semi-circular swing over the head of the angler, and the swing continued outward in the direction the cast is to be made. As the forward casting movement is made, the line is released and the tackle flies out. Very little practice is needed to find just how much casting force is needed for a given distance. If the rod is not a horridly stiff match rod, very little force is needed because the action of the rod helps. It will be found at first that there is a tendency to overcast. In the case of swims not very far out, a two-handed cast is not necessary. An underhand lob with one hand can send the tackle quite a long way.

When the tackle reaches the swim and drops into the water, the pick-up of the reel is still left in the open position so that the pull of the current draws the line off the reel at the bidding of the trotting down of the float. If a bite should come, the forefinger clamps immediately on to the edge of the spool to stop the line, the strike is made, and the pick-up engaged on to the line by a turn of the handle. All this is very easy to learn, very easy to do, but lacks the moment-to-moment cleanness and firmness of contact with and control of the tackle which a centre-pin reel gives.

But the centre-pin does demand more apprenticeship, though there is nothing of great difficulty about it. In the first place it is important that the rod shall be of a suitable type. It may be only a short one, say eleven feet, or it may be longer, say twelve feet; but it *must*, to work well, have a reasonable amount of action. It is that action which must add its spring to the free running of the reel.

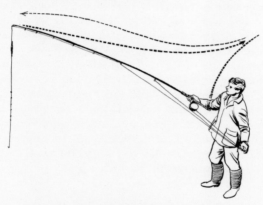

Fig. 45. Casting with float tackle and
centre-pin reel

Perhaps the swim to be fished is not very far from the bank, and in that case the free running of the reel need not be called upon. The rod is held in the right hand with the little finger against the rim of the reel, which is just behind the hand, down the butt. The tackle hangs from the rod top with the float just clear of the top ring. The reel is held station-ary by the little finger. Now enough line is drawn off the reel for a long loop, held by the left hand, to be between the reel and the butt ring. That will provide enough free line for a short cast to a swim quite near the bank. If the swim should be rather further out, another loop of line between the butt ring and the next ring above, should also be held in the left hand.

Now swing the rod back, either to left or right, according to con-venience in relation to growth on the bank, and, without pausing more than a moment, swing it out and forward in the direction to be cast. As the line swings out release the loops held in the left hand. That serves for near swims, and even further distance can be covered in the same way by taking *three* loops instead of one or two to be held in the left hand. For distances beyond that, as the line goes out and begins to pull on the rod, release finger pressure on the reel just enough to allow the reel to revolve in response to the pull of the line. *But* feel through the little finger so that the reel is not allowed to revolve too fast, faster than the line is being carried away; failure in this will cause an overrun on the reel, a tangle. As the tackle drops to enter the water increase the pressure on the reel so that its revolving stops.

Now the float will begin to go away with the current, and line must be fed out so that the float is not dragged unnaturally. With the left hand pull back a long loop of line from the reel in an outward and backward swing of the hand and arm, and let this be drawn away through the rings. Before it is all gone take another loop from the reel, timing it all the time so as not to pull on the float. Meanwhile the right little finger is in touch with the rim of the reel, just feeling it, ready to stop it at any moment. A bite may come, and then that little finger stops the reel completely at the same moment as the rod makes the strike. All this, this whole operation, undoubtedly sounds complicated and difficult; but, though it is not to be learnt in a moment, it is far less difficult than it sounds, and soon comes to be done without thought. It is certainly a much more positive and accurate way of fishing than by the use of the fixed-spool reel. It is well worth the learning.

## Laying-on

Both in still water and rivers of moderate current it sometimes happens that float fishing by the methods so far described does not give the results that the angler feels should come. Perhaps fish are being caught, but not such good fish as the water is known to hold; perhaps the water is more clear and bright than usual and the tackle looks very obvious. The feeling may come to the angler that the bait must seem too plainly suspended from an unnatural contraption. To these factors must be added that some species of fish, such as bream or tench, more often pick up their food from the mud of the bottom than take it floating with a current.

In these circumstances laying-on may often produce fish where none have so far been, or it may produce bigger fish, those bigger ones that are more attracted by a fairly substantial piece of food on the bottom than by a smaller one washing down with the current.

Think first of the still or scarcely moving water. The water is, so it has been found by plumbing, five feet deep. The float has been set so that the bait just touches bottom or is just off it. There are two shot on the nylon—one twelve inches from the hook, the other six inches higher. So then, if the float is pushed up thirteen inches, the hook, the nylon above it as far as the first shot, and the first shot itself, will lie along the bottom. Now, when the cast is made, the tackle will settle in that way with the float leaning over towards half-cock. The rod should be put in a rest after the cast has been made, and it may be a forked stick or a proprietary rod rest. If and when a fish takes, the first indication may be that the leaning of the float may become more pronounced, even to the point of lying flat. The strike may be made then or, as may often be the case with bream or tench, it may be better to wait until the float slides

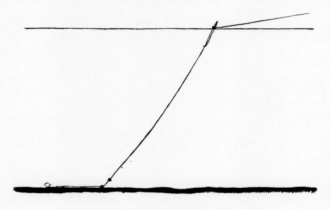

Fig. 46. Laying-on

away. As has been suggested above, it is often better to use a rather more substantial bait when laying-on. If the day or water is bright it may work to have even more of the nylon lying along the bottom, even both the shot, so that the float is leaning over rather farther than half-cock.

In the river of moderate flow laying-on will sometimes work well, though a current of any sort of strength will tend to make many bites undetectable. But in an easy current laying-on can be used, and the cast should be made down the current or down and across. By this means the line from rod top to hook can remain in a straight line, thus making it possible for bites to show on the float—it must be obvious that if this straight connexion between rod, float, and hook is lost, it becomes possible for a fish to bite without disturbing the float.

## The lift method

There is another and highly sensitive variant of laying-on which can be used in still water for fish that are found to be particularly shy; tench in quite shallow canals for example, or roach in similar circumstances, sometimes cannot be induced to take a bait firmly and decisively. It is then that this method may give an effective answer; it is what used to be called shot-leger but has, in recent years, been called the lift method. To use it is essential to be very accurate about the plumbing of the depth.

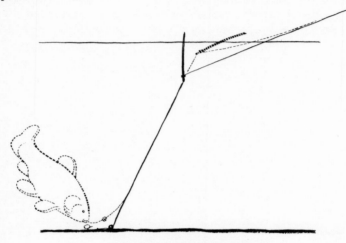

Fig. 47. The lift method

The float, which should be long and slim, such as a porcupine quill or long feather quill, is attached by the bottom only; a means is a rubber float cap, or two, at the end of the float just above the bottom ring. One large shot is used, say a BB or a swanshot, and it is pinched on to the nylon an inch (or at the most two inches) from the hook. The depth must be found accurately so that the float is cocked when the bait touches bottom. Now the float must be moved up three inches. The cast is made, the rod put in a rest, and the line just tightened. Now the inch of nylon from hook to the shot will lie on the bottom, and the nylon will slope up from the shot to the float at a slight angle with the float nicely cocked. Now, the instant that a fish picks up the bait (preferably a small one), the float will lift and lean over and the angler can strike. A very delicately precise and sensitive method this is. It can be varied as circumstances suggest; a gentle current may suggest a swanshot rather than a **BB**, or two **BB** shot close together, or even two swanshot for a slightly strong current—or sometimes, for deep water.

## Float fishing in fast water

The float fishing methods described till now have been those for waters in which there is no very heavy push of current; to attempt to take them, unchanged, to waters of strong current (as so many anglers do) is an unhappy experience. It is frustrating and unrewarding. The classic case is that of the so-called Hampshire Avon, a river of so fabulous a reputation that anglers are drawn to it with a sort of inevitability. A majority of them come from waters of an utterly different character, mostly needing the kind of techniques so far described; and a great part of that majority fail completely to come to terms with the Avon. They leave it declaring bitterly that it is greatly overrated.

But the Avon is not overrated. It is a splendid river that grows its many species of fish to great sizes; it is a river of crystalline water which flows with a very heavy current from which there are few easements. It has a very heavy weed growth; it provides very rich feeding for its fish. *But*, to one not accustomed to it, it poses a very difficult problem—to many the problem is insoluble, though there is no need for it to be so.

The first part of its problem is this staggering (to the newcomer) clarity of its water. For long distances every frond of its weed, and every stone of its bottom in the runs between the weeds, can be seen. The fish, usually, are not to be seen; they are in the weeds. The angler then has to find a means of presenting his bait to the fish without being seen himself, and, usually, this is done by fishing from far off. It is essentially water for long-trotting, often very long-trotting, thirty yards, forty yards, even seventy yards. Sometimes it may be done from a convenient shoulder of bank, sometimes from a boat, sometimes, to swims away from the bank, by long casting. More and more anglers now achieve their long casting by the use of the fixed-spool reel, which does make it easy. But though such a mode of fishing works well enough, the very smooth-running centre-pin reel is a better instrument in hands that are capable of using it; and it must be admitted that that is a far from easy skill to master.

The method of casting with loops drawn from the reel with left hand, already described, is practical for swims that are not too far away; and one very skilled in that method could use it for really long casting. But there is another cast, usually known as the Avon cast, which is better. Once mastered it gives very long fluent casts—but that mastery is hard to achieve. However, it can be achieved by practice; it is largely a matter of that smooth exact timing that practice may give. The angler stands facing the water with the rod in his right hand with the butt resting against the inside of his forearm. The reel is behind his hand with the little finger exercising control on the rim. The thumb of the left hand is hooked over the line between the reel and the butt ring; the terminal part of the tackle hangs below the rod top.

Now the rod is swung round to the left for about a quarter of a circle so that the weight of the terminal tackle swings out behind to pull on the rod. As it does so the rod is started on its forward and outward swing towards where the tackle is to be cast. At the same time as the

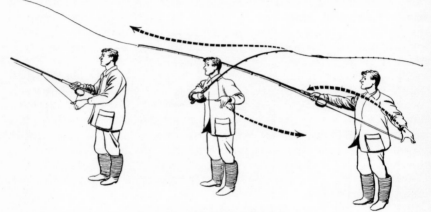

Fig. 48. Avon cast

forward swing is started, the left hand, with its thumb over the line, is swung downwards and backwards with a straight arm, thus starting the revolving of the reel against the gentle restraint of the little finger of the right hand. As the terminal tackle swings out forwards, the right little finger releases the reel so that the tackle can fly out, but still just keeping contact with the reel so that it shall not revolve faster than the line can be carried away—these centre-pin reels, let it be remembered, are *very* free running. Now the line is streaming away, and at the same time the left hand is brought swinging back towards the rod in a high arching sweep—not straight back, but with a quite high easy arch above the straight. This sweep is not a hurried one; the hand reaches the rod at just about the time that the terminal tackle is dropping to the water. The right hand little finger, meanwhile, has been increasing its restraint on the reel as the flying tackle loses speed and drops to the water. What is very important to remember in attempting this cast is that the reel will always try to revolve much faster than the line can be carried away by the cast. If it is allowed to do so the line will pile up on the reel into an impressive tangle—a 'bird's nest' as it is called. It is the right little finger that must be in command of the reel throughout the cast. It cannot be promised that this difficult cast will be learnt without some bird's nests. In making the forward swing of the rod, avoid swinging in a continuing circular movement across the front; the swing must go out in a pointing action to where the tackle has to be sent. It cannot be denied that these instructions sound rather frightening; but the learning is not nearly as formidable as it sounds.

This Avon mode of casting does depend upon the use of at least fairly heavy tackle, and that brings us to the second part of the problem of fast-water float fishing as exemplified by the Avon. This arises from the speed of the current, the sheer weight of it. As we know, a majority of the bottom-feeding fish do feed more often there, at the bottom, than elsewhere; we know it is essential to present the bait to them where they lie, close to the bottom. Light tackle cannot present the bait there.

If tackle of the kind that serves on the Thames, or the Great Ouse, or the Welland or Witham or Wensum, is used on the Avon (and too often it is), it never gets much below the surface before it has been swept down·to the end of the swim. So then, there must be enough weight of lead used to take the baited hook down to the fishing depth; because this sufficiency is vastly heavy by other standards, a vastly big float, by other standards, must be used to carry the lead. Avon floats are big fat floats. They may have to carry twenty shot.

We will suppose that the depth of the swim is seven feet; but do not set the float at seven feet from the hook. Give another eighteen inches, set the float at eight feet six inches from the hook, then concentrate the weight of lead at seven feet from the float. The shot may be bunched there, but there is another and better way based upon the fact that the more concentrated the weight is the more effective it is in getting the bait down to the fishing depth at once. At seven feet from the float, eighteen inches from the hook, have one shot with a barrel lead threaded on the nylon above it. Now, when this tackle is trotted down the swim, with just a little restraint from the finger on the rim of the reel, the lead will go just a little in advance of the float and the trail of nylon from lead to hook will wave ahead of the lead more or less parallel with the bottom. Thus it is possible to get straight down to the fishing depth *and* the bait is allowed to be responsive to the current, to have a natural seeming mobility in the play of water. The trail of nylon between lead and hook may sometimes be long, two feet or even more; but of course, the longer it is the greater its chance of becoming fouled in the weed beds.

In swims that must be cast to, far-off swims, the depth cannot be found by the use of the plummet; it must be found by trial and error. The depth must be guessed first; and, suppose the guess is seven feet, the float is set at seven feet. A cast is made and the tackle allowed to go down the swim. It may go straight down without a check of any kind; and in that case the float can be moved up a little, say two inches, and another run down the swim made. Still there is no check, and the float is put up another two inches. Now, on the next trot down, in two or three places the float checks and drags under. That shows that it is now set too high, there is too much nylon below the float. So it is set down an inch, and, this time, it goes down without a check. It is now known that the tackle is just clearing bottom.

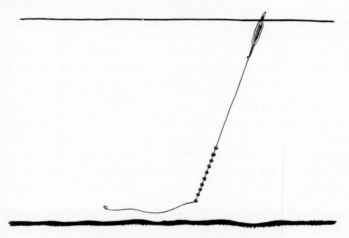

Fig. 49. Avon cast and float

When trotting tackle on rivers of less heavy flow than this the line had to be helped off the reel, fed out, by the left hand. There is no such need on the Avon. The strength of the current is quite enough to take out line with no help—and, indeed, the reel must be gently checked by the finger against the pull of the current.

In striking there is an equal difference. On the Avon the strike must often be made at great distances; there is a long length of loose line to take up and, if that line is nylon monofilament, the stretch of it has to be allowed for. The strike then must be a sweeping one, often right back over the shoulder; that imposes a further difference of tackle from what is used on slower rivers. The rod *must* be of that type described before, the Avon type, with plenty of lissome action in it to absorb the shock of a sweeping strike. The line must not be too light—it is the nature of the water that dictates the strength of tackle far more than the species of fish being angled for. For roach on a slow stream a line of two pounds breaking strain is usually ample; on the Avon a line of as much as five pounds breaking strain is more suitable for roach. A two-pound line could not really be expected to withstand such treatment—and, even if it did not break, it might not have the power to drive home a not too small hook at fifty yards. Monofilament lines are more used than anything else on the Avon, just as elsewhere; but a braided nylon or Terylene line is a great deal better. It is better for feeding off the reel, easier to manipulate, it does not stretch, it is easier to see on the water.

Those are important considerations. A skilled float fisher on the Avon is managing his float all the time, far away as it may be, and a line less slippery than monofilament is helpful. And to be able to see the line is of the greatest value. Errant currents between angler and float may put all sorts of bellyings into the line, and if they are allowed to remain even the most sweeping strike may never effectively reach the hook when a fish takes. A good float fisherman, when long-trotting, is constantly manipulating his line, mending it, as it is called—lifting the line by a movement of the rod and rolling bellies out of it as they begin to form, arranging and rearranging the line all the time so as to remain in constant contact with the float and hook. That may be done with a monofilament line; but a braided line is much more cooperative in doing it.

Groundbaiting on such water as that of the Avon is as different from all else on slower streams. Avon groundbait must be, like the tackle, heavy. It must be prepared in large quantities and made stodgy with a generous basis of stale loaves soaked till they can be mashed up completely. The water must be strained off and meal mixed in till a nearly dry puddingy consistency is reached. Balls about the size of a large orange are made up for throwing in, and, if maggots or worms or anything else not deriving from bread are to go on the hook, samples of them should go into a hole in each ball and sealed in. These balls must of course be put in well upstream of where it is needed they shall come to rest on the bottom. Several can go in at the start of fishing, and more should be put in at intervals through the fishing period.

# CHAPTER SEVEN

# Bottom fishing—legering

THE newcomer to angling, the bewitched novice, will probably take time to make his discovery of legering. At his earliest stages he will be so securely held by the spell of a float standing in the surface, so hypnotic a key to the mystery below, that he will have no attention for anything else. But by logical progression he will, sooner or later, come upon the wide scope that legering offers; then, probably, he will have a sense of revelation. The exploitation of the many forms of legering can become so absorbing that its devotees are prone almost to forget the float that lured them so deeply in earlier days. But both float and leger have their proper occasions.

Various situations make leger tackle essential. A very strong wind may make float tackle exceedingly difficult or even impossible, and then leger tackle with the rod top right against the water's surface, or even submerged, makes fishing possible. On such wide rivers as the Thames the fish sought, for example bream, may lie in deep swims in the middle of the river, and to fish with float tackle is hardly practicable; but legering serves well. Sometimes in rivers, but more often in still waters, a swim may be so deep that only a sliding float would make float fishing possible; and that is a mode of fishing to be avoided if there is a better alternative. A sliding float may have two rings, one about halfway up and one at the bottom. The line is threaded through both rings so that the float is free to slide up and down, and, at the depth at which it is desired to fish, say fifteen feet, a stop is tied in the line by a clove hitch. The best stop is a small slip of monofilament, small enough to go through the rod rings but just big enough to act as a stop against the rings of the float. Alternatively the line may be threaded through the bottom ring only of a normal float, with no use of a cap, and stopped in the same way. When the cast is made the float has slid down to rest against the shot, but, when the tackle enters the water and sinks, the float slides up the line until it is stopped by the slip of nylon. That is the method of its working, and sometimes it works perfectly well; but the behaviour of sliding floats *is* inclined to be a little unpredictable. They may sometimes be reluctant to come up the line to the surface. The same object, of presenting the bait in the right place, is much better and less troublesomely achieved by the use of leger tackle.

Often in the early part of the coarse fishing season, the second half of June and onwards through the summer, many fish, such as roach and chub and perch and dace, may live more in the very shallow or quite shallow runs between weed beds than in deeper water. In such places it is often as not hardly possible (or entirely impossible) to use float tackle. It is too difficult to manage there, and much too conspicuous. Again leger tackle makes fishing possible—and, often, very productive. Then to these cases must be added that some species are such confirmed bottom-feeders that it is more logical to offer them a bait that they can find lying on the bottom; and the bigger fish of some other species tend more to the seeking of food right on the bottom.

So look at leger tackle in its most basic form. The essential nature of it can be seen in its name—leger—so often erroneously spelt ledger. An

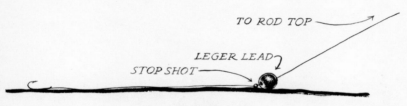

Fig. 50. Basic leger

accountant can define a ledger for you; but leger derives from the Latin *legere*—to lay out. That is what leger tackle does, basically; it is laid out along the bottom. The as-it-were copy-book leger has the hook at the end, and then at a chosen distance up the nylon, several inches, a foot, eighteen inches, what circumstances demand, there is a stop-shot pinched on to the nylon. Above this a perforated lead, say a round bullet perforated through the middle, is threaded on the nylon. The lead is free to slide up and down. The principle is that when the tackle has been cast and is lying out along the bottom, a fish takes the bait, thus drawing on the line and drawing it through the lead, which does not move. The pull passes up the line to the rod and there shows on the rod top, which is the signal to strike. That, in essence, is legering; but there are many variants to suit varying circumstances and fish. The first of them is float-leger; normal simple leger tackle is used, with a float set at more than the depth of the swim above the leger lead. So, when the cast is made and the line made tight, the float stands at half-cock.

All the variations may be separated into two main divisions—still leger and moving leger. Still leger is, naturally enough, used in still water—in gravel pits, in lakes, in reservoirs, in canals, and so on. The elementary leger described has caught a great many good fish in such waters, and will catch many more; but refinements and adaptations can be used. If the bottom is clean—not covered with a growth of weed for example, that filamentous algae known as blanket weed, flannel weed, and other names—then this simplest form of leger is effective.

But, often, the bottom *is* so covered. This weed, prone to be cursed by anglers, but indeed a good source of food for fish, lays a blanket-like cover over the bottom, a thick swaddling two or three inches deep. The elementary leger, cast on to it, sinks into it, bait, lead, all, and is there not only less likely to be found by the fish, but the whole is choked into uselessness by the cling of weed. Fortunately there are ways of overcoming the difficulty.

Fig. 51. Legering in blanket weed with
Arlesey bomb tackle

A splendid aid is a leger lead that has, since its introduction, virtually revolutionized legering, given it a virtuosity and flexibility that only float fishing had before. It is the Arlesey bomb, invented by Richard Walker. As its name implies, it is bomb-shaped, and in its head a swivel is inset (Fig. 8). It is an infinitely adaptable lead. Its streamlined shape makes it capable of being cast long distances, and in its various weights it can be used for a wide range of purposes, both in fresh water and in salt.

It provides an answer to the problem of a weedy bottom in still water. One suitable tackle may be made up thus; to the swivel in the head of the Arlesey bomb tie a foot length of nylon monofilament, and to the other end of that tie the smallest size of swivel. Through the other eye of that swivel thread the line. Tie on an eyed hook, and, two inches from it, pinch on a stop-shot between the hook and the eye of the swivel —that will act as a stop so that only two inches of nylon down to the hook is below the swivel. Now make the cast, put the rod in a rest or, better, two rests, and tighten up the line from rod top to lead. The lead will now be in the weed, with the bait, hanging on the hook from the main length, just resting on top of the weed.

The rod top may be watched for the sudden pulling down that will

Fig. 52. Swing tip

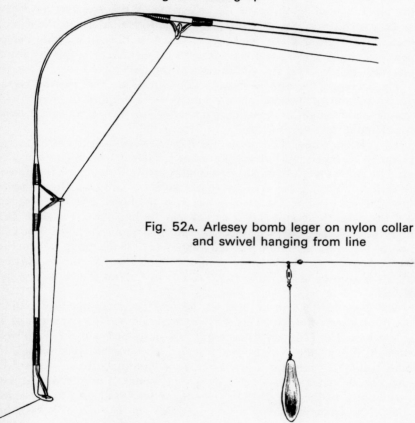

Fig. 52A. Arlesey bomb leger on nylon collar
and swivel hanging from line

reveal a bite, or another device can be used. An old and still practical one is to squeeze on to the line between butt ring and reel a small ball of paste, allowing it to hang down, pulling down the line below the straight. When the bait is taken the ball of paste will rise. In recent years a means of divining bites in legering has been introduced which is called a 'swing tip', and a remarkably sensitive one it is. Its practicability is confined to still or very slow water.

At the end of the top joint of the rod there is an extension of fibre-glass. The first part of it, about two inches, is limp; the next part, about six inches, is rigid and like a further rod tip, with an end ring and one intermediate ring. The whole thing, the top joint of the rod and the extension, is one entity, a spare top for the rod which is carried as well as the normal top. The extension, because of the limp intermediate part, hangs loosely from the top joint. The line is threaded through all the rings, including those of the extension. When the cast has been made and the rod put in a rest the line is tightened up to the extent that, though the line is straight from lead to rod, the extension hangs nearly straight down. The least touch on the bait by a fish is shown instantly on the swing tip, which rises to the pull.

The swing tip is not, perhaps, really suited to the legering tactic described above for coping with flannel weed because the line could not be made as tight as the method demands, but it is extremely efficient with simple legering.

The method, described above for flannel weed, works well with the majority of baits; but when that most excellent bait, bread crust, is used, it cannot work because crust is buoyant—it would not hang down. A different use of the Arlesey bomb gives an answer. The bomb is threaded on the line and, two inches from the hook, a shot is pinched on, and thus the bomb is free to slide on the line above the shot. The hook is baited with a piece of crust, the cast made, the rod is put in a rest or rests and the line tightened as before. Now the bomb rests in the weed, and the two inches from bomb to hook stand vertically, carried by the buoyancy of the bait, which stands just about the surface of the weed.

Still-leger tactics can be used in the moving water of rivers, and in the more slowly flowing rivers they are used in much the same way as in still water. The ordinary basic leger first described will often do well enough, though the Arlesey bomb will improve most leger tactics. In both still water and slow river water a soft muddy bottom, or a weedy one, can be defeated by attaching a short collar of monofilament, say two inches, to the eye of the swivel of the lead, and then to the other end of the collar attaching a very small swivel. Instead of having the lead itself threaded on the line and stopped by the stop shot, it is this upper swivel which is threaded on the line. The lead, then, is hanging below the line on its short nylon collar.

One of the greatest uncertainties of a beginner in legering is to judge the length that should be allowed between the stop-shot (or a swivel which is serving the same purpose) and the hook. In still or slow water about a foot could be regarded as standard; but various factors can suggest departures from the standard. Sometimes fish may be biting

Fig. 53

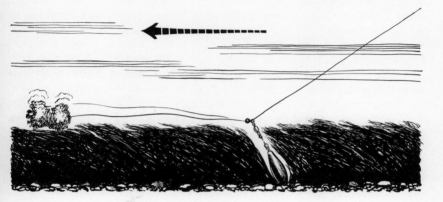

Fig. 54. This is another use for the Arlesey bomb to be used with a semi-buoyant bait such as flake, and it could be used with crust. To the swivel of the lead is a short link of nylon which has a swivel at its other end. Through the eye of the second swivel is threaded the line, and below is a stop-shot a few inches from the hook

Fig. 55. Arlesey bomb with nylon collar and swivel

shyly, taking the bait for only a moment, letting go before the message can reach the angler and allow him to strike; a shortening of the link from hook to lead will often cure the trouble. This shortening may be down to six inches or, even, to as little as an inch; the shorter the link the more immediate will be the message passed to the angler. But in a river swim with at least a moderate current it is often preferable to have a longer link between lead and hook, as much as two feet. If the bait is a light one the slight current can move it, make it waver; so it will appear more natural than one which lies inertly on the bottom.

A beginner is likely to be equally uncertain about the weight of lead to be used; one guide is that all must be proportionate—a very heavy lead is obviously disproportionate to very light tackle. But there are other considerations. When the lead is hidden in blanket weed it will not be conspicuous if it is big; and too light a lead would not anchor the tackle well. An ounce lead would do—and it has to be remembered that ordinarily the fish will not be lifting the lead as it takes the bait. The nylon slides through the lead at the pull of the fish. Suppose though that the leger tackle is being used on a clean gravel bottom in very clear water; then it may be judged that the tackle must be on the fine side. A big lead would be obtrusive and clumsy; one of a quarter of an ounce would be better.

In river fishing legering is normally done downstream and across— for the obvious reason that the current tends to prevent the tackle lying out in a straight line if the cast is made in any other way. Nevertheless this may sometimes be a disadvantage. When a fish bites, all is taut. If it is biting shyly it may respond to this tautness by dropping the bait so quickly that the angler has little chance to strike successfully.

If the river is a slow one legering upstream and across may give better results. When the cast has been made, whatever tightening up is done, there will be a slackness in the line; it will hang more or less loose. When a fish bites the line will be seen to move—it may become suddenly more slack, or it may tighten. Either way the bite is likely to be firm and leisurely and give the chance for a firmly effective strike. Fish so caught tend to be bigger than those caught by downstream fishing.

On fast flowing rivers still legering can be used; but it is less productive, and certainly less interesting, than moving leger. If still leger is used, the form already described, with the lead hanging on a collar of nylon, may often serve well. If there is a covering of silkweed (another filamentous alga) the method with a buoyant bait such as crust may do well. The bait will hover and waver over the weed seductively.

A moving leger method which can be very valuable indeed on fast rivers is that known as rolling-leger. It is an old method. Those of us who have fished for many years used to use lead wire wound round the line above a stop-shot, with as much as three feet of cast between the stop-shot and the hook. This was cast across stream and allowed to roll round with the push of the current. Sometimes the arc of roll would be a narrow one, just across a section of swim; sometimes it would be right across a wide gravelly flat over which the current ran hard. It may be imagined how greatly the Arlesey bomb has improved this mode of fishing. It has become a highly effective method of fishing the Hampshire Avon, and it may be as good in fast streamy swims on any river.

On rapid rivers good swims are often to be found running through weed beds, clean gravelly channels which may be only a foot wide. Such enticing runs (often well populated with fish in summer) may be fished with float tackle if they are not too shallow; but with moving

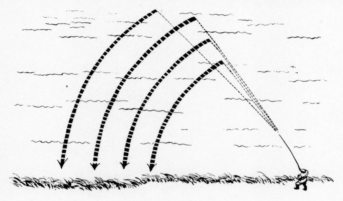

Fig. 56. Rolling leger

leger they may be far better fished. Again the lead is an Arlesey bomb, and the line is threaded directly through the eye of its swivel. The link from lead to hook should be at least fairly long because the bait must be as mobile as possible, responding to all the vagaries of current. On really fast rivers leads of half an ounce to an ounce are needed, but on less sharply flowing streams a quarter of an ounce will be found to be better.

The tackle is lobbed into the head of the swim, and the rod is lowered. While it is so held the lead will hold bottom. Leave it so for a few moments, then lift the rod top. Now the current will take the lead and trundle it down the swim. Let it go for two or three feet, and then lower the rod again so that the lead holds bottom. Going thus, work down the whole swim. A highly effective method this can be.

One more method of bottom fishing should be described, more specifically a method for perch. Perch, in summer, live much in the vicinity

of weeds; they weave through the labyrinths of weed beds seeking the
small fish that are their prey, and the many other smaller creatures that
live in the weeds. The weed beds are often dense, and it may be impossible to find a clear way through that could properly be called a swim.
Often the maximum access is small openings in the weed, small pockets
of open water.

The answer is the paternoster, as ancient a method as its name suggests. Paternosters of the past were elaborate, but those of today are
greatly simplified. To the bottom of the nylon is tied a pear-shaped lead
which has a ring in its top. Eighteen inches to two feet above the lead a

Fig. 57. Paternoster

loop is tied to project to the side, and to this is attached a hook on
about two inches of nylon. The hook, on its nylon link, stands out to the
side of the main line, and it is baited with a suitable perch bait—a worm
it may be, or a live minnow.

Now the angler works down the river (or about the lake) dropping
this paternoster into the open pockets in the weed beds, holding the
rod so that the line is straight from rod top to lead. In each place he
leaves it for a short time, two or three minutes perhaps, then goes on
to the next place. When a bite comes it will be signalled by a series of
staccato tugs, and then he will drop the rod top a little to slacken the
line. He will allow the slack line until he feels the pull become regular,
a steady pull away; then he strikes. Paternostering on a summer day can
be pleasant and, on its days, briskly productive.

# CHAPTER EIGHT

# Bottom fishing—baits

A FEW years ago the Wye River Board imposed a ban on maggots as bait for coarse fish on the Wye. Among the coarse fishermen who fish the Wye there was a great outcry; the ruling was declared to be a severe injustice. To protect the salmon, they said, they were to be deprived of their sport—and indeed the ban *was* imposed for the protection of the salmon. Many salmon parr (immature salmon in their river stage of life) were hooked on maggots and mortally injured. *But* the ban did not deprive the coarse fisherman of his sport. If he was so dependent on maggots as bait as to think his sport was ended without them it revealed that his fishing had become artificial, not really related to the natural history of the fish. He had been fishing by rule-of-thumb. Maggots are just one bait, a fair bait for the ordinary run of fish, but not a particularly good bait for big fish. And the scope of angling, its depth of interest and delight, are limited if it is restricted to the use of just one bait. Maggots are too easily got, too easily used; they can become a lazy bait, a habit.

The range of baits that can be used is great. Many an angler who has found himself without bait has been driven to experiment with what he could find by the water, and, quite often, has been surprised at what the fish would take just as freely as the more conventional baits to which he had been accustomed. The baits most constantly used are far fewer than could be used, but that is a convenience rather than a necessity. Let us look at the baits that, on their various occasions, will take fish—remembering that fish may show a fancifulness in baits. They will take this one day, that another day.

## Bread and its derivatives

Bread is the bottom fisherman's most valuable source of baits; it can be used in various forms. Of these one is *Paste*. The most generally useful paste is made from the crumb of a stale loaf. It is cut into slices, without the crust, and the slices are moistened. Then they are squeezed and pressed and amalgamated; the mass is split and moistened again, kneaded again. This is continued, never making the material wet but adding water a little at a time and kneading and kneading. In the end a soft rather glutinous paste is produced which allows the point of the hook to come through easily on striking. It is not an easy bait to keep on the hook—the hook does indeed usually need rebaiting for every cast—but it *is* a good bait for various fish. When paste is used for carp it must lie for long periods awaiting their attention, and then may be assailed by hordes of little fish which soon whittle it away. So a better paste for that purpose is made from the crumb of a new loaf; it is a stiff heavy paste which offers better resistance to little fish. By the time a carp does come to it, it will have softened enough for the hook to come through in response to the heavy strike which is used for carp.

*Crust* may often be a very good bait indeed, one for big fish. The traditional mode of preparing it is to use a stale loaf, cut the crust from it, moisten it, then leave it to be pressed under a heavily weighted board. To go on the hook it is cut into squares. Crust so used will catch fish; but it is better (or so the author has found) to use a new loaf, one which still has some rubberiness in the crust, and tear off pieces to put on the hook. From such ragged pieces fragments flake away in the water, greatly adding to its attractiveness.

*Bread cubes* are prepared by cutting a slice of bread into squares. This may be a good bait on its day, particularly as a floating bait for chub. But for other purposes *Flake* is usually far better. From a new loaf tear out a section of crust, then take from within, from the new moist crumb, a pinch. This will be flaky, soft, a little gluey. Pass the hook through it, and then, where the bend of the hook is, squeeze the flake a little. Where it is squeezed it will take on a glutinous pasty texture that will make it remain on the hook much better than might be supposed. The rest, still soft and flaky, will release little fragments in the water and, as with crust, this will be exceedingly attractive to the fish. Flake is one of the best baits.

## Worms

Worms, of various kinds, are baits of great importance to the bottom fisherman. All fish, at some time, will take worms; little fish and big fish share the taste for them. The king of them, a splendid worm for the angler's purposes, is the *Lobworm*. It is valuable whole, and just its tail is a good bait.

What anglers call the *Red worm* is as good a bait. It is small, up to about four inches in length, a bright clear red with a suggestion of iridescence on it. Old heaps of decaying leaves will often yield them plentifully; old sacks that have lain long and wetly on the ground often shelter them. A red worm will take any fish at some time or other.

The *Brandling* is also a small worm, small and red and ringed with yellow, about the same size as the red worm. It is to be found in great numbers in old manure heaps, and, as might be expected, is rather highly flavoured, exuding a yellow fluid. But it is a good bait.

The *Gilt tail* is found in much the same places as is the red worm, but is even smaller, often only about an inch long. It gets its name from what easily distinguishes it from the red worm—a yellowness on the tail. It is a very good bait for most fish, but it is undoubtedly the best of all baits for grayling.

All these worms, when first gathered, are soft and easily thrown off the hook in casting. They may be toughened by being kept for a few days in damp moss—not wet moss, just damp. The best moss is that long-fibred kind called sphagnum moss which is used by florists to keep flowers fresh in transit. Lobworms can be gathered in practical quantities by going on a lawn by night, on a not too cold night of good humidity. Go soft-footed and carry a torch, and the worms will be seen lying out with their tails still in the holes from which they have come. Sieze the worm firmly, then, not attempting to pull it out of its hole, hold on. Presently its strenuous attempts to withdraw will relax enough for it to be gathered. A store of worms for drawing upon can be built up by sinking into the ground a vessel such as a large crock or a tank, and filling it with a mixture of loamy soil, decaying leaves, grass cuttings, tea leaves. Keep it moist, and your worms will thrive. A pit filled in the same way will work too; and though there is nothing to prevent the worms escaping, the nourishment offered by the pit will keep them there. Crock or pit should be protected from frost; and it is as well to line a pit with small gauge wire netting to prevent the entry of moles—moles can wipe out a colony of worms with astonishing speed.

## Cheese

Cheeses of many kinds are good baits for several species of fish. Cheese may be used as it is made, or it may be incorporated into a paste; both make good baits. Strong cheeses such as gorgonzola, Stilton, Danish blue, appear to attract by their strength of smell; and processed cheeses prove that even they have a value for something by often being excellent bait. They have the virtue of staying on the hook well without too much hardening—cheese has a tendency to harden in water.

As good a way as any of making cheese paste is to cut bread in slices, grate cheese generously on each slice, and then go through the normal process of making paste. It has the quality of being a cheese bait which does not harden on the hook.

## Caddis

Here is a natural bait, one which fish are accustomed to take, and which they greatly like. So it is a bait which needs no groundbaiting—groundbaiting, after all, is merely doing what Nature has done already in the case of caddis—persuading the fish that the bait is good and natural. Caddis are the larvae, or underwater stage of life, of sedge flies. They live in cases of their construction, tubes made of pieces of grit, pieces of stick, pieces of weed, the mode of construction varying with the species. When the insect moves in its particular environment—in the weeds or on the bottom—its forepart, which is dark brown, emerges from the case so that the legs can be used. The case is dragged behind. The abdomen, which remains in the case, is dirty white.

**Fig. 58. Caddis, and the way of putting it
on hook**

Practical quantities for hook bait can be gathered from the bottom of clean ditches and sidestreams of rivers—anywhere indeed where there is easy access to the bottom. Trusses of weed can be sorted through and will yield plenty of caddis; and bundles of such shrubby material as gorse can be left in shallows to accumulate a population of them. They must be extracted from the case before they can be used on the hook, and the way to do it is just gently to squeeze the hind part of the case, thus inducing the grub to emerge from the front. Then a firm but gentle hold must be taken on the forepart while the squeezing of the back continues. Forceful pulling on the front will merely break the grub; it must be persuaded out. The hook should be nicked just under the skin of the abdomen, no more. Caddis can be kept alive in damp moss in a tin.

## Stewed wheat, stewed barley

These are baits that may, on their days, do very well indeed. Particularly they may sometimes take splendid bags of roach. Other fish will sometimes take them as well. The grain should be very slowly stewed in a saucepan till the outer husk splits to reveal a segment of the white interior. Too quick stewing will make them go pulpy and impossible to use on a hook. An alternative way is to half-fill a vacuum flask with the grain and then fill up with boiling water. This, left overnight, will provide grains stewed to just the right point by morning. If the flask is more than half filled with grain the expansion will burst the flask. Naturally this bait is a small one, even after stewing the grain has expanded it, and it must go on a small hook—say No. 16. The hook is nicked through the husk and out of the soft white segment of interior. Groundbaiting in all but water of heavy current is best done by throwing in a *few* of the grains at short intervals. On fast heavy water, obviously, heavy groundbait balls containing some of the grains must be used so that the groundbait may go to the bottom.

## Macaroni

This, boiled in milk till it is soft without being sloppy, is a good bait, more particularly for chub. It can be used threaded on the nylon and resting in the bend of the hook. Pieces from an inch to an inch and a half are the right size; smaller pieces can be used for groundbait.

## Potatoes

They should be boiled until soft but not crumbling, and are then a good bait for carp—if the carp have first been educated to them as food by, say, two weeks or more of groundbaiting with potato. They have a particular use in waters in which small fish attack and whittle away other softer baits put out for carp; they are proof against such attack. Small potatoes, golf ball size or a little larger, are best. The *Carp Catchers Club* found that in waters with a very soft mud bottom there was a tendency for potato bait to sink into the mud. Their ingenious answer was to use slices cut from bigger potatoes, so that, when the bait was cast, it planed down to the bottom and there rested on top of the mud.

## Wasp grubs

This, in its season, is so good a bait as almost to reconcile the sufferer to the wasp persecution that has to be endured in a good wasp year. August and September are of course the season of the bait. It is rather a troublesome bait to get and prepare, but rewards those ready to undertake the trouble. First the wasp nest, when found, must be killed.

Cyanide or one of the proprietary preparations is the means for killing, and the time for it is twilight when, at last, the wasps have ceased to plague for the day. The cyanide should be put in the entrance to the nest—and be *very* careful indeed not to get cyanide on the hands or to inhale its fumes; it can deal with humans as effectively as with wasps. By next day the wasps will be killed and the nest can be dug out—as it must be anyway if the nest is not to come alive again with the hatching of grubs in a few days.

Thereafter the grubs must be cooked in some way to toughen them for the hook—and to prevent them hatching. They may be steamed, baked, or boiled. Baking can be done in a slow oven, steaming in a vessel contained in another outer vessel holding hot water and kept simmering. To boil, put the whole nest in a saucepan and boil for five minutes. Use the soft white grubs for hook bait, and those already forming wings can go for groundbait. The whole should be dried off, preferably in the sun. Wasp grups should be only just nicked under the skin by the hook.

## Dock grubs

Here is another exceedingly good bait. To find it go among dock plants and look particularly for those showing some yellowing of the leaves. Dig them up and, with any luck, you will find among the roots these fat white grubs with mahogany heads. Nick them just under the skin.

## Other grubs

Gardening will turn up various succulent grubs, and most of them will take fish. Rotting trees often contain good fat white grubs that fish will like; they have a taste for caterpillars too. Waters below mills are good places to use meal worms which are often to be had from mills.

## Silkweed

Silkweed, in its proper place, is an exceedingly good bait for almost any kind of fish in the waters where silkweed grows. It is a filamentous alga that grows on the sills of weirs, on lock timbers and such places, where it makes a fine green silky covering, rather moss-like in look, a coating of tiny filaments. In its summer season fish eat it enthusiastically, and it is often said that it is for the tiny animal life that lives in it that fish love it. No doubt fish find these animals acceptable; but they like weed for its own sake. When it is gathered for bait it should not be left in contact with air, but should remain steadily in water if it is to retain its colour. It should be festooned on the hook by drawing the hook through it, and then trotted down those places in which it comes naturally—the runs below weirs, and indeed anywhere downstream of where it grows. Nature has done the groundbaiting. It should be remembered that it comes, in Nature, at all sorts of depths as well as close to the bottom; it may often do well fished at midwater.

## Slugs

They are always worth a trial, and sometimes do well, particularly for chub. Richard Walker, who knows as well as anyone, says they do well for carp—the black ones specially. He says that the slug should not be touched in the hooking.

## Freshwater mussels

Mussels are to be found in the shallows, on muddy bottoms. A blunt old knife can be forced between the upper and lower shells and passed round so that it severs the muscle controlling the opening and closing

Fig. 59. Freshwater mussel

of the shells. This done, the mussel can be pulled open. In the interior flesh there is a part which is tough and rather tongue-shaped; it is this which goes on the hook. The rest, cut up, can go for groundbait. A good bait at times.

## Bacon fat

A good bait for chub and barbel, sometimes for other fish.

## Sausage

Pieces of sausage, even up to half a sausage, can be a good bait for various fish. Sausage meat will do as well.

## Crayfish

On those rivers on which crayfish abound they are one of the best of all baits, and very particularly so for big chub. They can be got by putting a net on the bottom, on the gravel, and on that net a bait of fish offal, rabbit offal, meat, some such thing. To the net there is a string,

Fig. 60. Crayfish

and the string is tied to a stick which is held by one who watches. When the crayfish come on to the net, the net is lifted from the water. They may be found by an exploring hand in holes under the bank. For big chub a whole crayfish will not be too big, and claws, the tail, or the body will also make a good bait.

## Fruit

Various fruits are baits for chub rather than for other fish. Slices of banana, cherries, strawberries, or anything you like to try are capable of taking chub, and sometimes other fish.

## Elderberries

Elderberries on a small hook will sometimes take fish well in places where the fruits fall into the water in the course of Nature.

## Woodlice

They are a Kentish bait for roach, and there do well. So they might elsewhere.

## Flies, beetles

Bluebottles, various beetles, grasshoppers, any such animal, will sometimes take fish well. They are best used as surface baits, and of that more later.

## Maggots

What has already been said about maggots (or gentles) should not obscure the fact that they are a very useful bait. All fish will take maggots with varying degrees of freedom; what is chiefly against their use is the tendency for anglers to use them by habit, as if there were no alternatives. They have their occasions when they will give an answer hard to find otherwise—for example very shy tench in clear canal water. One or two maggots used by the lift method will sometimes take such tench when nothing else will. Chrysalids of maggots fished on or close to the surface can work well, particularly in bright summer weather. It is the practice of the true hardened maggot angler of the North and Midlands to use little maggots, those of the house fly, as groundbait— and in immense quantities. Squats, these little maggots are called. Maggots are a good bait, but not the best bait. Some other baits are much more likely to take big fish specimens.

CHAPTER NINE

# Spinning

WHAT is the general principle of spinning has already been described, that is the casting out and then the retrieving of a bait that imitates the natural prey of predatory fish. The fish that are to be taken by spinning, as well as by other methods, are pike, salmon, trout, sea trout, perch, chub, shad.* Perhaps the best way of further explanation of spinning is to relate it to the different kinds of tackle with which it can be done. In passing it should be noted that these methods have as good an application to sea fishing.

## With the centre-pin reel

When spinning had only one reel with which it could be done, the centre-pin reel, it was much less widely practised than it is now. The use of the centre-pin is not easy to learn, and, because of the rather sharp limitations of it, it was limited to a narrower field. The greater inertia of the spool of the reel, compared with the other two main types of spinning reel, needs a greater weight in the terminal tackle—the combined weight of bait and lead—to set the reel working. A certain minimum depth of water is needed as a result; and such tackle is too heavy and conspicuous to be used in very clear shallow water in bright conditions. Spinning with small baits, light lines, and very little lead (or none) was not possible as long as the only reel was the centre-pin.

There are still certain forms of spinning for which the centre-pin is more suited than other reels, though the majority of fishermen today manage to meet all their needs without it. There is indeed only one obvious form—spinning for big pike with a very big bait, one so heavy that it really passes beyond the true scope of the multiplying and fixed-spool reels. Big dead baits and very big spoons are such baits; for them the centre-pin and a correspondingly strong rod is the right tackle. It is relevant to point out here that up to a point the size and strength of the

* There are two shads, the allis shad and the twaite shad. Though sea fish, they run up certain rivers, notably the Wye and the Severn, from April to June, and give fine sport by spinning or bottom fishing.

104

fish determine the power of the rod, but only up to a point. What may be more directly important is the rod power needed to cast the weight of the bait being used. To cast a heavy bait may demand a much more powerful rod than is needed to cope with the fish; a much lighter rod might be perfectly capable of playing and landing the fish, but would be severely strained by casting the heavy bait.

To cast with the centre-pin, the angler stands facing the direction in which the cast is to be made. His right hand holds the butt of the rod near the top; his left hand holds the butt near the bottom. Just above the left hand is the reel, and his left forefinger is held against the inside surface of the drum of the reel. Assuming that the trace is about two and a half feet long, with the anti-kink lead just above the top of the trace, there will be three to three and a half feet of the terminal tackle hanging from the rod top. The rod is held pointing out in front above the horizontal position. Now the angler starts to swing the rod round to the right and to the rear in rather more than a quarter circle—say two-thirds. This movement is a sort of shallow scoop, starting high, going down into the scoop and finishing high to the rear. It is done with a springing movement towards the end so that the weight of the terminal tackle, flying back, pulls hard at the rod top, setting the spring of it. At the culmination of the back swing there is just a moment's pause to allow for this pulling back of the weight, and the forward swing is started, in the same shallow scoop as the backward swing. The forward swing too culminates in a springing of the rod, made straight out, not continuing the circular motion across the body. This final springing of the rod is given its fullest effect at the end of the forward swing by pulling in with the left hand and punching out with the right hand.

As the tackle starts to swing out and pull on the rod, the left fore-finger releases its pressure on the inside surface of the drum of the reel so that the tackle can fly out into the cast. The finger still keeps contact with the reel, just sensitively controlling it so that its revolutions are slowed just a little. Without such restraint on the reel, the drum would spin more quickly than the line is flying out. The result would be a bird's nest on the reel—*some* bird's nests are bound to occur in learning. As the terminal tackle begins to drop, the pressure must be increased because the line is now going out less quickly. Just as the terminal tackle reaches the water, the finger must stop the reel altogether.

Now, the bait being in the water, it must be wound back; but first it must be allowed to sink to the appropriate depth. That is dependent, obviously, on the depth of the water being fished; but the conditions under which this method is used mean that the bait should be at least fairly near the bottom. The retrieve should be made slowly.

Fig. 61. Casting with centre-pin reel for heavy spinning

## With the multiplying reel

The other two main ways of spinning are with the multiplying reel and with the fixed-spool reel. To have the best that both reels can give, the multiplier should be used for what may be called medium spinning (as against the heavy spinning done with the centre-pin), and the fixed-spool should be used for light spinning. Both terms are very variable in meaning, but are reasonable general definitions. The fixed-spool reel is used by many anglers for *all* spinning; but though this saves the cost of one reel, much else is lost. If you can afford only one reel, then let it be a fixed-spool with two spools—one for a heavier line and one for a lighter line. On modern fixed-spool reels spools are easily and quickly changed.

The range of weight of bait which is practical with the multiplying reel is a third of an ounce up to, say, an ounce and a half (this is in freshwater—saltwater multipliers have a much higher weight range). The range of line strengths for the multiplier, with those bait weights, can be regarded as being from eight or nine pounds breaking strain up to eighteen pounds breaking strain.

The range of bait weight for the fixed-spool reel takes over when baits become too light for the multiplier; this is not because the fixed-spool will not cast heavier weights—it will do so with appropriate increases in line strength. It is simply that at this point the advantages of the multiplier have to be lost. Spinning for pike and salmon more often demands the multiplier than the fixed-spool, but spinning with small baits for perch, trout, chub, sea trout, shad, needs the fixed-spool. How the spinning is done for these fish will emerge later, but at this stage some general help on spinning should be given.

Casting with the multiplier is not difficult to learn. The reel is put on the upper side of the butt of the rod—that means that the rod rings will be uppermost, not under the rod—and it is put near the top of the butt. Something like a yard of the terminal tackle hangs from the rod top. The left hand holds the bottom of the butt; the right hand holds the butt immediately under the reel, and the thumb presses on the actual line-filled spool. Now the right hand turns over so that the back of the hand is uppermost and so too are the handles of the reel.

Now all is ready to start to cast, and the first cast to master, the parent of all casting with the multiplier, is the overhead cast. The angler stands facing the direction in which the cast is to be made with the rod pointing out in front at a slightly upward angle. Now the rod is swung back in a movement that accelerates into a sharp springing of the rod top. The means of achieving this vital spring is by punching out with the

Fig. 62. The overhead cast with the multiplier and double-handed rod

left hand and pulling back with the right hand. It should be done fairly gently at first, until some sense of the timing comes. At the culmination of this overhead back stroke the terminal tackle will fly back and tug at the rod top. Now there should be just a moment's pause to allow that backward weight pull to bend the rod, to set the spring.

Then the forward stroke should begin, like the back stroke accelerating into a well-sprung snap-forward of the rod top—as if you were trying to flip a ball of clay off the rod top. Again the means is the use of the two hands; now the right hand punches forward and the left hand pulls in. As the tackle begins to pull forward on the rod, the right thumb releases its pressure on the spool so that the tackle can fly out, stripping out the line from the reel. *Some* touch should still be kept on the spool because, as with the centre-pin, the spool will otherwise revolve more quickly than the line can be carried away by the bait. And, again, as the bait's speed lessens and it begins to drop, increase thumb pressure till, just as the bait is about a foot above the water, the thumb stops the spool altogether.

Multiplying reels have a tension-setting knob which can be adjusted to different weights of bait, and at first this will help in avoiding overruns. Set it so that, with the rod held out horizontally in front with the bait hanging, the bait *just* drops, quite slowly, by its own weight without the thumb touching the spool. When mastery of the reel is achieved the tension knob can be left at zero so that, without its drag, longer casts can be made.

The point in the forward cast at which the thumb releases the spool is important. Beginners invariably leave it too late so that the bait, instead of going out in a high arc, slaps into the water not far in front. The point of release should be high, pretty well above the head—as the Americans say of it, 'aim at the moon'. Another point of importance is the use of thumbing when casting into a wind. The wind slows down the flight of the bait, but not the speed of the spool. Therefore, unless more thumbing is done on the spool, there will be a formidable overrun.

That then is the overhead cast with the multiplier. When it has been mastered variations come naturally, and of those the most often useful is what the Americans call the 'side swipe'. It is made to the right side of the angler, at about forty-five degrees above the horizontal, round the right shoulder. Underhand flips and backhand casts sometimes have their uses in confined places. But, with all these casts, the vigorous springing of the rod top at the end of the back cast, and again at the end of the forward cast, is all-important. It is that that gives distance, and the means for doing it is the punching out and pulling in of the two hands—on the backward cast pulling with the right hand and punching with the left, on the forward cast pulling with the left and punching with the right. With experience great accuracy can be achieved with the multiplier; the bait can be dropped to the square foot under the opposite bank. That is the multiplier's great advantage over the centre-pin and the fixed-spool. It is often claimed for the fixed-spool that it will cast further than the multiplier; but, in practical fishing (as apart from tournament casting) and within the range of bait weight that suits the multiplier, it will, in good hands, outcast the fixed-spool.

## With the fixed-spool reel

But there are many spinning occasions when baits must be used that are lighter than can be cast with the multiplier. This is the undisputed kingdom of the fixed-spool reel. Baits weighing from a third of an ounce downwards must have the reel's special ability if they are to be cast. Small Devon minnows, little spoons, natural minnows—these are baits that are used for perch, chub, trout (on some very specialized occasions), sea trout, salmon in some cases, shad—and for them the fixed-spool is essential. Lines of breaking strains from six or seven pounds downwards fit this range.

To learn to cast sufficiently well with the fixed-spool reel for ordinary day-to-day purposes is not difficult; most people would learn enough to start actual fishing with half-an-hour's practice. There are more advanced uses of the reel which are not as easily learnt, but the beginner will discover those with experience. Sometimes a short rod, seven feet usually, is used—this is for single-handed casting—sometimes a long rod, nine to ten feet, is used; that is for double-handed casting.

For the lighter kinds of fixed-spool spinning the short rod is generally used; and, sometimes, for heavier fixed-spool spinning on heavily bushed banks on which there is not room to use a longer rod. Again the overhead cast can conveniently be looked upon as the parent cast— though there is a very flexible range of casting techniques. So start facing the point to which the bait has to be cast with the rod pointing in that direction, and with the terminal tackle hanging two to three feet from the rod top. Disengage the bale arm which winds the line on the reel, and hold the line against the butt of the rod with the right forefinger. The pillar of the reel will be between the first and second fingers, or the second and third fingers, according to which is the more comfortable. Now bring the rod up and back overhead in an accelerating swing which culminates in a back springing of the rod, as with the multiplier. Again there must be that moment's pause which allows the weight of the bait to set up its backward pull to flex the rod. Now cut forward with the rod, accelerating into a forward springing of the rod top (as if flipping a ball of clay off the end). At a point overhead, not too far forward, release the line from the forefinger, and in this remember that a high trajectory is needed if the bait is not to hit the water a little way out. As the bait reaches the water, one turn of the handle of the reel will make the bale arm fling over and engage the line so that it may be wound in. That is the overhead cast.

A side cast is often useful, and it will be found that only quite a short swing back is necessary—indeed, in many places where growth presses closely, a mere outward flip of the rod top will be enough to send the bait flying out in quite a long cast. So freely does the line leave the spool that casts can be made from all sorts of tight places in which there is room for only the smallest rod movement. So it may be sometimes on small salmon streams in unfashionable places, and there the growth of alder may be almost unbrokenly continuous along the banks. Then there may be room only to poke the rod through between the boughs, with no room at all for lateral or upward swing. But, with the rod poked through, the bait can be set to swing back and forth, pendulum fashion, and then on the outward swing the line can be released and the bait will sail out.

As for the techniques of spinning itself, the retrieving of the bait after the cast has been made, the chief danger is that of settling into a monotonous mechanical way of fishing. These modern reels make the casting of the bait so easy that there is a tendency to cast, retrieve, cast, retrieve, with little thought of the behaviour of the bait under the surface. To fish so catches fewer fish, smaller fish (on average), and it can become boring. The bait should, so to speak, be seen (as in the mind's eye) all the time; all the time it should be remembered that the object sought is to persuade the quarry that this bait is a small fish, and possibly a slightly injured one, that it is trying to avoid being caught. Such real little fish do not swim evenly and quickly from one point to another and quite distant one. They pause, they swerve, they rise in the water and sink in the water, they hesitate and make sudden little spurts. That is the way the spinning bait, in most cases, should behave—the exceptions will emerge later, when dealing with specific fish.

So, in all circumstances that allow it, the bait should be allowed to sink to the appropriate depth and then be wound back at a varied pace. It may be brought slowly for a little while, then given a sudden brief spurt; the rod can be swung to one side or the other to make the bait swerve. Winding may stop entirely for a few moments so that the bait sinks, and then winding can restart with a sudden little panic dash. Sometimes a fish—a pike, a perch, whatever it may be—may be seen to be following the bait; it can often be induced to take by a sudden frightened spurt by the bait. Spinning can be a delightful form of fishing; it can also be a dully repetitive one.

# CHAPTER TEN

# Fly fishing—the dry fly

IT has been established, in an earlier part of this book, that the starting point of fly fishing is the fact that various species of fish feed upon natural flies in the progressive stages of their life history. It was pointed out that there are varyingly wide departures from the strictest adherence to this entomological basis, even to the point where artificial flies do not suggest natural insects at all, but are more suggestive of, for example, small fish. But the central principle remains—that the basis

Fig. 63. Typical ephemerid fly—the
medium olive, and this is the dun

of fly fishing is the fish's interest in natural flies. It is obvious then that schools of fishing that base themselves to any extent on entomology should be founded on a knowledge of the natural history of those flies that fish are likely to see and eat at all consistently. This explanation of fly fishing then should start with the flies.

There is one family of flies that exceeds all others in importance to the fly fisher; this is the upwinged flies, the *Ephemeridae* as they are called. On chalk streams, those that rise from underground springs fed

by rain which has seeped down through the chalk, and on many limestone streams similarly fed, the hatches of ephemerids may be copious
and constant. To have at least a broad recognition of the various
members of the family, and to be able to imitate them with the appropriate artificial fly, is necessary for anything like large success. The
illustration shows a typical ephemerid. The wings, it will be seen, fold
vertically over the back; there is an elegantly upturned body, and there
may be two or three tails according to species.

The start of the life cycle of an ephemerid fly is the egg, which
hatches under water. From it comes the larva which presently grows
and becomes what is known to the angler as a nymph. All the growth
that the insect makes is made during its nymphal life. With most

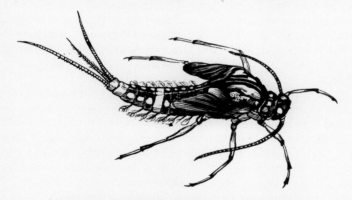

Fig. 64. Typical nymph—this is the nymph
of the medium olive

ephemerids the nymphal period lasts a year; but for the Mayfly, the
great and splendid Mayfly, it lasts two years. The nymphs of some
species live in weeds, some live in silt, some live among stones. Fish
eat nymphs avidly; anglers, therefore, study and imitate nymphs. A
typical nymph is shown in the illustration. The hump on the shoulders
of the nymph conceals the wings of the mature fly that will emerge
later. The tails of the nymph, it may be seen, are stumpy and three in
number.

In its due course the nymphal life ends; the nymph drifts to the
surface and splits at the shoulders. There, floating in the surface, the
next stage of life drags itself out of the nymphal shuck, and for a little
time floats down the current drying and stretching its wings—for now, at
last, it is a fly. It is a slightly downy dull fly; its wings are semi-opaque,
its colour subdued. As it floats thus, drying itself, it may be eaten by a

fish—the more so because nymphs hatch not singly but in numbers together, and this event is called by anglers a 'hatch'. The resultant concerted feeding of the fish upon the flies is called a 'rise'. This fly the fish are taking is called by anglers a 'dun'; and they, of course, must imitate the dun with the artificial fly.

Though so many duns meet so early an end to their aerial life, many more survive. Presently they flutter uncertainly from the water's surface and seek a resting place—under a leaf, in the grasses, on a fence. There they await their final metamorphosis, that one which will bring full maturity, enable them to breed. The wait may be short, a few hours in warmer weather, even a few days in colder weather; but finally it comes. The insect splits again and from the shuck comes that which the angler calls the 'spinner'—and a beautiful delicate and altogether perfect small creature it is. Its wings are glassy and iridescent; there is a translucency in the tender texture of its body. Its tails are longer now, and they bear a polish. The colour is delicate and lovely, pale at first but darkening with exposure. Life for the fly is nearly finished. There is nothing for it now but to breed.

The males perform a nuptial dance; in clouds they hang in the air, rising and sinking in the dance. As they dance there comes presently a female, and a male detaches from the dance, seizes the female and there in the air they mate. Now the female must go to the water, and she makes her way upstream to lay her eggs. Some species go thus, dipping to the surface dropping eggs there. Other species crawl down a post, reeds, such things, and lay their eggs underwater. Now the cycle is complete. The female spinner becomes a 'spent spinner' often called more. shortly 'spent'. She declines weakly upon the surface, wings outspread, and dies. Again now many are taken by fish, and the angler, therefore, imitates the spinner, and, particularly, the spent spinner.

That is the life history of ephemerid flies; now there should be given some key to the recognition of the members of the family.

## Large Dark Olive

When the season opens for trout in March (on many western and northern rivers), the fly most likely to be seen is the Large Dark Olive. It is about three-eighths of an inch long, and the dun, seen on the water, appears to be a rather dark slaty grey. Looked at more closely it is found to have rather dark dun-coloured wings, and a body which is leaden-coloured slightly verging to olive. Its spinner (the female, for it is a she who returns to the water) has a red-brown dead-leaf-coloured body with glassy wings which are colourless apart from the sparkle of their iridescence. This fly has two tails. Though it is known so specially as a fly of the season's opening, it can appear again in September. The Large Dark Olive dun can be imitated with Blue Dun, Blue Quill, Greenwell's Glory, Gold Ribbed Hare's Ear, Rough Olive. On northern rivers a justly esteemed wet fly is Waterhen Bloa. The spinner is well imitated by Pheasant Tail, Red Spinner, Lunn's Particular. Various imitations of the nymph, tied to imitate the shape of the insect, can be bought. A wet hackle Greenwell's Glory is a good imitation. It is worth comment, in passing, that many fly fishermen, who see the river only during the trout season, suppose that these flies now being described are creatures only of the spring, summer, and early autumn months. Such is not the case. In the depth of winter quite good hatches of, for example, the Large Dark Olive occur. There is some sort of hatch of fly right through the winter of good fly rivers.

## Medium Olive

Here is a fly that is very like the previous one, and is related. Though it is really about the same size, on the water it *appears* smaller—smaller, lighter in colour, slimmer. The Large Dark Olive dun looks a big dark lead-coloured fly when seen on the water; the Medium Olive looks much more yellowish olive, slighter. It has two tails. Its spinner too is a red spinner, red-brown in body. The Medium Olive usually becomes frequent on the water in April, and then continues throughout the trout season—and grayling will still be feeding on it in autumn. As the season advances olives tend to become smaller and lighter.

To imitate the nymph there are various patterns tied in nymph shape, and again a hackled wet Greenwell's Glory does well for the nymph. Tup's Indispensable tied as a wet fly is also a good nymph imitation. For the dun Gold Ribbed Hare's Ear is as good an imitation as any, and better than most. Other good flies are Olive Quill, Greenwell's Glory, and various patterns sold under the name of Olive. Again Waterhen Bloa is a good wet fly. For the spinner use Red Spinner, Pheasant Tail.

## Pale Watery

This is another of the generally olive flies; it begins to be seen during May, and then continues. It is small, only a quarter of an inch long, pale, fragile-looking, a very light yellow-olive that is more pale yellow than anything, but with pale grey wings. It is well named Pale Watery. It has two tails. The spinner is very delicate, very beautiful, an exquisite insect. The latter segments of its body are rich dark orange, the forward ones translucent. Its eyes are red or orange, its wings glassy and iridescent. A Ginger Quill or a Tup's Indispensable or a Lunn's Yellow Boy suggests the dun; a Pheasant Tail or Lunn's Particular suggests the spinner. All these flies should be on small hooks, size 00. For the nymph a little wet Tup's Indispensable or a nymph pattern named as Pale Watery are worth trying.

## Blue Winged Olive

Here is a fly of high summer, of June evenings and onwards. It may sometimes be seen by day, on some rivers, but it is typically a fly of evening, and particularly late evening. At this time, when the sun is down and the light gets less, trout often take it feverishly, slashing at it with a sort of double breaking of the surface, two rings merging, a figure of eight. The dun is a handsome fly, tall, looking bigger than it really is because its folded wings are so tall, so dark, so noticeable. Its true size is about that of the Medium Olive, about three-eighths of an inch. The body is green-olive—quite a bright colour compared with other ephemerids—and its tall wings are rather dark, a rather indigo blue. It has *three* tails. The spinner has a sherry-coloured body, and is indeed called the Sherry Spinner.

Various dressings to imitate the nymph may be bought, but for a wet fly to suggest the nymph about to hatch probably nothing is better (or perhaps even as good) as the dressing of William Law, recorded by Captain T. B. Thomas. It has a body of green wool ribbed with gold wire, and the hackle and tails are grey-blue hen hackle. Successful imitation of the dun was, at one time, apparently unattainable. Then it was discovered by the late G. E. M. Skues that an Orange Quill would be accepted by the trout, and so it has continued to be found ever since. Captain T. B. Thomas gives a pattern of his own for the Usk, and which will work on other rivers of the rocky type, which has a body of green wool, gold ribbed, hackle and tails of ginger cock, and a wing of light starling. Pheasant Tail does well for the spinner.

## Iron Blue

Here is a fly that trout prefer to all others. Its bulk cannot be the reason because it is tiny, the same size as the Pale Watery, a quarter of an inch; but if only a few Iron Blues are on the water in a multitude of other flies, the trout will pick out the Iron Blues. It is said to be a fly of the beginning and end of the season, of April and September; but it hatches well in May and often at other times too. Its name describes it well; it's a generally inky blue all over, with a suggestion of purple on the body. It has two tails.

Nymph patterns going under the name of Iron Blue usually do well, and Snipe and Purple does well as a wet fly. For the dun there are various patterns sold, and mostly they work well. The female spinner—and that is the one that returns to the water, not the male—has a dark red-brown body and clear wings. Pheasant Tail and Houghton Ruby serve well. All flies to imitate the Iron Blue must, of course, be on small hooks, size 00.

## March Brown

An early fly this one, usually late March and early April, and unmistakable when it comes. It is a fly of the faster rocky rivers, and does not occur on the chalk streams and those limestone streams which resemble the chalk streams. It is a big fly, about three-quarters of an inch long, with two tails; its name describes it well. The wings are veined and chequered with brown and the body is generally brown.

When the March Brown hatches it produces greedy rises—but they, these rises, are too often brief (that is a characteristic of early spring rises to any fly); the angler must make the most of them while they last. A good March Brown rise is something not easily forgotten; if the hatch is dense, as it may be on a good occasion, trout will rise frantically all over the river.

Various patterns of the nymph can be bought, and one that has a rabbit's fur body ribbed with gold, and a partridge hackle, will do well. There are many dressings to imitate the dun and going under the name March Brown. The spinner, so nicely named the Great Red Spinner, is of no real practical interest to the angler.

## The Mayfly

Here now is the king of the ephemerids, the great and splendid Mayfly itself. It is huge; the female, which is larger than the male, is fully an inch long; it has three tails. The wings of the dun are mottled with green-brown and so is the body; the prevailing colour of the fly is dull olive green. The spinner is a luscious and lovely fly, very black and white. The body is milky white marked with black; the wings are iridescent and marked with black—those of the male so heavily that they appear black at a distance. The tails are long and of dully polished black. The coming of the Mayfly, each year, has the sense of an event, a festival.

The time of its coming varies from river to river, lake to lake (it is a fly of great importance on the big Irish lakes); and it varies even on different parts of the same river. On the Kennet, a great Mayfly river, the lower river has its Mayfly well in advance of the upper river. But the whole span of the Mayfly season, on all waters, is within that period from the middle of May to the middle of June. When it does come, for the two to three weeks of its season, it rouses in the trout a steady gluttony that comes at no other time. The biggest trout, not seen at other times, now come to the surface to feed like the rest. This is the time for epic captures.

There is a wide choice of nymph patterns to be bought, and they mostly work well, and a wider choice of patterns for dun and spinner— the choice indeed is vast. Artificial Mayflies used to. be monstrous things with big fanlike wings, but those of today are sparser and kill better. Most of the patterns for the dun will take fish, but the biggest trout are usually better to be taken by a pattern that suggests the nymph just hatching into the dun. A pattern that is tied by the author has a body of olive silk over which is wound white horsehair ribbed with black horsehair (the olive just shows through the translucency of the horsehair, tinting it). The wings are a tuft of squirrel tail dyed yellow, and there is a ginger hackle and a badger hackle. The tails are three strands of black horsehair. The wing tuft is tied in to lean forward over the eye of the hook. This pattern has had great success. Patterns for the spinner usually have the wings tied 'spent'—spread flat on either side as the wings of the natural fly are at the spent stage.

Those are the main ephemerids that concern the fly fisher; there are other and not very important ones, but the angler who is prepared to imitate those that have been described will be well enough prepared for almost any occasion that ephemerids are on the water. Now the other principal flies of importance to the fly fisherman must be described.

## Sedge Flies

After the ephemerids, the sedge flies much exceed in importance any other group of flies. They are primarily flies of the evening, and particularly late evening, from May onwards. They will often come on just before twilight and still provide a means of taking fish when it has become too dark to see a fly. To fish then, at late evening, with a sedge, can be wildly exciting and often the nearest approach to a certainty in trout fishing. That is not the only time that a sedge will take fish; a few sedges hatch during the day, and it may be for that reason or not, but at the most apparently hopeless times an artificial sedge will often take trout. There are days when, though ephemerid flies are hatching freely, no trout will rise to them. A quite big sedge tried then, especially if dragged a little, may produce a firm rise. So it can be on a summer day, a July afternoon perhaps, and even, at such a time, a sedge will take a fish when no fly is on the water at all.

Sedge flies, in their larval stage, we have already met earlier in this book. Caddis grubs, so useful to the bottom fisherman, are larvae of sedge flies. Like the nymphs of the ephemerids, they spend their days of growth in the water, and, when fully grown, come to the surface to hatch, now, unlike ephemerids, they are fully mature. The recognition of sedge flies should give no difficulty at all. They have a rather moth-like look, with the same downy texture; but their wings are not flat as a

Fig. 65. Sedge fly

moth's are, they form a roof shape lengthwise over their backs, what is called 'penthouse' fashion.

There are a great many species of sedges varying in size from about a third of an inch up to the Great Red Sedge itself, which is over an inch in length. Fortunately quite a few patterns of sedge will represent the whole range. Little Red Sedge, Cinnamon Sedge, Dark Sedge, and Caperer should meet most contingencies.

## Alder

At a glance you might take the Alder for a sedge. It has the same general form, the penthouse wings. But those wings are dimly glassy, like old brown bottle glass, and heavily veined. The body is rather fat and nearly plum-coloured. During May is its time, and it and the Mayfly can often be on the water together; and, curiously, the artificial Alder will often take well while the Mayfly is on. It has often been said that it

Fig. 66. Alder fly

is the wet fly form of the Alder which does best; but that is far from having been the experience of the author. Many and many an occasion there has been when the Alder fished as a dry fly has been very success-ful indeed. Standard patterns of the Alder work well.


## Black Gnat

This is an inconspicuous little fly that comes about the water in summeı in clouds. It looks like a very small black housefly but, more closely examined, is as much brown and dingy olive as black. But imitations with suggestions of clear wings and black bodies do well. There are days in summer when trout will ignore all imitations of ephemerids but come determinedly to a little Black Gnat.


## Other Flies

Various other flies have their occasional days. Sometimes in August and September great falls of flying ants will come upon the water, and then, if trout start to take them, nothing but imitations of them will take fish. About the time the hawthorn blooms the Hawthorn Fly may be on the water in swarms—a small black fly with long trailing hind legs. It too may sometimes cause rises of trout for which nothing but an imitation of the Hawthorn Fly will do. The author remembers seeing such a rise on Tal-y-bont Reservoir in Breconshire, and then the whole water's surface boiled with trout taking the fly—and nothing would they look at which did not suggest the fly. On lakes great rises may be caused by Chironomids, which look like mosquitoes but do not bite—the Green Midge and the Olive Midge anglers call them. A small green fly that bears at least some sort of resemblance to the natural fly can do very well then.

The Grannom should also be mentioned, though it occurs only on certain rivers, particularly the lower Kennet. It is a sedge, but one that hatches in April, well before the time of the other sedges. When it does come it is greedily received by trout. A small pale fawn sedge this is, and the female carries at the end of the abdomen a small bunch of blue-green eggs.

Beyond all these flies there are others of minor importance, but hardly worth further examination here. It is not improbable that a new-comer to fly fishing may find a strong urge to further study of natural flies and artificial flies. To him may be recommended *An Angler's Entomology* by J. R. Harris, and a *Dictionary of Trout Flies* by A. Courtney Williams. The first is published by Collins, the second by Black.

## Casting

Now the point is reached at which the reader knows the tackle he must use for fly fishing, and he knows the natural flies upon which much of his fishing will be based; he knows a few artificial patterns that will represent those natural flies. He must learn to cast.

It is often said that it is impossible to learn to cast a fly from the teaching of the written word; that is only partly true. Much depends upon how logically, mechanically explicitly, the written instruction is given. An attempt will be made here; and let it be said in advance that any such attempt, in breaking up the action into its parts, cannot but make it sound more complicated than it really is. Anyone wishing to go beyond the teaching that follows here, could not do better than read the truly admirable and crystal clear instruction that is given—in fly casting and all other casting—in a book called *Casting* by Captain T. B. Thomas (to whom reference has been made earlier in this chapter). It is published by Allen & Unwin.

The first point to absorb and never for one moment forget is that the rod is a spring, and the line is the weight which, by flexing the rod, sets the spring. The hand and arm that control the rod and line enable the line's weight to set the spring, and then, at the right point, release the spring. See yourself then, facing the water, standing easily, not tense in any way. Fly casting is best done with an easy lissome kind of movement. The rod is in the right hand; the left hand does all the handling of the line. Draw a few yards of line from the reel and flip it out in front as

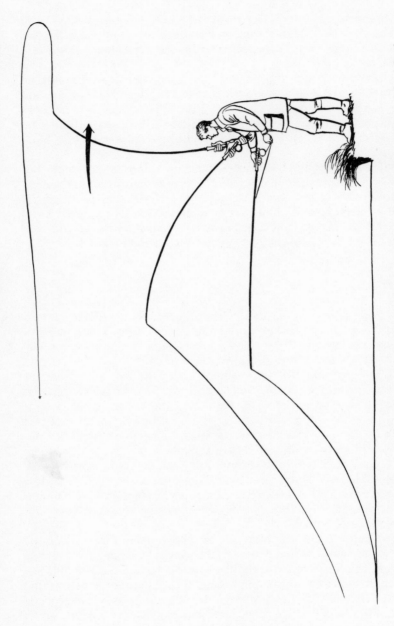

Fig. 67. Fly casting—beginning of back cast—line out in front—lift—quicken from 11 o'clock to 12 o'clock finishing with wrist-snap—line starts to fly out behind

you would flip with a coach whip. That gives you some initial weight out from the rod top to get the rod working.

Now, as you are about to begin a cast, your forearm, your wrist, the rod, are one piece. All in one line they are pointed out over the water at almost the horizontal. The line lies out beyond. Now the forearm, with the wrist and rod, begins to rise smoothly up towards, say, eleven o'clock. During this movement the wrist, and therefore the rod, lags a little behind the forearm; the wrist, that is to say, takes a slight downward arch. The smooth upward movement of the forearm is now quickening. It does so from eleven o'clock to a trifle past twelve o'clock, and at that time the wrist, which has been arched a little downward, snaps back to a position in firm line with the forearm. This has the effect of springing the *rod top*. On *no* account must the wrist be bent back past the line of the forearm; in that lies the whole essence of good casting. Now the heavy line will have been drawn from the surface of the water and will have started to fly out behind. The forearm and wrist, meantime, remain firm, *not dropping back at all behind*. The line up the back of the forearm continues in a straight line up the rear edge of the hand, up the thumb and up the butt of the rod. As the line extends behind, its weight pulls on the top of the rod, flexing it back—that is setting the spring of the rod. If all has been done as it should the line in this back cast will not drop below the horizontal. As the line completes its extension—which you can turn your head to watch—you end the pause you have made to allow the full extension, and begin to move the forearm forward again, increasing the tension on the line. This movement passes quickly into a forward snap of the wrist, into a quick downward arching of the wrist. This has the effect of giving a forward spring to the *rod top*. That sets the line flying forward, and by the time the rod reaches eleven o'clock the power of your forward wrist snap will be over. From there on the forearm follows through as the line extends forward and unrolls on to the water.

Now look back at what has happened and realize that the whole essence of it has been the firm anchoring of the rod butt. The spring that is your rod cannot properly be actuated by the weight of the line unless the butt *is* so anchored. If the holding of that base is loose, sloppy, the weight cannot set the spring. If the wrist is allowed to drop back behind the forearm at the top of the back cast, the anchorage *is* loose and sloppy. Then the line will drop low behind—that is a sign that the rod is not firmly anchored. If ever you find your line dropping behind, look at your wrist action. It is the forward snap of the wrist in the forward cast which releases the spring of the rod.

There is the principle of all fly casting. That is the heart of it. All else is built on that. You will find that in making the back cast it is well to

Fig. 68. Forearm and hand in straight line
as line goes out in back cast

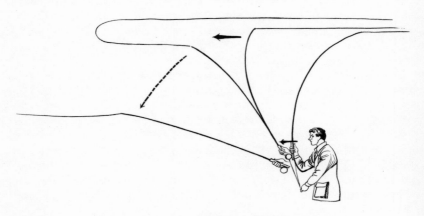

Fig. 69. Forward cast with fly tackle—
wrist-snap from 12 o'clock to 11 o'clock

make it in a very slightly convex curve out to the side so that the forward flying line does not slap into the rod.

Now you will want to lengthen line. As you make the back cast, throw your left hand (which is holding the line) out to the side so that more line is drawn from the reel. Hold it so until the forward cast starts to pull on the rod; then let go of the line and that which you have held

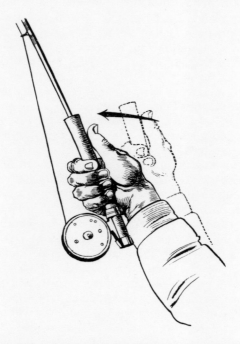

Fig. 70. Forward wrist-snap in forward cast
between 12 o'clock and 11 o'clock—
close-up

will be drawn away through the rings by the outward flying weight of the rest. That is what is called shooting line. If you want to continue lengthening line, as the forward flying line extends fully you go into another back cast, and, at the same time, repeat the movement of the left hand, thus drawing more line from the reel. This you can repeat until you have out as much line as you need. Casting in the air like this, back cast and forward cast, without allowing the line to drop, is called false casting.

Both shooting line and false casting have uses beyond what has been

already described. When a long line is being fished, to attempt to lift
the whole of it from the water to make a fresh cast may be impossible,
and even if possible, it may strain the rod. Some line therefore is
taken in through the rings by the left hand, and then shot when the new
cast is made. But indeed it is good technique to do this even if the line
is not a long one (particularly in dry fly fishing), because a fly delivered
by shooting line drops more lightly than one that is not. Anglers have
a phrase to describe how the fly should fall—'like thistledown', they say.
And similarly with false casting. In dry fly fishing the fly must be kept
dry if it is to continue to float, so, between each actual cast over a fish,
several false casts are made so as to flick off the fly such moisture as it
has gathered.

The casting technique so far described has been that with a single-
handed trout fly rod; but that used when casting two-handed, as with a
salmon fly rod, follows exactly the same principle. Now the left hand,
having first stripped a lot of line off the reel, grips the button of the rod
while its forefinger holds the line against the butt. The right hand holds
the butt near the top. Some line has already been flicked out, whip
fashion. Now casting begins, and when the forward cast is made the
left forefinger releases the line so that that which has been drawn from
the reel may be shot. Otherwise all is the same; the left hand anchors
the base of the rod while the right hand induces the line to fly out behind to flex the rod and then fly out in front to have the benefit of the
power of the rod released by the flexing. It will be found that a partial
turn of the body to the right helps in the making of the back cast,
followed by a turn back to the front for the forward cast.

Quite often in trout fly fishing overhead casting is impossible because
there is tree growth overhead. Such a situation demands horizontal
casting. The essential action is the same, but instead of being made in
the vertical plane, over the head, it is done parallel with the ground.
Horizontal casting is often a means of putting the fly under overhanging
boughs on the opposite bank, or, sometimes, upstream on the angler's
own bank. Trout, and often the best ones, may be found to be lying
under the overhanging sedges on the bank from which you are fishing.
A horizontal cast, made from downstream, is a means of presenting a
fly to the fish.

There is another means of presenting a fly under overhanging boughs
on the far bank. Use overhead casting in the normal way but, just as the
forward cast is made, drop on to one knee. This method can work with
the most satisfying neatness, popping the fly under what looks the most
formidable overhang of branches.

There are many occasions when a fish will be found rising upstream
of you when you are fishing from the right bank (the right bank is that

Fig. 71. Horizontal cast to fish lying under your own bank upstream

which is on the right when you are looking downstream), and growth on the bank is too close and high to allow a back cast overland. A development of the horizontal cast must be used, with the back cast made downstream over the water. Now, as the back cast is made, horizontally, the body pivots to the right and the right arm is thrown out in a downstream direction. The backward snap of the wrist is delayed until the body has turned and the arm has been thrown out. When the forward cast is made, the body pivots back to the left (or upstream direction) and the right arm is brought right round too and thrown out in an upstream direction before the forward snap of the wrist is made. It may often be that the fish is not lying straight upstream, but upstream and out towards the far bank, even right against the far bank. In such a case, when the forward snap of the wrist is made, the arm reaches out to point towards the fish and the snap is made towards it. This undoubtedly sounds complicated and difficult; but anyone who has mastered the basic overhead cast will soon master this too.

Fishing from the left bank, a fish lying upstream close to your own bank is a different problem; it demands a backhand cast. The cast is made, backhand, across the body from right to left, and it will be found that the greatest difficulty about it is not to lose the necessary forward arch of the wrist in the back cast. If the line is not to drop to the ground, the wrist arch has to be exaggerated by comparison with normal casting.

## Dry fly fishing

We will assume now that casting is sufficiently under control for serious fishing to begin. The beginning shall be dry fly fishing. Here is the river, and a hatch has begun and the fish are rising. One fish is rising steadily in the middle of the river. Your line has been greased to float (or it is a self-floating line which needs no greasing), your fly, selected to suggest the Olive Duns which are hatching, is tied on. Furtively you approach the fish from downstream—and judgement is needed in this; there is a general rule of fly fishing to cover it. This is the rule—never use a longer line to reach a fish than you need. That means that it is better to creep nearer your fish and cast a shorter line rather than to cast a longer line from a more aloof distance. For this there is good reason: every extra yard you allow between yourself and the fish means that much less direct connexion between you and the fly, that much less certainty in your strike being effective, that much more line to be under the control of the current rather than your control. So you creep to, shall we say, ten yards of your trout rather than fifteen yards. But why has the approach been made from downstream rather than upstream? In dry fly fishing it is the normal practice to cast over your fish from down-stream; but, as shall be shown, this should not be regarded as an in-flexible rule.

There are good reasons for the usual approach being made from downstream, and the most obvious of them is the fact that a fish lying in a current faces into that current so that water enters its mouth, passes over its gills, where oxygen is extracted, and then the water passes out at the back of the gills. The fish in fact breathes. If it con-sistently faced downstream it could not breathe. So there is the trout, feeding on surface flies; it is, as anglers say, 'in position'—it lies high in the water, close to the surface, at a place where the current brings to it the flies that float on the surface. To approach it from below ob-viously gives a better chance of avoiding being seen by the fish.

There is another reason as good. The dry fly fisherman's greatest enemy is what is called 'drag', and drag is more easily avoided by cast-ing from below than by casting from above. To know what drag is look at a natural fly as it is borne down by the current; it comes down with response to the current alone. Every small turn and inflexion of current affects the movement of the almost weightless fly. Now look at an artificial fly attached to a cast and line; see it cast across the river in which there are paths of current of differing speed and direction. Sections of line and cast between the rod and the fly are pulled at speeds different from the speed of the current on which the fly floats. The result is that line and cast pull on the fly, make it skate, make it move at a different speed and in a different direction from that of the current on which it floats. That is drag. Except in certain specialized cases, which will be mentioned later, no fish will take a fly which drags because it is unnatural; natural flies do not behave like that. The ex-ceptions, to be mentioned later, are cases in which drag is deliberate and imitates natural drag.

So here you are now, ten yards downstream of your trout, and you are about to try to cast your fly to the trout in such a way that it will not have drag, that it will float down over the trout with as close an approximation to the behaviour of a natural fly as possible. You get out line, false casting while you draw line from the reel until you have out enough line to reach—with a straight line—about a couple of yards up-stream of the fish. Your intention is to drop the fly about a couple of feet above the fish and just a little to your own side of the fish. The line you have out in excess of that need is for the prevention of drag. You use it thus—as you make the final forward cast that is to drop the fly on the water, and as the line is extending and beginning to drop, you pull back the rod just a little and then push it forward again. As a result the line and cast, which would have dropped in a straight line with the fly two yards upstream of the fish, now falls snakily with the fly about two feet upstream of the fish. Those loose and snaky curves of line will absorb the intervening differences of current speed and direction, and that enables the fly to float down at the bidding of the piece of current on which it floats. Because you have so made the cast that the fly floats a little to your own side of the fish, the fish is less likely to see the end of the cast leading up to the fly.

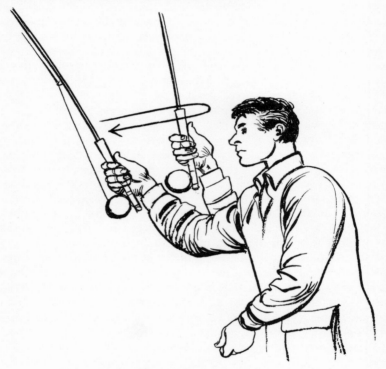

Fig. 72. Making a snaky cast to rising fish

And now comes that brief but apparently endless pause which is at the heart of the intense delight and excitement of dry fly fishing. You know the trout waits there, waits there to take the flies that float to it, and your fly is floating that small distance to come over the trout. It may or may not rise and take your fly. It may just lift in the water, just lift its nose—or, as anglers say, its neb—there will be a bubbly ring on the water and your fly will have gone. Your instinctive response will be an instantaneous and rather violently snatching strike; and this is about the hardest thing in dry fly fishing to overcome. Such a strike will probably snatch the fly straight out of the fish's mouth; it may just prick the fish and fail to secure a proper hold, and in that case the fish will be 'put down' and will rise no more for some time. What you have to school yourself to do is to pause at the taking of the fly so that the fish has time to turn down. Then, when you strike—or, more accurately, tighten the line firmly but not violently—the hook will be pulled into the angle of the jaws, into what is known as the scissors. Hooked thus a fish is well hooked. Successful striking is something that comes with experience; even the most experienced fly fisher strikes less successfully at the opening of the season than he does later in the season. A fish that rises close to the angler is plainly a different matter from one that rises fifteen yards away and at the end of a very snaky line. In the case of the near-to fish there must be a more conscious pause; the farther-away fish will not need so deliberate a pause because absorption of the curves in the line will translate a relatively quick strike into a sufficiently slow one.

Not all trout that rise to the fly do so in the way that has been described. It must not be assumed that if the fly passes over the fish without response there will be no rise—so let the fly float well downstream of the fish before picking it off. Sometimes the trout will let the fly pass over it, watching it, then it may drop back tail first, then lift and take the fly; or it may turn, follow the fly and then take it facing downstream.

But, let us suppose, this fish does not rise. The fly has to be picked off and offered again. If the fly is, as it were, snatched off the surface, some sort of splash will be made. That may alarm the fish and put it down (which means ceasing to rise); it will tend to make the fly waterlogged so that it will cease to float. So the left hand must draw line through the rings while the rod starts to move at first slowly and smoothly, quickening presently into the back cast. Then the fly will slide over the surface and into the air gently and without disturbance, and the line gathered by the left hand can be shot when the next cast is made. Before it is made several false casts are made to flick moisture off the fly, and it is better that they should be made downstream of the fish so as not to alarm it. Now the fly can be presented again.

So far, in this dry fly fishing, we have been thinking of a fish that lies not only upstream but also across. Very often—indeed, more often than not—the fish will be sufficiently upstream that the floating back of the fly will present the difficulty of an accumulation of slack line as the fly floats back. If this is allowed to happen the amount of slack will go beyond what is necessary for the avoidance of drag, and will mean that if the fish rises and a strike must be made, the strike will be lost in the slack. It will not reach the fish and the fish will not be hooked. The loose line must be gathered as the fly floats back so that contact with the fly is maintained. There is a means for this.

The left hand holds the line between finger and thumb with the palm downwards. Then, as the fly floats back, the left hand turns over and to the left, drawing the loose line through the rings into the palm. There the other fingers take it and hold it against the palm while the hand turns back to the first position to take more line through the rings. This too it turns over into the palm and the hold of the other fingers. Thus, as long as the fly floats back, the left hand is kept easily and smoothly turning through this movement and gathering the loose line into the palm—*but* not taking it faster than the fly is floating back. The fly must not be pulled.

We will hope that when the fly is presented to a rising fish it, the fish, will take it forthwith and all will end in triumph. More often than not, of course, this is not the case. The fish fails to take the fly, and we must, if we can, diagnose the reason and make the proper correction. The fly, then, floats over the fish without response but the fish continues to take natural flies. We can then be reasonably certain that we have not scared the fish. First, was the fly dragging? It appeared not to be, but there is such a thing as 'invisible drag', drag so slight that we cannot see it, but enough to create a dubiety in the fish and make it too suspicious to take the fly. We can present the fly again with even more care not to have drag. Still the fly is refused. Perhaps it did not see the fly the first time, or even the second time, but at another cast it is still refused. That cannot be the reason then. Perhaps another fly chosen to suggest the natural fly which the trout is taking will be more convincing to the trout.

Suppose the fish is taking Medium Olive, and suppose we have been offering it a Greenwell's Glory. Now we change the fly to a Gold Ribbed Hare's Ear—and now possibly all is well; the trout is convinced and rises to the fly. But, perhaps, nothing so fortunate happens. The fly is refused but the trout still rises to natural fly. It may be now that you, watching that tantalizingly rising fish, notice that though Medium Olives are coming over the fish regularly, another sort of fly is also coming down, not as often, but is being taken when it does come. You realize that it is not the Medium Olive which the trout is taking, but this other fly. Such a thing may quite often happen if that other fly is an Iron Blue Dun. Trout like Iron Blue Duns, very specially. Now you change your fly to an imitation of the Iron Blue Dun, and you rise and hook the fish.

Sometimes though you find you are casting to a fish that remains unconvinced by the best that you can do; even when you, now rather desperate, make a careless cast, flop line and fly on the water, that trout still rises. This is a fish better left, unless it is very big. It is one of those fish so hardened to anglers that it ignores their flies but continues to rise. Time is being wasted and you do not know how long the rise will last. This is particularly a consideration in the early part of the season when rises tend to be very short. They usually start suddenly and end suddenly; they may last only half an hour. Better then to turn your attention to another and possibly less difficult fish.

Different speeds and directions of current are not the only hazards that may lie between the angler and the fish to which he wants to cast. Weed beds often come to the surface, and there, just the farther side of such a weed bed, you may see a good trout rising steadily. A snaky cast, accurately made, can be the means of rising such a fish. Get out generously more line than is needed to reach the fish, and, by the pull back and push forward of the rod that has been described, drop line and fly so that a snake of line and cast lies across the weed with just a few feet of cast lying on the water beyond the weeds, and with the fly a mere foot upstream of the fish. That will give just freedom enough for the fly to come over the trout before drag sets in. If the fly is refused, picking the fly off for another cast may be difficult; there will be a risk of the hook fouling the weed. A flip of the rod top can be made to send a wave down the line which will free line and fly from water and weed bed. Before the effect is lost go straight into the back cast.

A fish that lies directly upstream of you, close to your own bank, is often a difficult problem—and may be all the more so if something, perhaps a bush on the bank, prevents your making a cast from downstream. The cross-country cast may take this fish. You must mark precisely where the trout lies—relating it to a tussock on the bank, or some such thing. Then, keeping very low, you go inland a few yards and upstream until, crouched on one knee, you are directly opposite the fish. Now you must get out enough line to go well beyond the fish, and then make the cast so that the line lies over the intervening bank, over the sedges on the bank edge, and the cast and fly drop loosely just upstream of the fish. The fly will not be able to float far without drag, but, with luck (and skill), just far enough to come over the fish and be taken. You, of course, crouched there, will not be able to see the rise. You will hear it. You may also see the edge of the rings spreading out, and, if you strike at that, you will have given enough pause. Retrieving the line and fly for a fresh cast is less difficult than might appear. Do not attempt to go into a back cast in the ordinary way; draw the line gently by hand, and it will usually come through the sedges without becoming caught up.

These trout that lie close under the bank are seldom easy; and so often it is the better fish that lie so. The shepherd's crook cast may take such a fish that otherwise would be inviolate. What is aimed at is to make the end of the cast, near the fly, double round in a crook just as cast and fly are dropping on to the water. Then, you see, it is the fly that will come to the fish first; the fly will engage its attention before it has had a chance to see the following cast. This is specially relevant to the problem of these bank fish because, casting directly upstream as you must, the cast will come straight over the head of the fish before it sees the fly. You will, as anglers say, 'line the fish'. This is what the shepherd's crook cast seeks to avoid.

So get out line to reach upstream of the fish, deliver your final cast, and then, just as the fly and line are dropping, push out the rod to the river side, away from the bank. That is rather a simplification of the movement; but experience will soon demonstrate further. Once the shepherd's crook is mastered it has other very valuable uses—for example a fish that lies straight upstream of you and just in front of a weed bed that comes to the surface. By pushing out the rod to the right a left crook can be made; by a push to the left a right crook can be made.

The foreshortening that arises from looking along the line at a rising fish may sometimes be misleading; this is often specially so in the case of a fish that lies close to the far bank. You make your cast; you see your fly beautifully cocked and, high on its hackles, float down. It appears to pass right over your fish; but there is no rise. You may satisfy yourself that the fly is right and the fish ready to take; but no rise comes. The truth is, so often, that your fly is really passing a yard to your own side of the fish; another yard of line taken from the reel will probably rise the fish at once.

It was said earlier that, though upstream fishing is the general practice in dry fly fishing, there should not be too rigid an attitude to this. Upstream casting is, in a majority of cases, the more convenient and practical way of approaching a fish, but there are far more cases than might be supposed in which a downstream cast will do better. Some such cases are obvious. A fish is rising, we will suppose, in a place to which no approach can be made from downstream—there may be bushes on the bank, or the fish may be lying just under the upstream end of the arch of a bridge. If such a fish is to be cast to at all it must be from upstream. But there are also many occasions when a fish that can be cast to from downstream would be better cast to from upstream. In times of bright sun and clear water trout may become more acutely sensitive to the cast coming over them or near them before the fly. The author remembers a July afternoon on which no fish could be induced to take a fly cast from downstream, but seven big fish were taken in an hour by casting from upstream. The difference which produced such solid results was that, casting from upstream, the fly came first. On stretches of river that have a broad even flow, big trout may often cruise during a heavy hatch of fly rather than remain in position. They move slowly upstream, moving to left and right, picking a fly here and a fly there; then they drop back, then move up again. Those fish are more easily taken by fishing from upstream than downstream— or so it often is.

Drag is the obvious difficulty in fishing from upstream. How are you to present an undragging fly when the current bears the fly away from you, not towards you? You false cast until you have out enough line to reach well downstream of the fish, then, as you make the final delivery of the fly, you pull back the rod and then push it forward again just as line and fly are falling to the water. The result is that line and cast fall in a loose snake upon the water; the fly goes down at the bidding of the current, entirely drag-free.

Something should be said about the playing of fish on fly tackle. Look first at the situation in which you are likely to find yourself at the moment a trout is hooked. The trout rises, you strike, and your first and very urgent need is to get a tight line. So, as you strike, take a step back. This is in any case an insurance against giving a slack line in that first moment when a trout may easily shake itself free of the hook hold; but, quite often, a hooked trout will make a first run either straight towards the angler, or partially so. In such a case that first step back can lead easily into several such steps that will avoid a slack line. If you are, as you should be, using your left hand on the line all the time, you will meet the early part of the trout's fight with that left hand, stripping in line through the rings if need be, then, if the trout runs from you, yielding line through the slight restraint of the left hand. This restraint can be increased if the fish is clearly heading for a dense weed bed or some other snag.

But, as soon as you can, you need to get the fish on to the reel. To play it entirely on loose line controlled by the left hand is apt to lead to unmanageable amounts of loose line which may catch in bankside growth or get under the feet. After the first desperate moments the trout will come under at least some control and give at least some short pause during which the rod can be transferred to the left hand, which will also hold the line against the rod butt. Then the right hand can rapidly wind up the loose line on to the reel. *Now* you can feel more secure. You can give line, or take it up, directly on the reel, and this is a much happier and more solid position. To the inexperienced it may sound complicated and clumsy to make this transference of the rod, but in practice it comes to be done without conscious volition. If the trout is big and strong be in no too great hurry to use the net. It may be brought to the bank but still be inclined to thrash and plunge; a premature attempt to net it may send it off on another wild run at a critical

moment. When the fish is ready, sink the net in the water on the downstream side of the rod if that is practicable and draw the fish over it;
then lift.


## Nymph fishing

On chalk streams and those limestone streams that are also gently
flowing and have a richness of fly life, there is a form of fishing which,
though it is truly wet fly fishing, comes more naturally within the orbit
of dry fly fishing. It is nymph fishing, and it is so much complementary
to the dry fly that it must be considered with it.

It has emerged earlier in this book that trout feed upon the nymphal
or underwater stage of life of aquatic flies as well as the true fly stages—
they do indeed feed upon nymphs a great deal more than upon the
surface fly. They take nymphs in the open water as they ascend to the
surface for hatching, they seek them in the weed, they find them on
the bottom. Just before a hatch of fly, and during the early part of the
hatch, and to a varying extent all through the hatch, trout are to be seen
lying poised about middle water turning this way and that, opening
their mouths as they do so. They are taking nymphs; they are catch-
able but they are not, broadly, to be caught on the dry fly. It may sometimes occur that throughout the duration of a hatch of fly, no trout at
all (or few) will rise to the surface fly; those non-rising trout are taking
nymphs below the surface.

To fish for them the same dry fly tackle is used, and, up to a point,
the same method. The main difference is that though the dry fly *must*
float, the artificial nymph *must* sink. So let us suppose that it is diag-
nosed that a trout is nymphing—in the crystalline water it may be seen
doing so; or there will be a disturbance of the surface that the beginner
will probably take to be a rise to the surface fly. But then he will notice
that this is happening where no fly is floating down, and the surface is
not being as completely broken as it is with a true surface rise. It is
more of a humping of the water, with or without a breaking of the
surface. Anglers say the fish is 'bulging'. The bulge is the transmission
to the surface of the fish's movement below.

So you tie on your nymph—a generalized pattern or one that imitates
a particular nymph. If you see Medium Olives hatching, it is reasonable to suppose that the fish are taking Medium Olive nymphs. You
make your approach to the fish from downstream as you do with the
dry fly and your line is greased to float or it is a self-floating line—the
last two or three feet of such lines, incidentally, do need greasing. You
wet the fly in your mouth so that it shall start wet, and to keep it wet

you do not false cast in the air as you lengthen line, but let the fly enter
the water on each lengthening forward cast. Thus it is anyway with un-
weighted nymphs, but more commonly now nymphs are dressed with
weighted bodies, and these sink well and are valuable for deeply-lying
fish. This way of nymph fishing, based upon the weighted nymph, was
developed by Frank Sawyer. His Pheasant Tail Nymph, which is very
successful, has the thoracic hump built up with copper wire, with
pheasant tail herl making the stubby tails, being brought up the body,
and over the thoracic hump.

You will have greased the cast down to about two or three feet from
the nymph, according to the average depth of the water, and this last
part can be smeared with a paste of fuller's earth and water so that it
shall sink, and now, when you have out enough line to drop the nymph
about four feet or even more upstream of the fish, the ungreased part
of the cast, with the nymph, will sink at once. Now cast and the nymph
will drift down to where the trout waits. Perhaps you can see the fish,
and you may see it open its mouth and turn to the nymph; if so strike
instantly and gently. You may see a humping of the surface, and if so,
strike. As often as not you will not be able to see the fish, nor will you
see a surface disturbance; but you may see a sudden drawing under of
the greased part of the cast, and on that you should strike. Sometimes
the warning will be no more than a glint under the surface as the fish
turns, and for this too you should strike.

Probably the above sounds difficult, as if the evidence of an offer
from a fish is too far from being positive, and at first it may be found so.
This is a thing to which the eye becomes trained by degrees—the time
comes indeed when you find you have struck successfully without
knowing quite why—and in the earlier days of nymph fishing it will be
found to be very helpful indeed to tie into the cast with a clove hitch,
at the bottom of the greased part of the cast, a wisp of white feather.
This can be watched for signs of an offer.

Frank Sawyer, to whom reference is made above, is the greatest
living exponent of nymph fishing, and he has greatly enlarged its scope
with his patterns which are weighted with fuse wire or copper wire. An
explanation of his methods and dressings can be found in his admirable
book, *Nymphs and the Trout*, published by Stanley Paul.

References have been made from time to time in the foregoing parts
of this book to chalk streams and limestone streams as being a kind different from other trout streams. There should be further explanation of
the difference. A chalk stream and a true limestone stream have in common that they do not depend upon surface water running off the land.
Moorland and mountain streams (as they are called), rivers that rise on
high moorlands and mountains and run down to the lowlands, are

generally of a type that is fed by such surface water; and as a result they
vary greatly in level, running low in times of drought, and being subject
to floods in times of rain. Because they are subject to scouring by flood,
because their current is often fast and sometimes tumbling, there is a
tendency in them not to have much weed growth, and for their fly life
to be on the sparse side. They are also often acid in nature, and that too
tends to a less high scale of life.

Chalk streams and limestone streams are fed from underground
springs. Rain falls on the high chalk or limestone hills, and, in its slow
quiet way, seeps down and down into the secret heart of the hills, down
through the porous chalk or limestone until it reaches an impervious
layer underneath. From there the springs break, pure, crystalline, six
months after the rain that feeds them fell on the hills above. These
provide birth for rivers of the chalk and limestone kind, and from this
origin the rivers are gentle and wonderfully clear. They do not, as other
rivers do, rise angrily and sink badly. Their flow is at most times constant and full, and the life in them is profuse and fat. Because they are
alkaline their weed growth is luxuriant and their fly life rich. Their fish
grow big and splendid, and lie above the yellow sparkle of the gravel
bottom waiting for the endless generosity of food.

# CHAPTER ELEVEN

# Wet fly fishing

To speak of wet fly fishing is to cover a wide range of techniques. There is downstream wet fly fishing; there is upstream wet fly fishing, and that divides again into more than one mode of fishing. So it is on rivers; on lakes and reservoirs there is wet fly fishing of a different kind. It has often been said in books on fly fishing that the beginner, seeking the easier way into it, should start with wet fly fishing, more specifically downstream wet fly fishing, and from there graduate by degrees to the supreme heights of dry fly fishing. The beginner will not find this curious belief supported by his experience. Great as are the skills which may be developed in the dry fly, to be a really good wet fly fisher demands a greater skill. It is odd too that the downstream wet fly should be selected as the easiest way; to catch little trout that none but the newest beginner would want to catch *is* relatively easy by downstream wet fly fishing, but to catch good trout by downstream fishing demands considerable skill.

It has also been written, many a time, that the decisive factor for downstream or upstream fishing is the direction of the wind. If there should be a strong wind blowing downstream, so it has been said, then the fishing should be downstream. If there is no such wind, or the wind is blowing upstream, then the fishing should be upstream. The wind *can* compel the fishing to be upstream or down, but that is a poor reason to be the only reason for choice of upstream or down. Other factors provide good reason for this way of fishing or that. The fish may be high in the water and active on a soft and pleasant day; they may be dour and skulking against the bottom on a hard-looking dull day. It may be warm or it may be cold; it may be evening or morning. Plenty of things provide reason for choice of a way of fishing.

## Downstream wet fly, short line

But, perhaps, there is something to be said for starting off the new fly fisher on downstream fishing of some sort. It makes less demand on his still none too polished casting powers. What is usually recommended is that he should start by casting a long line downstream and across;

but that is more truly a method of a specialized kind; as has been said, it demands skill for worthwhile results. So let our beginner start with short line fishing downstream. That, circumspectly practised, can give reasonable results at an early stage.

At once this fishing almost certainly introduces a new factor—that of wading. A majority of rivers to which wet fly is most suited are of the fast rocky sort. Their typical conformation goes broadly like this; you may come first upon what is called 'a flat', and this is a broad flow of fairly even but not deep water, one to four feet perhaps. Its bottom is usually stony, and here and there its surface will show a boil or hump which signals the presence of a larger rock on the bottom. A flat quickens presently, as the bottom starts down an incline; the current becomes faster, the water shallower, and it streams down among the stones, creaming and chattering. This is a 'stickle'. The stickle boils down its last few yards, pours over in a smother, and enters a 'pool'. A pool, in varying degree, is deep. At the top is the throat of the pool, and that is still fast and heavy. Soon the water's pace steadies and broadens, and there is the main body of the pool, the 'dub'. Now the water has an even pace, usually smooth because the water is too deep for bottom irregularities to rumple the surface. Now comes the tail of the pool, and the current quickens into a fast 'glide'—shallower than the dub, but smooth and glassy. The tail becomes shallower, its surface begins to show breaks and boils, and we are into another flat or into a stickle to the next pool. That, broadly, is the pattern of the typical stony wet fly river, such rivers as are to be found in Scotland, the North, Wales and the West, the South-West.* Without wading the greater part of such water could not be fished.

To the beginner wading comes as a new and often overwhelming pleasure, one sufficient in itself. On not too cold days the delight of it can lead to unwise indulgence. Without wishing to deprive the beginner of any part of his pleasure, it must be stressed that wading is a means of approaching fish not otherwise approachable, and to wade too widely, too unconsideredly, with careless joyful splashing, will prevent the catching of fish, not aid it. Wading, done without care, can also be dangerous. So let it be a principle that the least wading that can be done for a given objective, the better the chance of taking fish. When wading move gently, slowly, without splash, without a scraping of iron-hobbed feet on the stones of the bottom.

Consider carefully the sort of waders to wear. Good waders are good friends; bad waders can be bad and dangerous enemies. There are two main kinds—thigh waders and trouser (or belly) waders. Salmon fishing

* For a precise analysis of the mechanical behaviour of such a river see *Salmon Taking Times* by R. V. Righyni, published by Macdonald.

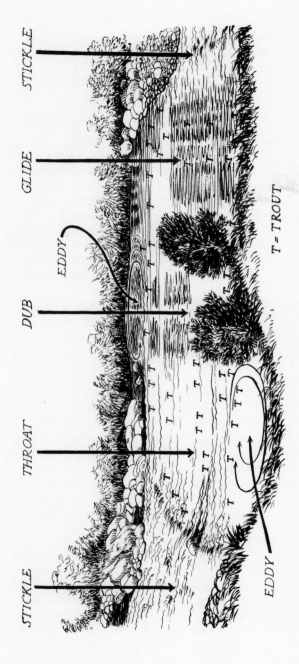

STICKLE     GLIDE     DUB     THROAT     STICKLE

EDDY

EDDY

T = TROUT

Fig. 73. Typical wet fly river

usually demands trouser waders; trout fishing usually needs only thigh
waders, but there are trout rivers on which chances are increased by
trouser waders. Such a river as the Usk has wide reaches on which
trouser waders can give much more fishing water to the wearer. The
best kind of thigh wader is that with leg and foot made in one, with a
lace-up instep to make the foot more firmly snug. A loose sloppy foot fit
is uncomfortable and may be dangerous. Rubber soles can be dangerous
too; their grip on wet rocks is too insecure. The best all-round sole is
one of leather or composition with iron hobs. Compressed felt soles are
also to be had, and they do serve quite well on wet rock, but have not
quite the general usefulness and toughness of hobbed soles.

So now here is the river, the typical wet fly river, and here is the
angler ready to wade and fish with a short downstream line. A flat will
be a good place to try; many trout live in the streamy well-oxygenated
water of flats. Rod, line, and cast are set up; now flies are needed. One
fly may be used because for the beginner that is less prone to tangling
than more than one would be; but it is more profitable to use more, say

Fig. 74. Downstream wet fly cast

three. One can go at the end of the cast, and in that position it is known
as the point or tail fly. A good general choice would be a Greenwell's
Glory. A yard up the cast comes the first dropper; on its two- or three-
inch link of nylon, a Partridge and Orange is tied on. Another yard up
the cast, on another dropper link, the top dropper or bob fly is tied on.
It can be a Pheasant Tail.

Now the angler wades quietly, gently, a little way into the edge of
the river, moving very slowly and with the minimum of movement. He
goes just far enough to be able to cast over a band of streamy water that
comes down on his side of the flat—and he will soon notice that this flat,
which may appear at first to be one broad quite even flow, has really a
number of different paths of current. Now he, standing in the slack
water between the stream and the bank, gets out a fairly short line, not
more than about twice the length of the rod. He does this with as little
movement as possible, trying to confine movement to his rod arm—and
with that short line little arm action is needed. His arrival there will
probably have caused some first alarm; but as he stands, heron fashion,
the fish soon forget that he was not always there. He becomes accepted
as an object.

He makes his cast, little more than a flick across stream, even a little upstream, and with his rod held at rather an upward angle, lets the flies come round with the current until they are at the dangle straight below him. As the flies come round he moves the rod round slowly to keep in touch with them. For a few moments he leaves them there, hanging in the current; then he lifts the rod slowly, perhaps trembling the rod a little, till the flies leave the water and he casts again to the same place as before. Fishing thus it is perfectly possible to take several trout, even more than several, without moving; the virtue of it is that he does *not* move. Some fish may take at some point on the way round, some will take when the fly is at the dangle, or is being slowly retrieved for the next cast.

Sometimes it will be found that every time it is the same fly that is taken; and in such a case it may be worth while to change the other two flies to the same pattern. Perhaps, for a time, trout come well; but after a few have been taken, no more are risen and hooked. Then the line, which so far has been the same length, can be lengthened a few feet, though still remaining quite short. An important part of the success of this way of fishing is the very direct connexion between the angler and his flies, with very little line in the water. But a few more feet will cover fish that have not seen the flies before. If that too soon produces no more fish, the angler can back slowly and unobtrusively towards the bank, move down, then out again to another place of vantage.

Many of the fish will hook themselves, but quite often a small splash in the surface will be seen in the vicinity of the flies, and at this the angler must strike instantly and gently. On the hooking of a fish he must, as far as he may, steer it out of the stream and into the slack in which he stands. There, quietly and furtively, he can net it.

## Downstream wet fly—long line

And now we come to that method which has so often been set as the fly fishing beginner's first exercise. 'Chuck it and chance it' the method is called by its denigrators; but they are usually those who have had little experience of it or have never realized its proper purpose and potentialities in good hands. It has been represented as a sort of broadcast throwing of flies upon the water, so that any trout that happens to be in the path of the flies can take them. So used, downstream fishing will take a few trout, but seldom good ones. There is a more specialized application of the method.

You may separate fishing days in a very generalized way into soft days and hard days. A soft day may have a certain amount of light cloud, some fitful sun; its air is moist rather than dry, the light is soft rather than sharp and hard. There is the sense of happiness and pulse in Nature; fish show, there is fly upon the water and fish move freely to it. Such days are good days for fishing. On a typical hard day of the worst sort, the air is dry, the sky clouded with sharp leaden or steely-looking cloud. The light, even if dull, is sharp and metallic. If there is a wind it will not be a soft zephyr as it is on a soft day; it will be sharp and chill upon the face. That is a bad fishing day of the extreme sort, and fish will be dour and will remain close to the bottom, showing no sign of themselves. Some poor days are less obvious in cause, but have the common factor that there is no movement in the fish; they hug the bottom dourly.

These are the days for the long line downstream mode of fishing. You can use a team of three wet flies or you can use one fly; and in this connexion Captain T. B. Thomas has pointed out something which, if it cannot be explained, can be happily proved. It is that one fly is specially successful for this fishing; it is March Brown with silver body— March Brown and Silver as it is usually called. It should not be too small—size 4 perhaps, New Scale.

Start at the top of the water to be fished; and that may be a long flat. Get out a long line, and let it be a sinking line, ungreased; cast it downstream and across at an angle of about forty-five degrees. According to those who belittle this way of fishing, that is all it is—a steady raking of the water, casting, letting the flies swing round till they are at the dangle below, moving down a couple of paces, casting again, and so on, right down the water. Dull fishing they say it is, and so it is if so done. Fishing thus the fly or flies spend most of the path they make in swinging round hanging on a taut line, skidding unnaturally against the current, behaving very suspiciously in the sight of a big fish that has lived long enough to learn suspicion.

The good downstream fisher has a keen eye for water. As he fishes he studies the current, judges where trout could be expected to be, does all he can to bring the flies to those places in the best way he can. He notes where there are easements between two paths of current, where submerged rocks and rocky ledges and holes in the bottom make turns of current, small eddies, hangs of water—all those places indeed where a trout may have no difficulty in holding position, but where the current will bear food down. He will do what he can, by management of rod and line, to bring the flies to these places with as little drag as possible.

When he casts his long line, he will have a further couple of yards stripped from the reel and held in his left hand. When his line falls to the water, he will note if fast current between him and the fly will make a downstream belly in the line. If that is likely, as soon as the line touches water he will roll a belly of line upstream with a rolling movement of the rod; 'mending line' this is called. This, by preventing the intermediate fast current dragging the line, will give the flies more chance to move without drag and to fish more slowly. So, for the first part of fishing out the cast, though the flies have begun to move down and round, they will still do so with some appearance of free movement. At the point when this initial advantage is being lost—and particularly if at this point there is what looks to be good holding water, the left hand releases its spare line and encourages it out through the rings. Then, at this crucial stage, the flies will be given a fresh lease of free movement. Then the swing round will pass to the last part; they will be swinging round to the straight downstream stage, straight down from the angler. As they come to this, the right arm can gradually lift the rod so that by the time the flies are straight downstream the rod is vertical, and, even, the arm may be held high. Now there will be a belly of line hanging down from the rod top, and again there will be more chance of living-looking movement in the flies.

When the flies have come to the dangle, leave them thus for a short time, hanging on that aerial belly of line. A fish may often take them. But now another cast has to be made; before it is the angler pulls in some line through the rings in short plucks. He does so for more than one reason. One is that a fish may respond to the darting, fidgeting, living-looking movements the flies then have. Another is that he must take up some line before casting so that the rod top may not be strained. He will take up thus the amount of line he fed through the rings during the fishing out of the cast, and some more. Now he moves down his couple of paces and casts as before, shooting line taken in, but retaining the couple of yards for feeding out during the fishing out of the cast. So he works down, searching out all the likely trout lies and fishing them as well as these tricks will let him, bringing his well-sunk flies to the dour trout close to the bottom. Sometimes he may see a humping of the water that tells of a moving fish, and to that he must respond instantly by striking. Much more often he will see nothing, but feel a pluck to which, if he is good enough, he can strike quickly enough to hook his fish. Sometimes his fish will hook itself. It may now be apparent that a good downstream fly fisher is very good indeed.

On less dour days downstream fishing with a long line may also be rewarding, using the same tactics but with a greased or self-flowing line. Thus the flies will work near the surface where, on this more favourable day, the fish may be expected to be.

## Upstream wet fly—single fly

At some time during most trout-fishing days, except very hard ones, on rivers of the typically wet fly kind, there will be a marked movement of fish to feed high in the water. Flies will be seen to be hatching, and, though some will be taken at the surface as hatched flies, a much greater number will be taken just in the surface, just under the surface, and approaching the surface; they will be taken as nymphs just before hatching. The frequency and length of these periods of activity is largely variable with the time of the year (apart from weather conditions). In the early part of the season the periods are likely to be short—in March and April they may last only half an hour and come only once in the day, though they may be longer and may come more than once. But as the season matures so the frequency and length of the periods of activity increases. There may be recurrent periods at odd times through much of the day in May and June. In July and August activity is likely to be lessened, but September may see a return to something like May and June.

When hatches of fly do come, and fish are seen to be active—by surface rises and by the taking of nymphs in and near the surface—that is the time to use a single wet fly fished upstream. Now the fishing will not be done, as it is in so much of wet fly fishing, by reading the water, but by casting to an individual fish that has been seen to move. To some extent it may be mixed with casting to places that look as if they should hold a trout; but mainly this is a form of fishing very like the fishing of the dry fly and the chalk stream nymph. The angler works very slowly, very circumspectly upstream—or even, if fish are rising well, he may stand in the river in one place and from there cover one fish after another within casting range, only moving when he has caught or failed to catch them. The choice of fly must be controlled by what is hatching. If olives are hatching the artificial fly may be, for example, a Greenwell, a Gold Ribbed Hare's Ear, a Rough Olive; if Iron Blue duns are hatching the artificial fly can be a Snipe and Purple.

When a fish is seen to be taking fly an approach is made from downstream to reasonably short casting range—one and a half times the length of the rod perhaps. The cast is made and the fly dropped a yard or yard and a half upstream of the fish. As it is borne back, just submerged, the rod is raised, and, if necessary, the left hand draws the line; thus the fly is made to move back just a *very little* faster than the speed of the current and close contact is maintained between fly and rod.

When the fish takes some sort of rise form will usually be seen, a humping of the surface, a small splashing, and if need be that can be the signal to strike. But quite often the fish will have hooked itself.

## Upstream wet fly with a team of flies

Sometimes the difference between long line downstream fishing with a team of flies and upstream fishing with a team of flies can be just the way the wind is blowing and how hard it is blowing. It is better to have a strong wind blowing from behind than to have to cast into it. But one way or the other can justly be chosen without the pressure of wind. The day that demands the downstream method has been described—the hard unpromising day—though, as has been established, long-line downstream fishing has other uses. Upstream fishing with a team of flies also searches the water on the basis of judgement as to where trout can be expected to lie, but does it on normally hopeful days when weather conditions are not noticeably hard. The most generally useful and manageable number of flies is three; the point fly can be one with a good entry, a sleekly shaped fly such as a winged Greenwell, the first dropper can be one of the broadly useful hackle flies such as Partridge and Orange, a black hackle fly with a silver rib to the body such as William's Favourite, or, if Iron Blues are likely to be about, a Snipe and Purple. The bob fly has a special function in this method and needs to be of a buzzy form, a fly with a good buzzy hackle, preferably a hackle right down the body.

The angler wades very quietly and slowly upstream, casting a short line so that, most of the time, only the cast will be in the water. The line will be in the air between the cast and the rod top. As he goes he will be searching ahead with his eyes, seeking out all the places that his knowledge and experience tell him should hold trout. This method is at its most effective in quite shallow water, running over submerged rocks with, here and there, a rock showing above the surface. In one place he will see ahead of him two minor currents that divide; and he will divine that in the V between them there will be an easement in which a fish can lie to receive the food brought by the two currents. Such a place will usually have a smooth surface between the more rumpled surface on either side. Two minor currents coming down to join will also have between them such an easy profitable place. The slacker edges of currents will often have trout waiting in them for the same reasons. Rocks cause the current to be turned this way and that, and in the turns, between the small splits of current the rocks make, it will be possible to pick out little smooth-surfaced areas where there is an easement. A rock that stands above the surface will make the current divide, and the current pushing down from either side of the rock will gradually converge again. A few feet or yards below the rock, where the current is veering in to rejoin, trout will lie in the V of easy water, waiting to pick up food from one side or the other. A trout may also lie in front of the rock.

Sometimes the river falls down a series of large or small steps of rock, and within the semi-cup in the surface of such steps there is often a small area of smooth water, though these places have a keen flow through them. Trout lie there; they also lie in the little basins out of the main current formed in angles of current in the drop down the steps and past upstanding rocks. Even where there are none of these more obvious signposts, it may be seen that the running surface of the water is rumpled and humped unevenly, thus demonstrating that stones of varying sizes form the bottom. Among these stones all sorts of minor eddies are made, not only lateral eddies but vertical ones as well. Through all such areas the flies should be made to search.

How then *are* the flies made to search? The angler is wading very slowly upstream, making his short nervous casts—nervous in the sense

Fig. 75. Upstream wet fly cast
coming down

that they are not mechanically repetitive, but are sensitively combining with the eyes to pry out the trout from the riddle of the water. Each cast is made, and the point fly and the first dropper submerge. But the rod point is kept fairly high so that the bob fly, instead of submerging, is made to bob on the surface. As the current bears the flies back the rod point is raised to keep pace, and the left hand does any necessary drawing of the line for the same purpose. So the flies are brought back at perhaps *very little more* than the speed of the current, with the bob fly bobbing on the surface and often bringing trout up from below to splash at it.

When trout take one of the two submerged flies, it may be divined by the flash of the turning of the fish, by the splash of it, by the humping of the surface, or by the sudden drawing of the cast; and to any of these signs a responsive strike can be made. But, as with the previous method described, the fish will often hook themselves.

## Sedge time

Any time throughout the season, from the second part of May onwards, when the daytime fishing is not as successful as could be wished, the angler can say to himself, 'Never mind, wait till sedge time comes.' Sedge time comes as the light begins to lessen; warm twilights are the times for the sedge, and they can be magical. The river smells more excitingly at this brief lovely time; the dank soft smell of it fills the senses. The light fades and fat plops begin to sound over the river, and most particularly so on the quiet slack water at the tails of pools, in the glides. Rises start to show all over the water. Over the water come the sedges, downy-winged, fluttering, dibbing on to the surface; some of them are great flies, an inch in length. The trout slash at them fiercely.

Now the angler ties on a sedge fly, no little fly, but a really big buzzy sedge, a wet one. It may be as big as anything that is tied on a trout hook for British waters. He stands just in the water probably, at a point that commands a broad area of slackly flowing water, and from there he makes his casts, short casts, longer casts, upstream, downstream, across stream, any direction to where a trout is slashing at the sedges. He makes his cast well beyond his fish, and as soon as the fly is in the water he starts to strip in line through the rings with the left hand. His fly comes towards him in fussing small skating movements, just as natural sedges go. In the short time till it is finally dark he may take trout after trout. Enchanted fishing this is, and a wonderful redeemer of bad days. It is not confined to these fast rocky rivers, the typical wet fly rivers. On chalk streams too, at the crepuscular ending of the day, a big sedge dry fly will take many a trout that has been inviolate by day, and all the more so if the fly is plucked in by hand.

## Still-water fishing

Pressure on fishing space grows quickly now. For all those who would fish for trout, there is no longer river space enough. So still waters—reservoirs, gravel pits, various ponds and lakes—are stocked with trout to multiply opportunity. The great lakes of Scotland and Ireland provide fine fishing for trout. But the virtue of still-water trout fishing is not limited to this purely opportunist factor; trout in many still waters grow very big and give sport that, if it lacks some of the atmospheric delight of river fishing, can be desperately exciting on its occasions. Reservoirs have bred a new race of trout anglers.

Fishing from the shore on reservoirs lays a strong accent on long casting. The best feeding a trout in big still waters can have it finds in the shallows. There the sun penetrates, there the weed grows, there the insect life is, there the snails and shrimps are. So there the fisherman goes. He wades into the shallows and casts a long line with, often, a big fly bright with tinsel. He lets it sink well, and then brings it back towards him with plucks of the left hand. Sometimes, particularly at evening when there is a calm on the water, fish come to the surface to feed; and then he casts to them with a dry fly. He has to estimate the cruising pattern of his fish, mark the usually circular route the fish follows, and then put his fly down in advance of the fish's coming so that it shall find the fly waiting. There may be hatches of hawthorn fly, that black fly with long trailing legs; there may be hatches of green midges, and these he will match with a rather small green artificial fly.

That is the general pattern of shore fishing in reservoirs, and it is similar on gravel pits and other large still waters. Usually favourable places are points of shore that stand out; large bays may be good too.

## Boat fishing on still waters

On the big lakes, or on big still waters generally, one method of boat fishing is more used than any other; that is drifting. The whole fishing is done in a series of drifts. The boat is taken, by rowing or by outboard engine, to the upwind extremity of the water to be fished—and it is sought that as much of the drift as possible shall pass over shallows. The boat is put beam-on to the wind, and the two anglers in the boat sit at either end. As the boat drifts thus downwind they cast before the drift, down the wind and across it to some extent, using quite a short line so that mostly only the cast shall go upon the water. Three flies are usually used, and the top one is a bob fly to skip and bob on the ripples—and, let it be well marked, some sort of a wind is essential to this fishing. Flies of the fancy kind are more used than anything more naturalistic. So the drift goes; the anglers cast, draw the flies back with the bob fly working over the ripples, then cast again; and so on and so on. When the downwind limit of the water is reached the boat is taken upwind again and put on to another drift parallel to the first and adjacent to it. One drift after another is made, moving over a drift at a time.

A flat calm may fall sometimes, but if luck is good there may be a rise to surface fly; and then a turn can be made to dry fly fishing to any fish within reach of the boat—again marking if possible any cruising pattern the fish may show.

Though drifting is the most used of boat techniques, the boat may be taken near to the shallows, particularly off points of shore or outcrops of rock on the bottom, and casts made in towards the shore, over the shallows. The wind-facing side of a lake is more profitable, because it is to that shore that natural flies are blown.

## Dapping

On the great lakes of Ireland one of the greatest events of the fishing
year is the dapping season. There are indeed two such seasons, of which
one is the more important. The greater one is the Mayfly season; the
lesser one is the daddy-long-legs season. The former comes during May
and into June; the latter comes in September. In late summer too dapping is done with the Murragh, a very big sedge fly. These are no
business of delicacy with an artificial fly. The natural flies are collected
and are used several together mounted on a large hook. Above the hook
is a short length of stout nylon, and above that a line of floss silk. The
rod is long, fourteen feet usually.

The water is covered by drifts in the way already described, and the
anglers hold their rods high so that the wind takes the light floss line and
arches it out downwind of the drift of the boat. The fly-baited hook, so
hovered, bounces and dibbles on the surface. To this, in a good season,
come many of the best trout in the water, slashing at the copious gobbet
of fly. This is a rather crude and easy way to fish, perhaps, but greatly
loved by those who do it. Its excitement and success cannot be denied;
and it has something of a festival about it.

Scottish lakes have their own variants of dapping, but there it is done
not with natural flies but with very big and buzzy artificials. Brown
trout can be the quarry, but often it is sea trout—and a desperate spell
this fishing puts on its devotees, and some splendid baskets it may
produce.

# CHAPTER TWELVE

# The Fish

## The Roach

IT is almost inescapable that a description of the fishes that are the quarry of British anglers shall begin with the roach. In British waters it has a wider occurrence than any other fish—except perhaps the perch; it is more fished for than any other fish. To its devotees it is almost a reason for living.

The roach is a member of the great carp family to which a majority of our freshwater fishes belong, and it is one of the smaller members of the family. More roach of half a pound and under are caught than are

Fig. 76. Roach

caught upwards of half a pound. On a majority of waters a roach of a pound is a good fish, and to most roach fishermen a roach weighing two pounds is a lifetime's quest, and those who are successful in the quest are in a minority. The roach can, in favourable circumstances, grow bigger; in recent years the list of roach weighing three pounds or more has grown much more quickly than formerly—tackle has improved, the average level of skill is higher, there are vastly more anglers than there used to be. At the time of writing the British record for roach stands at three pounds fourteen ounces, and there it has stood for a long time. Many have thought that the almost mystical weight of four pounds could never be attained; but one angler, Nat Holmes of Omagh in the

County Tyrone, *did* catch one of that weight in Fairy Water which runs
not far from Omagh. It was, unfortunately, never officially verified.

From all this it might be hard to perceive the reason for the imagina-
tive grip of the roach on so many anglers. But, undoubtedly, the roach
does exercise such a grip; there is a powerful fascination in it; there is
a special delight in the fishing for it. It is hard of capture in its larger
sizes, subtle and shy and evasive; its capture demands experience and
accomplishment in the angler. When it is caught, it is such a very
satisfying and delighting creature to draw from unseen places beneath
the water's surface.

It is brilliantly silvery, prismatically glancing with colour, with red in
its eye and coral red for its belly fins. Its dorsal fin and tail fin are sepia
to greenish brown, its back dark with deep blue or greenish blue; its
belly is white. A handsome fish, a lovely sight for wondering eyes. There
is a rather elegant yeoman solidity about it.

Predominantly the roach is a feeder at the bottom. There, as a
member of its shoal, it eats snails, grubs, insects, freshwater shrimps,
caddis, worms. It eats much vegetable matter too, and most particularly
those filamentous algae which are known as flannel weed and silkweed.
If there is a gravel bottom available it will live on it for preference,
avoiding mud if it may be avoided. It will always live in weed or in the
vicinity of weed if there is weed, and, generally, only reaches its finest
size and condition when it has weed and gravel. The most notable
exception is the reservoirs of the Metropolitan Water Board. In these
roach grow phenomenally—and it was from one of them that there
came the roach that holds the record; Bill Penney was its captor. It is
an indication of the wide variety of waters in which the roach is to be
found that it grows to its biggest sizes in two such dissimilar environ-
ments—these great reservoirs and the gravel-bottomed, heavily weeded,
crystal-watered chalk streams. These chalk streams have their fame,
in the main, for the splendour of the trout fishing they give; but Nature
made them mixed fisheries. Coarse fish, and most particularly roach,
thrive magnificently in them if allowed to. The Hampshire Avon, largely
a chalk stream, is indeed (and most fortunately) preserved as a mixed
fishery in its lower reaches, and its roach are splendid.

But the roach gives its delight in many other places, in northern
canals, in the labyrinth of waters that comprise the Norfolk Broads and
the rivers which connect them, the fen countries of Lincolnshire and
Cambridgeshire and of north Somerset, and most other places that
coarse fishing may be done. The finest roach fishery of all (apart, perhaps, from the London reservoirs) is that fishing in Northern Ireland
near Omagh already referred to. Until 1957 it was unknown, with no
fisher for its wonderful roach but Nat Holmes—and he, against his

better judgement, was authoritatively told that the fish were rudd. This was significant because it was believed that there were no true roach in Ireland except in the River Blackwater of Co. Cork. But, in 1957, the author, on a tour for the discovery of new fishing in Northern Ireland, came to Omagh and went with Nat Holmes to Fairy Water. It was then that he, the author, made the discovery that these fish were true roach, that they were in these waters by Omagh in huge numbers, and that they grew to unprecedented sizes.

More roach are caught by float fishing methods than by any other means; the particular form of float fishing depending upon which of the very wide variety of roach waters is being fished. In the still or very slow waters of the fen country and in many northern canals, the commonest method is to use a constant feeding-in of cloud groundbait so as to keep a milky cloud in the water, and casting into the clouded water with very light float tackle baited with one maggot. Little balls of the cloud are thrown in often, and into the cloud a few 'feeder' maggots are also thrown to go slowly sinking. The hook is usually size 16 or smaller, the nylon from one to two pounds breaking strain, the float very small, and the shotting very light. Thus the baited hook sinks slowly, and may be taken at any depth as it sinks. But it has been shown that even on canals on which this is the established way of taking large numbers of rather small roach, an angler who uses heavier tackle, baits with a big bait such as a lobworm, and is prepared to wait with his bait legered on the bottom, may take a really big roach—if infrequently.

On such rivers as the Thames and the Great Ouse, rivers of slow or medium pace, the fixed-line method already described is much used, as is also the Thames method of trotting down from a punt or boat anchored across the current. Fishing with a bait laid-on with float tackle, or with leger or float leger, will often take bigger roach than will float fishing with the stream. Such fish come less often but are much more likely to be the so greatly desired two-pounders.

On really fast rivers, most particularly the Hampshire Avon, it is the nature of the river rather than the fish which dictates methods. The heavy float tackle already described must be used, long-trotting down swims that have been heavily groundbaited. Legering, again, is likely to take big fish, and especially that form of legering in which the bait is worked down a run between the weeds by stages, leaving the lead in one place for a little while, then working it a little farther down, and so on.

The fishing of such still waters as reservoirs is dominated by the depth of the water, which is beyond the convenient use of float tackle. Legering with big baits will take more of those fine reservoir roach than other methods will. Because groundbaiting is not allowed in the Metropolitan

Water Board's reservoirs, such a bait as bread flake or a flaky piece of crust often does better than other baits. Fragments of the bait flaking away serve, to some extent, the same purpose as groundbaiting.

In slow- or medium-paced rivers roach in summer are to be found in quite shallow swims, even as little as a foot between weed beds, or between weed beds and the bank. Where such swims bank up at their downstream ends is often a good place to look for roach. If a quite shallow run between weed beds falls away at its downstream end into a deeper hole, that too is likely to hold roach. Often a swim may be found in a not very deep trough against a reed-fringed bank, with a weed bed along its farther edge; that too may be a good roach swim in summer. In winter roach move into deeper water, and water out of the heavier push of winter current. The easy edges of currents will often hold them then, and so will gentle currents against the bank, if they are not too shallow. In weir pools currents that eddy back in a direction opposite to the main rush of water will often hold roach—and this both in summer and winter.

On the fast rivers, those of the Avon kind, roach must be looked for in currents far faster, far heavier, than could be expected to hold them in other rivers. In summer the fast shallow runs between weed beds, and in winter the steadier deeper swims. Anglers coming from slower rivers often wander wistfully looking for 'the slow water' when coming newly to the Avon. There is no slow water; the fish live in the fast water.

Roach fishing, by and large, is dominated by the use of maggots as bait. The result is too high a preponderance of small and medium roach. Many other baits will take roach, and many of them will take bigger roach. Flake is exceedingly good, so is crust. Worms are good, and the very biggest roach are to be taken on lobworms. The tail of a lobworm is a good roach bait, and a whole red worm or brandling often works well. Stewed wheat may sometimes be very good. In season elderberries can be good where they fall from overhanging bushes. An excellent summer bait, in places where it occurs naturally, is silkweed. Natural baits such as caddis have their fine days.

The roach may be caught throughout the season, but autumn and winter fishing gives better sport (in terms of size and condition of fish) than does summer.


## The Bream

The bream, also a member of the carp family, is a fish of placid places; it is a slow ambling sort of fish. Like the roach, it is a shoal fish, and its shoals may sometimes be enormous. Slowly, tranquilly, the shoal browses over its aqueous pastures, not staying in one place long—often indeed moving all the time. The waters in which it lives are also slow, slow or still; or so it is in most cases. There are some cases of bream that live in more rapid waters, and the most notable case is that of the colony of bream that lives in the fast, clear, gravel-bottomed water of the Royalty Fishery on the Hampshire Avon, only just above the estuary. But, most typically, the bream lives in the slow mud-bottomed waters of Norfolk, of the fen country of Lincolnshire and Cambridge-shire and that similar country of north Somerset. It occurs equally notably in the meres of Shropshire, in the lowland lochs that surround the town of Lochmaben in Dumfriesshire. It is to be found in a multi-tude of creeping lowland rivers and willow-margined millponds and

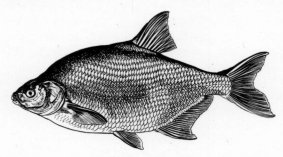

Fig. 77. Bream

such quiet waters. It also grows to splendid sizes in some of the Metro-politan Water Board reservoirs. The Thames produces some of the finest bream caught anywhere. Ireland has a multitude of very fine bream waters; in a majority of its rivers, in countless lakes, large and small, in the canals, in all these, the bream team and grow big. And, broadly, these Irish bream tend to greater vigour, more capacity for fighting than most of those met in English waters. The biggest bream of all, the record fish of thirteen pounds eight ounces, was caught in Chiddingstone Castle lake in Kent.

There are two bream, two species. One is the common bream (or bronze bream); the other is the silver (or white) bream. The common bream is the bigger one, and the only one with which anglers are willingly concerned. It is caught on the majority of only moderate bream waters at weights that average about two pounds; but on good waters, such a one as the Thames, fish of five pounds, six pounds, up to nine pounds or thereabouts, are not uncommon. The silver bream has a close resemblance to the young common bream, but seldom grows to more than a few ounces in weight. It *can* grow to weights of three pounds and more, but it seldom does. To most anglers a silver bream is indistinguishable from an immature common bream.

The common bream cannot be called, even by its devotees, a fish of elegance or grace. It is deep, high in the back, deep in the belly, narrow from side to side; its dorsal fin is rather peaked up in front, and its anal fin is very long. The lower lobe of its tail fin (or caudal fin) is longer than the upper lobe. The colour of it has a silvery base, overlaid by a bronzy tarnish that deepens on the back to a brownish olive. It has been said, and justly said, that a bream is like a tarnished pewter dish standing on its edge. With such a shape, and the ease of temperament that goes with it, the bream is not a stirring fighter. His best attempts arise when he is able to turn his awkward broadside shape side-on to a current of some strength.

The bream is most at home in its sluggish waters, when it has a muddy bottom in which to forage—there is no fish which may more properly be called a bottom-feeder. It sucks and sifts through the mud, seeking the organisms that live therein, and a muddy clouding of the water is often a sign of its presence. It eats all sorts of water insects, snails, worms, grubs, and great amounts of such tiny creatures as tubifex worms, the larvae of mosquitoes, daphnia.

Fishing for bream is very much concerned with location of the shoal. In two swims, a few yards apart, one angler may catch bream steadily while the other angler has not one bite. Location of the shoal is complicated by the roving habits of bream, and, when a shoal *is* located, it must be an immediate object to retain the shoal in that place by lavish groundbaiting. In bream fishing you cannot over-groundbait. Nor should the groundbait be insubstantial in its ingredients. Quantities of stale loaves soaked till mashy soft, then drained and mashed up and mixed and dried off with meal (such as layer's mash), make good bream groundbait.

So important is the location and holding of bream shoals that Peter Stone of Oxford, as good a bream fisher as there is, has devised a system with his friends. They start at the upper limit of the water in which they expect to find bream (on the Thames), and fish as a team, spaced out down the bank. If no bream are found presently, they move down one stage to try for a time in the water immediately below. So they go on till one angler finds bream, if only one fish. Then, at once, all those fishing move in to close, very close proximity to he who has found fish. They groundbait at once and heavily and concentrate on this area which now is carpeted with groundbait.

Float fishing is a great deal used for bream with the bait, in moving water, just tripping bottom. This may be effective for the taking of numbers of bream rather than for the biggest single specimens. For them, the bigger bream, a stationary bait lying on the bottom is usually better. Such fishing may be done with float tackle laying-on, with leger tackle, or with float leger tackle. In the deep swims of such a river as the Great Ouse, which may be holes in mid-river fourteen or more feet deep, a sliding float is sometimes used; leger fishing is however often better.

On shallow still waters, most typically the Norfolk Broads, the shoal is located by the muddy clouding of the water, and there held by heavy groundbaiting. The boat—and this Broads fishing must be by boat—is anchored well off, a long cast off, and float tackle is cast up to where the fish are feeding. The fixed-spool reel is a great advantage for this fishing.

On reservoirs, because the fishing is necessarily in deep water, legering is more used than any other way; and, similarly, the greater part of Thames bream fishing is in deep water in the middle of the river. Legering then is obviously better because float fishing would be difficult, even with a sliding float, and the weight of the leger lead makes long casting to the swim easier.

There is a form of float fishing for bream, devised by Jan Roelfs, that most successful Dutch angler, which is based upon the premise that the biggest bream often hover higher in the water, over the heads of the smaller bream throng feeding on the bottom. A very long slim float is used, as much as ten inches long. In its centre is a small cork or balsawood body in which is a ring for the threading of the line. At the bottom of the float is another ring. Thus the float can be used slider fashion for deep water. The cast is so shotted that the long upper half of the float, above the body, stands above the water, and this light shotting also allows the bait to sink slowly.

So, when the cast is made, the bait does not at once sink to the main shoal on the bottom, but goes down slowly while the long float cants over gradually. During this descent the big bream have their chance to take the bait without competition from smaller fish. Jan Roelfs's results, and those of his followers, have shown how often they do so take it.

Though many small bream are caught on fine tackle and tiny hooks, and this more particularly in fishing matches, fishing for worthy sized bream demands bigger tackle. Big bream prefer, on the whole, bigger baits; and bigger baits demand bigger hooks if those hooks are to take hold. Most bream fishing can be better done with hook sizes from, say, No. 10 to No. 4 than it can with smaller hooks. And, though nylon of two pounds breaking strain is used for the catching of multitudes of small bream, five or six pounds breaking strain is more sensible stuff for big bream. Stiff tip-actioned match rods are often and very mistakenly used for bream; a rod of the Avon type is far more suitable. A longer rod may sometimes be dictated if float fishing is to be used in deepish water,* but still, if big bream are expected it is preferable that the rod shall have its action going right down it—and in that it will be unlike most of the rods which are sold for this sort of fishing.

Probably maggots are more often used for bream than any other bait; but the reason for that is no product of reason, but simply that a majority of anglers think only in terms of maggots. Maggots will catch bream, more particularly small and medium bream; but they are not the most likely bait to take big bream. Bread in its various forms is as good a bream bait as any—crust, paste, flake, will all serve the bream fisher well; and for big bream the pieces used should not be too small. Many a big bream has taken the golf-ball-sized lump of paste put out for carp.

Worms are good bream baits, and for the biggest bream a lobworm is more likely to be successful than one of the smaller worms—though this should not be too thoughtlessly accepted. In a clear shallow canal, for example, there may be days of bright light when the smaller worm may work better than the bigger one. Worms have the disadvantage, sometimes a considerable one, that they attract eels, those pestering small eels that gorge the bait, tangle the tackle, waste much good fishing time.

Stewed wheat will sometimes have its days with bream, though, it must be admitted, the bream it takes are more often small and medium ones than big ones. Freshwater mussels can be a good bait for big bream.

Like the roach the bream is an all round the season fish. Autumn and mild winter days probably see the best bream fishing.

## The Tench

You may sometimes catch tench in winter; but the whole atmosphere of tench, the whole fat happy beauty of it, the whole true context of it, is summer, warm dewy placid summer. The time for tench, the proper time for the truest enjoyment of tench, are those warm still mornings of mid-summer when from dawn to breakfast time not an air stirs the satin of the surface, and the sinking scented summer evenings when moths fly and hay smells sweet in the meadows. Sometimes, on some waters, you may catch tench through the day; but the purpose of fishing is the delight it gives, and the purest delight of tench fishing is in the early and late hours.

Most generally indeed it is only in those hours that tench are to be found feeding freely; during the heat of summer days they tend to

---

* A sliding float would still allow the benefit of the shorter livelier rod in such a case.

drowse away the hours close to the surface, lying among the leaves of the lily pads. There they may sometimes be tempted with small baits on light tackle, but always of course with a high chance that the light tackle will be broken in the fight that follows.

It is a deceptive fish, this tench, so sleepy seeming, so lusciously fat, so round, so much an idling browser, that it might be expected to respond lethargically to being hooked. How far indeed it is from doing so. Sometimes it may give tentative warning of its bite for minutes, even much longer, stirring the float, making it lean and shiver, sidle on the surface, before it does at last slide away. But then, when the strike is made, its first run will be long, heavy, astonishingly and delightfully powerful, and it will not give up quickly.

The tench is another member of the carp family, a solid robust member, a beautiful member. It is often called the green tench, and some

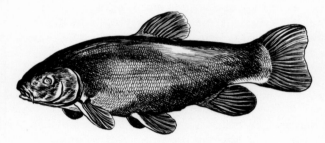

Fig. 78. Tench

tench are greenish; but the most typical tench, and the most beautiful ones, are brownish with a suffusion of gold, a buttercup gold that pricks out the edges of the tiny scales. At its best, its well-fed best, it is quite a deep fish, tending to roundness in section, very smooth, very varnished looking. Its eye is small and crimson with a fine small ring of gold round the pupil, and its great broad fins are spatular and rather bluish.

It is not among the biggest of fish, but it is not small. A three-pounder is a fair fish, a five-pounder a good one. The record stands at nine pounds one ounce (at this time of writing). Bigger ones, ten pounds, even eleven pounds, exist, but, so far, no one has found a means for their deception.

It is sometimes to be found in rivers, slow creeping ones, mostly; but it is more typically a fish of still waters. Old willow-grown mill ponds, reedy meres, are characteristic tench waters, so are neglected canals, and it is now much to be found in the increasing gravel pit lakes.

Wherever it is, it is much more often than not in close association with weed; the denser the weed jungles the more plentiful and bigger will be the tench.

In these weeds it finds its food, tiny creatures of the ooze which it sucks from the mud bottom among the weeds, snails and their eggs which it finds on the weeds, insect larvae, caddis particularly, water hog louse, beetles, worms, and some of the weed itself it eats too.

So swims in which to fish for tench should be chosen close to weed beds. Openings in weed beds are good; and, for the best chance of good fishing, there is often advantage if the swim is prepared in advance. The weed may be so dense that there is no space big enough for fishing, and one must be made. Some sort of weed cutter can be used (two scythe blades bolted together make a good weed cutter), and it can be dragged through the weeds till an open area a few yards square is made. It will be the better swim if lanes leading to it from several directions are also cut. All this should be done at least several days in advance of fishing. Then, on each of those days, groundbait should be put into the swim and along the lanes leading to it. Plenty of groundbait should be used— the bread and meal mixture as for bream.

But this is ambitious preparation; it needs much access to the water before the fishing day. It is preparation such as may be used on club or private waters, and, once started, may pay very well indeed if the swim so made is maintained. For many tench fishermen it is not possible; but they, if they can possibly do so, should groundbait their swims for at least two or three days before fishing. The swims to choose for this summer fishing should not be too deep; from about three to five feet is usually deep enough,* because the tench in summer does not like to be far from the sun and light—it is they which produce the proliferation of the organisms which it eats.

On the fishing day more groundbait can be put in, and it can be put in with no fear of frightening the tench. On the contrary the disturbance and clouding of the water attracts them—it is indeed an old practice to rake the bottom of the swim before fishing. The tench come for what is disturbed from the bottom.

As to the choice of fishing method, more anglers than not will float fish because there is such pleasure in watching a float at the starting of a new season in June. There is such a delicious excitement in seeing the first stirring of the float when the tench begin to feed. The bait is best put right on the bottom, using the float tackle with laying-on tactics. The tackle should not be too light. A rod of the Avon type is as good as any, with its shock-absorbing action going right through it; and a

* On some gravel pit lakes it may be that there are no swims as shallow as this, and thus a swim must be chosen which is relatively shallow.

line of less than five pounds breaking strain is not practical for tench that live near weeds and may be big. Hook sizes should suit bait sizes.

Paste is as good a bait as there is for tench, and in most cases a piece as big as a walnut is better than a smaller one. That needs a size 5 or 6 hook—certainly no smaller. Crust is good, so is flake; those bread baits, and worms, may be said to be the best bait for tench. Maggots will take tench, and there are circumstances in which they may work when bigger baits will not; there are days when the tench are sifting through the bottom mud for tiny creatures and cannot be induced to take an interest in bigger things. One or two maggots on, say, a size 12 hook, and lying on the bottom, may be successful. Loose maggots should be scattered to lie on and in the mud.

Though the use of float tackle for tench is so deeply engaging, it has to be admitted that leger tackle is often more likely to succeed with the bigger fish—either as simple leger or as float leger. If the tench should be particularly reluctant to bite, in very clear water perhaps, both float and lead can be discarded. For this mode of fishing the fixed-spool reel is undoubtedly preferable to the centre-pin. The hook is tied to the monofilament reel line, and with nothing more at all between rod and bait, the cast is made and the rod put in two rests. The line lies along the bottom, and the pick-up arm of the reel is left in the off position. When a fish picks up the bait and moves off with it, the line is seen to be slipping off the spool of the reel. Then the rod is picked up, the pick-up flicked on with a turn of the handle, the strike is made.

Tench in clear water canals of no great depth often have their own special problem. They may be very finickily suspicious and selective, and be entirely proof against normal fishing with float or leger. The lift method with a small bait, a maggot, two maggots, a small piece of crust or paste, may very well work. There are indeed many times when the lift method is more successful on any tench water, and with any bait.

As late summer slips into autumn, the early and late habit of tench tends to change. The middle hours of warm dull soft days will often give sport with tench then, and it may be in deeper swims than those of summer. Specially mild days of winter will bring tench on to feed too, and, if you want sport so unseasonable in atmosphere, they can be caught.

## The Rudd

Rudd, it is sometimes said, resemble roach. Perhaps, in poor mean waters, waters lacking the best that is needed for the well-being of rudd, such a comparison is justified. Where rudd live in waters that are happy for them, the comparison is a poor one, hollow and misleading.

The rudd is similar in size to the roach, and, like it, a member of the carp family, but heavier for its length because it is so sturdily, even massively thick about the shoulders, so stoutly humped over the back. Its dorsal fin is set well back, farther back than that of the roach. The roach's mouth has a weak and timid look, with its lower lip barely in line with the upper one; it has almost a retreating look. The rudd's mouth is upturned, jutting, with lower lip aggressive-looking. It is really no difference of character, the one timid, the other bold, that this expresses; it arises from the roach's bottom-feeding habits and the rudd's tendency to feed more from the surface than lower down in the water.

But all this is not the most essential part of the difference of impression received from roach and rudd. No silver blue-backed fish the rudd,

Fig. 79. Rudd

not as the roach is. The roach is modestly coloured, sober, if it is compared with the rudd. The rudd is a beautiful fish, chunky, stout, coloured like a banner. The silveriness of its flanks is heavily over-plated with gold, a rich yellowness of gold (though, in some waters, this may be darker, a bronzy colour). A roach's dorsal and caudal fins are dull; those of the rudd, and all its fins, are a glowing orange vermilion, verging to scarlet. In those more darkly coloured rudd this red deepens to a smoky wine-like colour.

There is as much difference in habit between them too, the roach and the rudd. While the roach haunts its bottom swims, the rudd, except in winter, is near the surface. Through summer and much of autumn it is a fish of the upper water, a seeker of the sun, and it is on sunny days that it is most active. On the surface, or close to it, it finds much of its food—insects floating on the surface, insects freely swimming near the surface, snails, grubs, all sorts of aquatic animals in the weeds that grow to the surface.

Rudd are sometimes to be found in rivers, usually the slower ones, and they are particularly so to be found in Ireland (the rudd is very widely distributed in Ireland). But the rudd is more characteristically a lake fish, and, in Britain, a rather locally distributed one. It is a common fish of the Norfolk Broads and the Lincolnshire and Cambridgeshire Fen Country; it is in Slapton Ley, that rather strange mere that lies narrowly between the hills and the sea beach in South Devon. It lives in the fen district of north Somerset, and it is scattered rather sparsely in other places.

A rudd of two pounds is quite a good one; a three-pounder is good. The record rudd weighed four and a half pounds, and was caught in a Norfolk mere by the Rev. E. C. Alston.

To catch rudd in a lake one method stands in easy predominance. A boat, standing off a long cast's distance, is taken along the face of the reed beds. At several points a slice of bread is thrown to lie on the water close to the reeds—and there it may be anchored with a string and a stone. To this bread the rudd will congregate, nibbling at it. Light float tackle is used—a fixed-spool reel for ease of casting, a small float, the hook set a couple of feet or so below the float. Only very light shotting is used because the bait should sink slowly—and, indeed, this is better achieved by having immediately under the float enough lead to cock it, leaving the bait to sink slowly by its own weight. The bait may be one to three maggots on a hook of appropriate size, say size 10 or size 12. This tackle, so baited, is cast up to the floating bread, and, very often, the float will shoot off before the bait has fully sunk. If such is not the case, the bait should not be left long idle. It should be retrieved and another cast made. Crust is also a good bait, but, of course, a shot will be needed near it to overcome its buoyancy. The same method can be used without the floating bread, moving very slowly along the reeds making prospecting casts. Bays in the reeds can be very pleasantly and effectively fished by tying up the boat right against the reeds and fishing out into the bay.

In those slow rivers that hold rudd similar methods will work well. If maggots are the bait a few can be thrown in loose and often, and the same self-cocking float tactics used. If two feet from float to hook does not work, the gap can be experimentally increased till the rudd's depth is found. Sometimes it may be found that a setting equal to the full depth of the water is best, though the rudd will mostly be caught at about half depth as the bait sinks slowly. Stewed wheat is sometimes effective for such fishing, and so are small worms or paste.

Rudd in summer are loving takers of flies; dry fly fishing or wet fly fishing will take many of them. The fly rod indeed gives a good way of bait fishing for rudd. Rod, line, and cast can be as for fly fishing, but with an eyed hook, say size 12–14, instead of a fly, and on the hook one or two maggots. They can be cast like a fly and allowed to sink by their own weight.

In winter rudd go deeper; they become much like roach in their habits. In lakes they may be fished for as for roach, on or close to the bottom in swims against the shore towards which the wind is blowing. Worms are often a good bait.

## The Barbel

The barbel, also a member of the carp family, is altogether a formidable fish, big, strong, a liver often in strenuous places; it is a most dour and powerful fighter. As completely as any fish is, it is a river fish. Not for it (if it is left to Nature and not artificial stocking) the slow river, the placid gentle current. Its natural habitat is the river with at least some

Fig. 80. Barbel

strength of flow, and there it will be found as often in the heavier pushes of water as it will in the easier places. Look at the shape of the barbel and you can divine something of the sort of water for which it was devised by Nature; it has its own very specialized streamlining. Along its belly it is nearly flat, but from the rather flattened snout to the tail there is one sweeping curve, right over the back. Then imagine this fish, so specializedly shaped, lying closely on the gravel bottom which it loves; imagine the strong current sweeping over that arch of back. Not only would the force of current not inconvenience it, not dislodge it from its position—it would hold it down, hold it easily in its position on the gravel, and that is a clue to the barbel's way of life. Its colour too is that of the gravel, amber, darker on the back. Under the current it lives on the gravel, finds its food there. As to how it finds its food, look at the barbules round its mouth; there are four of them, organs of taste. With them it searches, by taste, among the stones, and so finds its food.

That food is partly animal, partly vegetable. It eats insects, crustaceans, snails, worms; it also eats the silkweed that is brought down by the current from the weirs below which it often lies. And, quite often, particularly in the summer, and particularly as it grows bigger, it eats small fish.

As you might expect from the places in which it lives, the barbel is strong—though it is often to be found in places of gentler current, it does spend much of its life in heavy currents. Some say that the barbel is the most heavily powerful fighting fish of them all, and there is something to be said for this claim. The fast streamy rivers of Yorkshire, the Trent, the Thames and its tributaries, were the barbel's main original homes, but it is now acclimatized in many other rivers, and of those most dramatically in the Avon of Hampshire and the Stour of Dorset. In them it has grown big and prospered. In a good barbel river you may call a fish of nine or ten pounds a good one, a twelve-pounder a very good one. The record stands at the moment of writing at fourteen pounds six ounces, but, because bigger barbel are not rare, that record will not continue unbroken.

The nature of float fishing for barbel is variable with the sort of water in which the fishing is done. England's most famous barbel water now is on the Hampshire Avon, and there the barbel swims are strong and urgent. They may be four feet deep or they may be eight; but they are all heavy in their flow. The tackle must be what the water dictates. The rod must be strong with plenty of action right down its length, and that length is best at ten or eleven feet. The typical Avon rod is as much used as anything, but its power could be rather inadequate for a barbel of, say, eleven pounds or more. An angler setting himself particularly to the pursuit of big barbel would do better to use such a rod as that designed by Richard Walker for carp, the Mark IV Carp Rod. It has the necessary capacity for casting not very heavy baits, but also the power for coping with big strong fish in heavy currents.

Lines should match. Though one of six pounds breaking strain will manage well enough with the average run of barbel, one of nine or ten pounds breaking strain is better suited to big barbel. Floats, as they must usually be on the Avon, are big, very buoyant, able to carry the lead necessary to get down quickly to the bottom. Hook sizes depend on bait sizes, and the range of sizes is more likely to be from 4 to 8 than anything smaller—though here a proviso must be made. Sometimes in bright weather in summer, Avon barbel in hard-fished reaches become shy and finicky, and may then need quite small maggot baits on suitably smaller hooks.

Fairly copious groundbaiting is needed, pressed into firm balls, orange-size, so that they may go quickly to the bottom; they must be thrown in well above the swim to be fished. The common bread and meal basis is right, but, if baits other than bread are used, samples of them should be included in each ball. Cheese, for example, is a highly successful barbel bait, so are quite big pieces of sausage; lobworms sometimes work well. The groundbaiting works best if it is done for a day or two in advance of the fishing, and then continued during the fishing. But if it is done only during the fishing it can bring results. On the Kennet, incidentally, there is a school of barbel fishermen who use no groundbait; though they make no big bags they catch plenty of barbel.

The float should be set at, say, a foot to eighteen inches more than the depth of the swim, and, as the tackle is trotted down, it should be retarded just a little to induce the trail of nylon from the lead to the hook to go in advance, going more or less parallel with the bottom and very close to it. This mode of fishing can be scaled down in weight and modified to suit other slower types of water. Barbel swims on the Kennet for example, though usually quickly flowing, lack the heaviness of Avon swims. On the Thames, though barbel are often to be found under the push and disturbance of weir pool currents, they are also to be found in the gentle flow of backwaters.

Many barbel do fall to float fishing, but there is no doubt that leger-ing is more often the better method. It can be done in several ways. The least successful is the stationary leger, done with a lead heavy enough to hold the bottom in one place, with the cast made downstream and across and then left to fish in that one place. Barbel are caught thus, but a moving leger will catch more and often better barbel.

The rolling leger is the best known way, and it takes many barbel. The best lead is the Arlesey bomb, and it should be used as described in the chapter on legering. There is another way of using it which will often take barbel that are shy of taking a bait on the, so to speak, standard rolling leger method. The lead should be of such a weight that has been found just able to hold bottom in the force of the current. Then the cast is made upstream and the tackle just persuaded to roll back towards the angler, he, meanwhile, taking up on the reel the slack line gathered. This method overcomes the fish's suspicion of a taut line. The other method of moving leger fishing, already described, of working the tackle down runs by the lifting and lowering of the rod, is also a good one.

But, quite often on summer days, barbel are to be found lying in fast streamy but quite shallow currents that finger through the heavy trusses of weed. If a leger lead that is at all heavy is used for the searching of such water, the lead is likely to become immovably entangled in the weed—and, yet, it is through the weed that the bait must be fished. It may be done by bending over the line above the stop-shot a piece of nylon monofilament so that the doubled hang of it is, say, two inches.

On this can be pinched two or three swanshot, the upper one being close to the line so that the loop of nylon round the line is too small to pass over the stop-shot. This makes a leger lead that will allow the bait to find its way through the labyrinth of weed with only a small chance of entanglement. It is a means of catching barbel that otherwise might be inviolate.

Those baits which have become standard for barbel are likely to work very well in water where the barbel are much fished for; the fish have become used to regarding them as food. But the angler fortunate enough to be able to fish for barbel on waters not commonly open to coarse fishing may find that barbel are aloof to such baits. A dead minnow fished on the bottom is then likely to do much better; and, indeed, it is probably a better bait for the biggest barbel anywhere. A drawback is that eels are even more likely to be interested—but that is a chance that must be taken.

Barbel can be caught throughout summer and mild autumn, and on soft days in winter. But when frost and very cold water come barbel stop feeding.

## The Perch

There is a splendour about the perch, a dashing, glowing, painted look; there is something piratical about it. It is an aggressive marauding fish, and that is what it looks. It has two dorsal fins, and the first one has exceedingly sharp spines; the action of the fin reflects the fish's mood. As its prey is sighted and draws near the fin is erected; when the fish is quiescent the fin lies back. The whole shape of the perch indeed is a key to character; it has a large fierce head with a large fierce mouth, its back is aggressively humped, its scales are rough to the touch. Its colour is beautiful, almost soldierly. On the back it is deep rather bronzy green, and down its flanks it shades into a lighter colour that is pricked with gold. Its belly is beautifully contrasting white, and the belly fins are clear coral red. Down its sides, from the back nearly to the belly, there are black stripes, usually six of them; the one that originates at the junction of the two dorsal fins is usually bifurcated at the top, and occasionally, others of the stripes may be so too. A splendid handsome thrilling fish the perch may look, and that is how the beginner usually sees it, because, in far more cases than not, it is the first fish he sees.

That this is so is because perch, mostly, are specially bold and freely biting, and most particularly this is so of smaller perch. So, when the beginner, with no art, no tactics born of experience, just drops into the water his rough tackle baited with worm, it is invariably a perch which seizes the worm if it is seized at all. Then what a dazzled spell of fascination falls upon the beginner—here is this fierce brilliant little fish a-bristle with life, a wonderful creature to be drawn from green depths. It is thus that many lifelong anglers are made. And, where this happens once it may happen a number of times because perch, except for the very biggest ones, are shoal fish. One after another of the shoal may be caught. It has always been said that if one perch of a shoal should be hooked and lost, no more of the shoal will bite; but often fact does not bear this out.

It is another advantage of the perch that only the roach is as widely distributed. In a majority of rivers, in most lakes, in canals, in reservoirs, in old green mill pools, in gravel pits, the perch is to be found. In rivers, when the season opens in June, it is usually in the shallower water, in the runs between the weeds, in the shallow more easily flowing

Fig. 81. Perch

areas beside big main currents. As the season goes on to early autumn the perch moves to deeper quieter water, and then is soon in those places that all anglers know as 'perchy'. These are deep holes most often, out of the current, in the elbows of sharp bends in the river, against the piers of bridges, against lock structures, against camp sheathing, under deep banks. There they are often congregated in great shoals, ranging mostly from about midwater to the bottom.

In lakes summer will find the perch in the weedy shallower water; but there too autumn will send them into deeper water, and in winter they will usually be in the deepest water. Thus in gravel pits, which are often very deep, they may be in the deepest parts throughout winter.

Though the perch is so obviously a predator, a preyer upon other fish, through much of its life its diet is wider than this suggests. It is much given to hunting through the weed beds for caddis, for snails, for all sorts of grubs and insects, eating all these things as well as the minnows and gudgeon and young of other species. It is as it becomes really big that it turns more and more to the pursuit of other, smaller fish. Even then it does not give up entirely its taste, always strong, for worms. The oldest biggest perch may be caught on a big lobworm.

In a majority of waters a perch of a pound is quite a fair fish—in some enclosed waters indeed which are densely populated with perch, they may never grow beyond a few inches in length. In waters which may be called good perch waters a perch of two pounds is a fair fish, and one of three pounds is a good fish. Anywhere a perch of four pounds and more is a very good fish, but there are plenty of perch, as yet uncaught, which are heavier, even as much as ten pounds.

Far more perch are caught by float fishing than by any other method, and a very pleasant undemanding form of fishing it is. Almost any rod will do, though one of the Avon type is best, and the reel may be a centre-pin or a fixed-spool. What the strength of the line is is dependent upon what is known of the size of the fish in the water being fished, and upon the presence or absence of strong weed growth.

For much perch fishing a breaking strain of three pounds is adequate; but should the fish run very big or the snags be fierce, then five or six pounds is better. Hook sizes should match bait sizes, but it is always an advantage, bait size allowing, for the hook to be larger than smaller. The perch has a big mouth and it is a fierce fighter. If a lobworm is the bait the hook cannot be smaller than size 6, and for a red worm or a brandling size 12 is the smallest which is practical. A live minnow is an exceedingly good bait for a perch, and so is a gudgeon, and for them a hook should not be smaller than size 6. A minnow should be hooked through the upper lip, *not* both lips; if hooked through both lips it cannot breathe and will die. If a gudgeon is small it too can be hooked through the upper lip; but a bigger one is better hooked with a treble hook nicked through the back just in front of the dorsal fin.

In summer float fishing the tackle should be adjusted so that the bait is at midwater or rather lower, and worked in the weedy shallows. So it may be both in rivers and still waters. But, with autumn, it is the 'perchy' places that should be so fished in rivers; in still waters that are not too deep, the deeper places can be fished. Those still waters which are really deep dictate that winter fishing must be with leger tackle. A big lobworm on leger tackle can be cast to lie at the bottom of the deep water.

An angler using float tackle will soon recognize the typical perch bite, quite unlike any other. The float will bob sharply, down and up; then it will do it again, perhaps several times. As it does so the angler must wait, and presently the float will go under and away in earnest; it is then that the strike should be made. In rivers too leger tackle can be used, though it is a less delightful dallying sort of fishing than this typical float fishing for perch. In those shallow places where the weed is dense, and only small holes are to be found in the jungle, the pater-noster must be used.

Spinning with light tackle, with the fixed-spool reel and a light line, may be a prolific way of taking perch, more particularly in places relatively free from weed. No bait is quite as good as a dead natural minnow, and a newly killed one is better than a preserved one; it can be killed by a finger flip on the head. Many artificial spinning baits will take perch well—spoons and Devon minnows are the best, and they should be about an inch in length.

Sink-and-draw fishing with a dead minnow is an exceedingly suc-cessful way of taking perch. Use a size 6 hook on nylon, and, with a baiting needle, thread the nylon through the mouth and body and out at the tail. Then draw the nylon through till the bend of the hook rests in the corner of the mouth. On the shank of the hook should be pinched a large split shot. Cast the minnow so that it sinks almost to the bottom, darting erratically this way and that, and then draw it nearly to the surface and let it sink again, now nearer to you. Continue so until it is brought back, and then make another cast at a different angle and work it back in the same way. Worms mounted on weightless or only lightly shotted tackle can be worked in the same way, and they too, so used, can be very successful.

One other way of taking perch, which, if not so abundantly produc-tive, is pleasant, is wet fly fishing. A quite big fly should be used, one of the bright flashy flies that are used for sea trout—Peter Ross, Zulu, Butcher, Bloody Butcher. Cast the fly, let it sink well, then retrieve it by short plucks with the left hand.

## The Chub

Perhaps there is a method of fishing that could not be used for the capture of chub; it is hard to think of one, and this is a clue to the nature of the chub. Omnivorous the chub is called, and this is a tech-nical way of saying that it is a perpetually greedy fish, an earnest full-time seeker of food in any form that bountiful Nature may send it. On the bottom, in the weeds, on the fry-haunted shallows, at and near the surface, everywhere in the water indeed, its slow, watchful, wary-eyed quest for food takes the chub. The careful watcher, cat-footed, going ghost-like, can often see the chub floating slowly through the clear green water, its full round eye with jewelled gleam rolling as it pursues its lazy ceaseless search for food.

It is, pre-eminently, a river fish, this chub, a member of the carp family; sometimes it may be found in lakes, but that is accidental,

untypical. Its natural home is in the easier gentler currents of rivers.
Early in the season, in high summer, it may be much in shallow water, in
the enlivened paths of water that thread between the weed beds where
the sun goes through to the gravel. When summer wanes and autumn
begins to cool the water, it will turn to deeper places and then the great
shadowy shoals of chub are to be found congregated in all those places
that are so eloquently 'chubby'. There you may see them, if you are
quiet, ranks and ranks of fish, seeming very dark of tail; indigo those
tails look as they just fan faintly in the gentle current. These chub-
haunted swims may lie between two major paths of current, between
great weed beds on the broad flat wide reaches of the river; most
typically of all they lie where easy currents come down close against
the bank, and it is those banks that have an overhang of trees and
bushes that are ideally fit for chub. So it is with the general run of

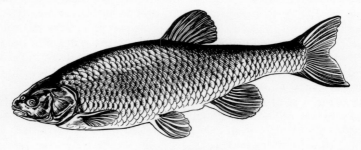

Fig. 82. Chub

chub, from that size when it becomes reasonably safe for them to
associate with their rapacious elders, up to what might be called the
biggest medium sizes—four pounds, four and a half pounds. After that,
as they become greater and greater in size, they fall away from the
shoaling habit, become solitaries, inhabitants of lonely holts under the
bank or in nearly impregnable corners of weed or root labyrinths.

In most good chub rivers you can call a three-pound fish a quite fair
one; so it is on Wye and Thames. On the great chub waters—the
Hampshire Avon, the topmost waters of the Great Ouse—a four-pound
fish is fair. Anywhere a five-pounder is a good fish, and in many places
an epic fish; after that, going upwards, all chub are epic fish. For many
years the record hung between eight and nine pounds, and there was
at first astonishment, even unbelief, when Dr Cameron caught a chub
of ten and a half pounds on the Annan, that Scottish border river only
valued till then as one for salmon and trout and sea trout. This wonderful chub was little enough esteemed among the river's game-fishing

habitués, but it caused a thrilled stir in coarse fishing circles south of the border. That record, till now, still stands; there may be bigger chub, but probably not much bigger.

To eyes not prejudiced by love of salmon and trout, the chub is a beautiful fish, sturdy, chunky, having an appearance of being carved in jade, inlaid with silver and bronze and brass, with a rather dusky patina as it matures. Its back is dark and very jade-like in its texture, a deep softly polished colour, dark olive green. Its flanks have a metallic shine, with the big bold scales chased and enamelled, and each with a dark centre. Its belly is white and the belly fins, which are large and bold in shape, are a clear soft coral. The dorsal fin and the tail fin, though they look indigo in the water, are umber. The chub's head, that so characteristic head, is big; it is a solid carved jade lump with a great mouth that shows white when the thick rubber-textured lips are opened. The eye is large and rolling, a slow cautious pawky sort of eye, the eye of a fish not easily deceived. Because there has always been, and always will be, confusion between big dace and small chub, let it be remembered that the chub's mouth is so big, goes so far back in the great head. The mouth of a dace is small in a neater smaller head. The rear edge of the dorsal and anal fins of the chub have a convex, outwardly rounded line; those of the dace are concave, hollow at the edge.

And now the food of the chub! On the bottom it eats caddis, insects of any kind, snails, grubs, swan mussels, leaches, silkweed. And, in those alkaline rivers in which they are found, crayfish. All those it will eat and anything else that it should find. In the weeds it hunts out anything living and it pursues the minnows, gudgeon, and the young of any fish including its own. In its swims under the overhanging boughs it takes the flies, caterpillars, beetles, that drop from above; it takes all worms, slugs, grasshoppers, bluebottles, cowdung flies, or anything else that comes accidentally into the water. If a cherry tree should overhang the water, it will eat the falling fruit, and so too it takes elderberries, plums or what you will. The chub is, if ever animal was, omnivorous.

To fish for chub discard all idea of light stiff rods and filmy lines. Chub tackle should be stout. That this is so emphasized is because the nature of the chub is so very cautious, so very suspicious, so shy. Let just one step be put down heavily, let just one glimpse be given of the angler, let any sudden movement be made, all those chub that till then have been so evident will fade from sight. They will not rush away in panic; they will sink and vanish, dissolve away. To answer this, many an angler, mistakenly, has had recourse to fine tackle to overcome the chub's coy caution. And, quite often, he has hooked his chub. But the chub, the cautious chub, seldom lives far from fierce entanglements of root or growth, and on the instant of hooking it plunges into the tangle and there breaks the inadequate tackle.

The truth is that chub are not frightened by strong tackle; what alarms them is any sight or sound of the angler. So providing he goes about his fishing with infinite pains against vibration of the bank or showing of the least part of himself, the angler can choose his tackle to match the needs of his quarry's strength in tight corners. The Avon type of rod suits this fishing well, for all the general run of chub; for very big solitary chub the rod had better be something of the kind of the Walker Mark IV Carp Rod. The line, for almost any chub fishing, should not be less than about five pounds breaking strain, and for very big chub it had better be eight, nine, or even ten pounds breaking strain. The first plunge of a big chub is *very* testing.

For long-trotting, and much float fishing for chub must be done so, the centre-pin reel is best, though the fixed-spool reel can be and often is used. Hook sizes must be dependent upon the size of baits; but it is unwise ever to use a smaller hook than may be used. The chub's mouth is big, and a secure hook hold can be a crucial factor.

The nature of float fishing tactics for chub must vary to some extent with the water being fished; but far more often than not it is better done from a distance, by long-trotting, with, sometimes, stret-pegging. On such a river as the Thames or the quieter parts of the Wye which chub prefer, or the Severn, floats need not be very big because they will not need to carry any great weight of lead to get down to the fish. But on the Avon there is almost no water that is not heavy and fast by the standards of other rivers. In these heavy swims floats then must be big to carry the big weights of lead needed to take the bait immediately down to the proper fishing level.

Legering in several forms is often successful in the taking of chub. Still legering works well, more particularly in the less fast waters. A characteristic chub bite then is a violent wrench of the rod top that may almost snatch it out of its rest; and such a bite quite often fails to lead to a hooked fish. The chub has struck and gone before the angler can act. If the angler rests his rod in one rest and continues to hold the rod, he will sometimes see the rod top just begin to move, an inch perhaps, two inches. His responsive strike will usually send the hook solidly home. A higher proportion of slow bites leading to hooked fish can be had if the legering is done upstream or upstream and across—if, of course, the current is slow enough to allow that. The sign of a bite may be a tightening of the line, or, as often, it may be a sudden slackening of the line.

In the faster water, such as the Avon, moving leger tends to work better (though still leger will work too). That method by which the

tackle is worked down the runs between the weeds or right down a swim
by the alternate raising and lowering of the rod is usually the best
method. In most waters, when the holt of a very big chub is known or
suspected, a still leger put to lie against that holt is often better than
anything else. Quite big chub are often to be found in quite small
brooks, and there moving leger and still leger work well, and so does
that way of fishing that has come to be known as floatless leadless
fishing. Just the line with a hook tied to it and carrying a bait is cast
into the appropriate place. This mode of fishing indeed may be a very
good one for very big and very cautious old chub. On these brooks, and
on any chub water, a square of bread or a big piece of crust can be
floated down the current on just a hook tied to the line—no float, no
lead. To this surface bait chub will rise with a slow opening of the great
white mouth.

Baits for chub, of course, are innumerable. Crust, flake, paste, bread
cubes, all work well, and they are best used with mashed bread and
meal groundbait—and this, on fast rivers, should be fairly copious.
Maggots, worms, slugs, crayfish (whole or in parts), sausage, macaroni,
cheese (very specially cheese, strong cheese), cheese paste, bacon fat,
are all good. Samples of them should be included in the groundbait,
except in the case of crayfish; they come in the ordinary course of
Nature. Cheese and sausage pieces are often best groundbaited by
throwing in continually odd pieces of the same size as those on the
hook. Elderberries, cherries, strawberries, plums, pieces of banana,
pieces of apple, will take chub. Elderberries should be used downstream
of an elder bush that overhangs the water; in the case of the other
fruits groundbaiting should be done by the throwing in of specimens
fairly often.

Spinning will take chub. For the general run of chub a fixed-spool
reel with a line of three or four pounds breaking strain serves well. A
dead minnow is as good a bait as there is, though artificial baits can also
do well. For very big chub a quite big bait, on appropriate tackle, can
be spun through the water where such chub may be supposed to live.
Live baiting with minnow or gudgeon is often deadly for chub—and,
indeed, many a big chub has taken a quite big live bait meant for a
pike.

Fly fishing for chub, in summer and in autumn, is pleasant fishing
and often very productive. Wet fly fishing with big bushy flies will take
plenty of chub, but the greater delight is in dry fly fishing. Flies are
better if they are big, and good patterns are those that have an effect
of buzz and fuss—so as to suggest the moths and caterpillars and sedges
that fall upon the water with a fussing of wings or hairs. The various
Palmer flies—Red, Soldier, and the rest—are good; so are the Bumbles

in all their colours, so is Coachman, so are Sedges of various kinds. This fishing works well by day, but is at its best by evening. The trout fisher, as we know, seeks to put his dry fly down softly; but the fly fisher for chub goes along the banks where the willows hang—often doing so by boat—and casts his fly to fall with a flop, just as those animals do which fall from the boughs. When the chub rises, takes the fly, there must be a distinct pause before the strike is made. The chub is slow; he tilts up, takes the fly with deliberation, tilts down again. Then is the time to strike.

There is one other and often desperately exciting way of fishing for chub; this is dapping under the overhanging boughs. The angler, going softly, silently as a ghost, peers through the tangle of bush and bough and sees below him the shadowy drifting chub. He has a strong rod, a strong line, and on the end of the line is a foot or so of strong nylon. Not far above the hook a split shot acts as stop to a perforated bullet. The hook is, perhaps, a No. 6. He has collected, it may be, grasshoppers, bluebottles, something buzzy and alive. He puts the hook through the shoulders of the bait, and winds round the rod top enough line to reach the surface. Now he works the rod top gently through the tangle till he can unwind the line so that, presently, the bait is suspended just over the water. Then, as he sees a good chub near, he allows the bait to dibble on the surface. Then he sees (and his heart is thumping) the chub tilt up, open its great white mouth, and the bait is sucked in. Now he *must*—and how difficult it is—wait until the chub has turned down. Then he strikes; and he must just hang on in the subsequent uproar till the fish escapes or is beaten and he can push the landing net through to receive the chub. Only one chub, obviously, can be caught in each place that is fished. This dapping is most especially a method for those simmering days of hot summer when the shade in which he waits trembles with the hum of insects and the quiver of sun-drowsed air. And there is another thing about the chub—on those hot days, and on every other sort of day all through the season, there is always a chance of catching chub.

## The Dace

That the dace is easily confused with small chub has already been established. A chub, when young, lacks the bronzy tarnish that it has later. It is silvery, and most dace are silvery. 'The silvery dace' indeed it is often called; but, to make confusion more possible, very big dace in some rivers, notably the Kennet, deepen greatly in colour, thus increasing the chance of confusion. But, typically, the dace is a small fish, a

member of the carp family, far more often under half a pound than over
it; and it is brilliantly silvery with watery coloured fins. Only very big
dace in some rivers have a deepening of colour on the flanks with a
tendency to some red on the belly fins. And, though the shape of dorsal
and anal fins is a positive difference between chub and dace, there is the
more general one that the dace is altogether lighter, daintier, slimmer
than a young chub. The head is noticeably smaller and lighter, and the
mouth very distinctly smaller.

The dace, like the chub, is essentially a river fish, a lover of lively
currents, a frolicker in the upper water near the sun in all the warmer
months. In high summer it will be more in shallow streaming water
through the weed beds than anywhere else, and never will it be in dead
water. But, as autumn cools the river and then winter comes, dace leave
the lively shallows and their shoals are likely to be found in the same
deepish swims that the roach inhabit.

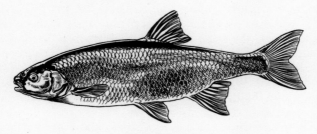

Fig. 83. Dace

In a majority of rivers dace are so small that they are scarcely worth
the trouble of the angler; one of a quarter of a pound may be quite a
respectable size. But there are some rivers—the Kennet, the Hampshire
Avon, the Suffolk Stour, the Thet in Norfolk, for example—in which
dace grow greatly bigger. These dace are a different angling matter;
they fight with dashing brilliance, almost as a trout fights. These more
worthy dace may be considered quite good fish at half a pound; one of
three-quarters of a pound is a good fish. One of a pound or more will
be called by the angler 'a specimen'. Above the pound they are very
infrequent, and at the moment of writing the record stands at one
pound, eight ounces, five drams. That record is seldom challenged, and
when it is it is more often than not a small chub mistaken for a dace.
The author did once catch a dace that weighed one pound eight ounces,
but that was taken on a mayfly while trout fishing two days before the
coarse fishing season started.

The dace's food is mainly insects, freshwater shrimps and water hog

lice, snails, and such small animals; it also eats such vegetable matter
as silkweed. But, very particularly, it is a taker of flies at the surface.
The flyfisher for trout often finds dace in his bag.

Bottom fishing for dace has been much confused by the dace's
reputation for being a lightning-fast biter. Those little dace that teem in
their shoals on the summer shallows do so bite; but so do the young of
various species. Big dace are reasonably leisurely biters; and they do
not insist, necessarily, on the tiny baits that they are supposed to like.
When they, the bigger dace, are in their summer swims, shallow ones
through the weeds, light float tackle may be swum down to them, just
clearing bottom. Very light moving leger is often better; a quarter-
ounce Arlesey bomb can be used, and the tackle worked down the swim
by the method of lifting and lowering the rod already described. The
sport to be had from such fishing is naturally closely related to the
tackle used; a line of two pounds breaking strain is amply strong
enough. Hook sizes must, as always, be related to bait sizes; if the bait
is two or three maggots a size 12 hook will serve. Crust is a good bait,
so is flake, and stewed wheat will take good dace if a few grains are
often tippled down the swim to engage their interest. In places where it
occurs naturally, silkweed will do well. With the seasonal change to
deeper steadier swims, float fishing close to the bottom, as if for roach,
will take dace well. With all dace fishing groundbaiting should be light;
too heavy groundbaiting may well make the fish full fed, and, therefore, disinterested in baits.

On rivers where dace are big, fly fishing, and more particularly dry
fly fishing, is a light-heartedly enjoyable way of fishing. The cast should
be light, tapering to nylon of, say, two pounds breaking strain. Flies
dressed on hook size 0 will usually serve, and dace are not very particular as to pattern. Whickham's Fancy, Greenwell's Glory, Gold
Ribbed Hare's Ear, Olive Dun, Red Tag, Pheasant Tail, will all be
successful.

# CHAPTER THIRTEEN

# The Fish, continued

## The Eel

To the eyes of many the eel has hardly the seeming of a fish at all, so serpent-like is it. There is indeed a creeping evilness of look about it, repellent rather than engaging, a coldly sinuous aspect which is made more potent by the oddly human look of its face, closely viewed. Its way of life makes no friends for it; it eats most things, but is most attracted by carion. Nothing is more likely to lure it than a dead fish, or, even, the remains of some land animal. The angler, fishing for any other fish, has a friendliness to that quarry; but if he fishes for eels he is as often as not impelled by a repelled fascination.

Fig. 84. Eel

The smaller eels are an accidental scourge of those who fish for other fish. Farinaceous baits the eel will leave alone; but if the angler baits with worm he will often be plagued with small or smallish eels that swallow down his bait, tangle his tackle, lap their slimy twists through everything, and waste good fishing time. The only practical way to deal with them is the brief harsh way—a foot stubbed firmly on the neck and the head severed with a strong sharp knife. To attempt to extract the hook from the writhing enemy is vain.

Small eels are one thing; big eels are another. Small eels vary from tiny 'bootlaces' to fish of perhaps two pounds or so. Above that they begin to become big. But your convinced seeker of big eels will not

179

think them worthy until they are about five pounds at least; and, though
the record stands at this moment at eight and a half pounds, there is no
doubt that fearsomely bigger eels exist in our waters, twenty pounds,
even thirty pounds. These are the goal of the true eel fisher.

For them no delicacy of approach is the thing, no matter of fluid skills
of light tackle and deft hands. The attraction of the fishing lies only in
the possibility of extracting the shivery menace and great strength of a
monstrous eel. Any but the strongest tackle is useless for the huge unseen force below. So the rod is strong, very strong; the line is certainly
thirty pounds breaking strain, and it may be more, because there is no
question of playing the fish as it is ordinarily understood.

There is just one bait to suit this fishing—a dead fish; a dead roach or
dace of perhaps a quarter of a pound, even more, or a fresh herring.
Thread the nylon of the line into the bait against the tail and bring it
out through the mouth; then tie on a big eyed hook, say a size 3. Now
pull the hook and nylon back so that the hook just projects from the
corner of the mouth of the bait, and secure the nylon to the tail of the
bait with a tie of thread. Push the baiting needle through the belly of
the fish upwards to the back, thus piercing the swim bladder; only so
will the bait sink. Now cast the bait with a long cast, well away from the
bank, and put the rod in rests. If the reel is a fixed-spool, tighten up the
line and then leave the pick-up in the open position so that the line can
run out freely to a pull. If a centre-pin reel is used, coil up a few yards of
line on the ground—and do that on some sort of groundsheet to avoid
tangles. Now wait.

When a bite comes the line will slide away; let it slide. If more goes
than is coiled on the ground, feed more out by hand. The eel must feel
no resistance. Usually an eel will pause at the end of its first run. When
it goes off again, strike; and now is the time for brute force. If the eel
is truly big it will pull with heavy power, and, if you give it the least
respite, it will knit the line through every available snag. So pull, wind,
and continue to do so until the eel breaks your tackle or you draw it to
the bank. When it does come to the bank continue to pull, and walk
back as you do, pulling the eel on its slime up the bank and well back
from the water.

And for this contingency you have ready a sack, and into it you
drop your great eel, then cutting the nylon and tying the neck of the
sack.

Sometimes you will catch eels for which your heavy tackle is grossly
strong; but no matter. When your monstrous eel comes, it will need
all that strength. For this fishing for very big eels, night is a better
time than day; but an eerie and troublesome business it could be to deal
with such a quarry in the dark. Perhaps, indeed, it would be wiser to

attempt it only with the aid of a companion who could hold a strong torch at the crucial time. And, let it be remembered, big eels *can* be caught by day.

## The Carp

Now, as some see it, we are coming upon almost holy ground. There is that about the carp that puts a hypnosis upon those who come within its spell. It is a big fish, capable of becoming very big indeed; it is often an obvious fish—obvious in the sense that on lazy summer days it is to be seen cruising or floating hugely just under the surface of those placid pools in which it thrives best. But this bigness, this summer day obviousness, adds to the sense of mystery, almost of unattainableness, that

Fig. 85. Carp

works so potently upon the imagination of the fisherman. So it must always have worked, and the evidence of it is the web of legend that has surrounded the carp. Moats of royal chateaux often had their carp, huge wallowing fish that would come regularly to be fed (no fish tames as easily as the carp); these great fish, so legend said, had been there for a hundred years, two hundred years, the selfsame fish, growing slowly bigger and bigger. That legend has always been persistent about the carp, that it had this immensely long slow span of life. The truth is that a carp that lives to thirty years is an old one, but, during that quite short time, it can grow astonishingly quickly if its environment is favourable.

The appearance of wisdom, of unfishlike sagacity, which the carp wears, has no doubt aided the growth of the legend. Thwarted anglers over the centuries have been prepared to swear that this fish possessed powers of thought and reasoning that put it beyond the danger of the angler's wiles. Until after the Second World War the biggest carp that had ever been caught in Britain weighed twenty-six pounds, and at that weight it seemed to most anglers to be something more of fable than of fact. Only a very few anglers had ever caught a carp of more than ten pounds, and those few were as men who had had an almost mystical experience; they were, to other anglers, men apart.

This slightly eerie sense of more than fishlike being was increased by the extraordinary explosion of speed and power revealed by the odd carp that *was* hooked. Imagine the scene, some retired and secret-seeming pool, probably girt by tall dark trees that allowed only an occasional ruffle of wind to reach the surface. There, during the day, the carp could be seen, looking deep blue on the back, with a trellis pattern of big scales on the flanks, great bulky fish hanging poised high in the water. Seen thus in the common hours of day, they had always been found to be inviolate; if there were to be any chance at all of hooking them the angler must come at evening. So then he would come, at the time of sinking light, when the big soft moths were on the wing, and the bats began to fly, on one of those warm scented summer evenings that are drenched with dew. As he put up his tackle there would be huge eruptions of the silk-still water, and great amber-coloured fish would jump and fall back in smothers of water. In such haunted peace, such stillness, these events were unnerving and the angler's trembling fingers would fumble with his knots.

But presently his cast would be made, his float would stand as if painted on the surface. Then, this being one of those rare occasions, after he had waited as he had waited so often before, the float would stir, sidle a little in the surface, then shoot away. The loose line which he had coiled upon the ground would be gone and he had struck. Now an unimaginable power would wrench his rod into a painful curve. The unseen fish would tear away fifty yards, a hundred yards, an irresistible power that could not be stopped. If the attempt should be made to stop it the line would part like cotton. It was this uncanny outburst of so much unseen power in such still and silent circumstances that drugged the imaginations of fishermen.

But these occurrences were rare. Far more often no unreckoned hours of waiting, no subtleties, could broach the queer security of the carp. So suspicious was it, so shy, so apprehensively sensitive to the angler's approach, that big carp were thought to be, and said to be, uncatchable. To overcome their cunning fine tackle was used; but if a carp were hooked, it broke the tackle instantly and contemptuously.

So it was until after the Second World War. Then Richard Walker began his impassioned but coolly logical concentration on the carp. He showed that big carp could be caught, and that big carp could be far bigger than had ever been suspected. He devised techniques and designed tackle for carp fishing that have been the foundation of all the very successful carp fishing that has been done in the years that have followed. His own fishing' culminated in the catching of a carp of the hitherto unbelievable weight of forty-four pounds. That fish is still to be seen, alive, in the aquarium of the London Zoo. The methods now to be described are largely those initiated by Walker. There are those who say now that the difficulty of carp fishing is greatly exaggerated, and in some waters carp are not very difficult to catch if you are prepared to be thorough and to wait; but those carp would still be inviolate if Walker had not done his pioneering. And, indeed, let no fisher of those easier waters think that all carp are now to be had with no more trouble. In the pool from which Walker took his great fish there are other and huge carp that have till now defied all the concentrated attempts of all the best carp fishers.

But before going to methods and tackle we should look more closely at the fish itself. It is, so to speak, the head of the carp family, the first and greatest of all the carps. This, the common carp, has various forms, but they are all just the one species. Though it was originally an introduced fish, brought here, so it is said, about six hundred years ago —though there is far from being certainty about that—its residence has been long enough for it to be, in what might be called its standard form, a wild fish. This true wild carp is fairly racy in form, a long though very solid fish. The four barbules on its upper lip, two on either side, reveal that it is largely a bottom feeder. Its mouth shows the same tendency; it is prehensile—it can be extended in a kind of funnel form to suck up from the silt of the bottom the small organisms that live there. Its scales are very large and very clearly defined with handsome dark centres. The general impression of its colour, seen side on, or when it jumps, is amber, often a rather greenish amber, with the back dark. It is that dark back that looks so blue as the fish cruises just under the surface, almost ultramarine.

So the wild carp; but the carp to be found in many waters are often either fish that have been put in from artificially raised stock, or are the descendants of such stock. These fish are often either what are called mirror carp or leather carp; both are known collectively as king carp— and there is an aptness about that latter name. They have a majesty, these king carp. The mirror carp have only a few and greatly enlarged scales, and most of those are along the lateral line, with the rest of the body naked. Leather carp are entirely naked, with no scales at all—but indeed, fish intermediate between both types are common enough, and it is simpler to use just the term king carp.

These king carp are immensely deeper, bulkier from side to side, altogether more massive than the wild carp; they are splendid fish. All carp have the capacity to grow fast in an environment which feeds them well; but the growth rate of king carp can be astonishing. A rate of four pounds a year increase is not at all uncommon in water rich in food, and far greater growth rates are possible in very rich waters. Quite often in waters holding king carp fish may be found that have the same bulky majesty of form as the king carp, but are fully scaled. It may be assumed that these are fish that have reverted to the basic form of scaling.

It might be thought that so big a fish, with so fast a rate of growth, would be a steady eater of the largest available forms of food, but this is not so. Though carp do eat such things as worms, snails, and others of the bigger food animals to be found in water (and are prepared to take *very* big baits), a large part of what they eat consists of very small organisms. They spend much time browsing on the mud of the bottom, sucking from it tiny tubifex worms and similar insubstantial things; they eat a great deal of the plankton—those tiny free-swimming creatures such as water fleas. Those waters which produce the fastest growth in carp are invariably rich in plankton. It is this preoccupation with such insubstantial food which is often the despair of carp fishermen. A carp that is deeply immersed in such feeding is exceedingly hard to deflect on to feeding on what the angler can offer.

Carp that are feeding in this manner, nuzzling in the bottom, are to be identified by the great eruptive clusters of bubbles that come to the surface. Finding carp in that mood is easy enough; to get them to take a bait may often be impossible. The feeding of carp is, generally, closely related to water temperature. It is within only quite a narrow band of temperature that they will normally feed—say from the upper fifties Fahrenheit to the upper sixties. It is this that dictates the times of day at which carp fishing is to be done with reasonable hope of success.

Warm summer weather is, broadly, the most hopeful of conditions; but the middle hours of day are seldom productive. It is early and late that the carp fisher must expect his sport, and he tends to become largely nocturnal in his habits. During the day he will see the carp, because they enjoy living just under the surface to feel the sun; he will see them in the small clear spaces between the lily pads, or just very slowly cruising from weed bed to weed bed. So they will be through the heat of the day; but on this typical fine carp day of summer, as the sun goes off the water at evening, the water temperature will begin to fall till it comes within the optimum range. Now the angler fishes in the fairly shallow water, say from four feet to eight feet.

Then twilight comes, then darkness. If it is a warm evening the shallow water may still remain within the right temperature range, and may be so till midnight, one o'clock. This is a time of major opportunity. But even on midsummer nights a cooling comes thereafter, and as it comes the shallow water may fall below the right temperature. The carp will retire to deeper water, and there, perhaps, continue to feed, because the deeper water is slower to cool. It must be remembered too that air temperature falls more quickly than water temperature. When a slight shiver has come to the air, the water may still lag at a warmer level. But when these small hours come when even summer nights can become surprisingly cold (to those who have never before fished by night), all activity will die from the water. Unless, and unusually, this sharp fall into cold does not come, there will be no more carp for a time.

But then dawn comes, and as the sun comes upon the shallows, warming them to life, there the carp will go, and there feed. Many and many is the big carp that has been caught at this time—from soon after dawn to about eight o'clock.

Now all this is a general pattern, a typical one; but necessarily, it has all sorts of exceptions. Sometimes a carp *will* be caught at 3 a.m., sometimes in the first faint light of dawn. And, too, carp are sometimes caught by day when the conditions serve. The constant key is water temperature, and, what is related to that, the amount of dissolved oxygen in the water. Dull quite warm days are likely to produce daytime carp; soft days in October before the first frost has come to end practical carp fishing may well produce carp catches—it was indeed on such an October day that Bob Richards of Gloucester caught a carp of $31\frac{1}{4}$ pounds which held the record until it was beaten by Richard Walker's 44 pound fish.

So far only one rod has been produced which precisely meets the needs of carp fishing. It is that rod, designed by Richard Walker, which is known as the Mark IV Carp Rod. It is so designed that it is capable of casting quite light baits, but will also cast up to an ounce, and has the power to handle the biggest carp. Beyond dispute the only fully satisfactory reel to use with it is a good fixed-spool with a large line capacity—that being essential because big carp may sometimes make an initial run of quite extraordinary length and speed. To try to stop this run would be almost certainly disastrous. To be quite safe the reel should hold two hundred yards of line and its breaking strain should be about eleven pounds, *certainly* not less than nine pounds.

All sorts of baits have been used for carp, all sorts of mysterious elaborations of smells and flavours have been lovingly added to them; but just a few simple baits will take carp when they are to be taken at all. None is more generally successful than paste. The normally prepared paste made from stale bread has the disadvantage of yielding easily to the attacks of small fish; they can soon whittle away to uselessness the big ball of paste that is likely to interest a carp. A paste made from new bread overcomes this to a large extent. This paste is very stiff and resistant, and, for most other fishing, would have the disadvantage that the hook would not come through it sufficiently easily on striking. But carp bites are very seldom quick in coming, and by the time one does come the paste has softened just enough to allow the sweeping carp strike to send the hook through the paste.

Bread crust is a splendid surface bait for carp, and of that more later. Lobworms work well in some waters, but have the disadvantage of attracting eels. On those waters where small fish very persistently and troublesomely attack paste baits, potato has been found to provide an answer; but it is a bait to which the carp must be accustomed over a long period, by previous baitings-up of the swim. Three weeks of such pre-baiting is not too much, done day by day.

Now to the water, and, almost certainly, it will be a still water. Carp *are* to be caught in slow rivers in some places, but they are seldom as big as still-water carp—or so it is in Britain. In France, if nowhere else, there is at least some divergence from this. Bertin, the barman at the Paris Ritz Hotel, the keenest of anglers, told the author of his consistent catches of carp into the teens of pounds in the Dordogne in southern France. But our carp fishing will be typical carp fishing; it will be done in some deeply retired pool, and we will come to it as the sun leaves it, and the dew begins to fall. Before this evening at least several days of pre-baiting will have been done in the swim to be fished; now the approach is made with the most exacting care to make no heavy footfall, to show not one glimpse of ourselves. The first thing is to throw in again a heavy mixture of mashed bread and meal. It is not thrown to fall in a round patch, but rather in a long broad path of bait extending in the line the cast is to be made. It is so done so that if the cast should fall a little long or a little short, the baited hook will still fall on the groundbait.

The bait is paste, and it is better for it to be really big, so that it may resist other smaller fish better; and all experience shows that a big ball of paste is more attractive to a carp than a small one. The size of a golf ball is often used, but the author has used balls the size of a hen's egg and found the carp have had no difficulty or reluctance to take it into their great mouths. Such great baits, obviously, must have a hook to match. It is an eyed hook, and it is tied directly to the monofilament line with no float and no lead on the line. Just the line and the hook, and the hook is size 2, or at the smallest size 3. Now the cast is made, the line tightened up so that it is straight from bait to rod, and the rod is put in two rests. The front rest should be of the type illustrated so that the line shall not be pinched and thus prevented from running freely. Now the pick-up arm of the reel is put in the open position, so that that too allows line to slip away freely. The line is now lying along the bottom. Between the reel and the butt ring a large fold of silver foil is put over the line, sagging it down a little. Its duty is to signify bites, and on the darkest night it will be visible.

All is now ready; now the angler must wait. He may wait only an hour; often he will wait several hours. Quite often he will wait until he goes home. But let us suppose a carp does come to the bait. There may be a few warning twitches of the silver foil; they may come, cease, come again—or there may be no warning. But, then, suddenly the silver foil lifts, shoots up against the butt ring and there jams. The line is streaming away, sometimes just steadily, sometimes ripping away. The

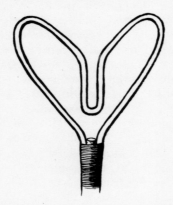

Fig. 86. Head of rod rest—it was designed
by Richard Walker

angler, whose heart is near to bursting, picks up the rod, flicks on the pick-up, pauses just long enough to feel the pull of the fish to make sure that it is running from him, not towards him, and strikes, a sweeping strike over the shoulder. The fish is hooked, and it surges away on a run that seems as if it will never end. When it does, line must be recovered by pumping—pulling the rod back slowly up to the shoulder, then dropping it forward and winding up the line gained. This is repeated until the fish runs again.

If all goes well the fish will at last (probably long last) be tired and drawn towards the bank. Now the very big net must be sunk vertically into the water and the fish drawn up to it. As often as not the fish will dive into it, taking it for a snag. To lift so heavy a fish by the end of the handle is asking too much, so when the net has been brought to the surface, the angler puts down his rod and, so to speak, climbs down the net handle and takes the net by the rim, or by the net itself, with both hands and lifts out net and fish.

In the majority of cases when a carp picks up the bait and runs, it will do so in a direction which allows the angler to feel its weight as soon as he picks up the rod, thus leaving him free to strike. But it may happen that the fish runs towards him, producing a slack line which does not allow him to strike. In such a case line must be taken up on the reel as quickly as possible till the weight is felt and the strike can be made— the angler hoping meanwhile that the fish will not sense his winding and, consequently, drop the bait.

This method of carp fishing has become what may be called the basic or standard method, and it does catch a great many carp that, before Richard Walker devised the method and the tackle, would have seemed uncatchable. But, as has already been said, there are waters in which the hordes of small fish so often present in carp waters, often rudd, or roach, whittle away a ball of paste so persistently that it becomes useless to use it. It is for such cases that potato as a bait may prove a working alternative. The not-*too*-well cooked potato, golf-ball size or rather bigger, has the nylon line threaded through it with a baiting needle; then the hook is tied on, and the hook pulled back into the potato so that it is entirely covered—it is, incidentally, usually essential with any bait that the hook shall be so covered. The hard touch of metal is apt to alarm the carp so that it drops the bait. And, let it be noted again, the use of potato as bait usually necessitates at least a fairly long period of pre-baiting to induce the fish to accept potato as food. A Walker development of potato fishing was made for a lake with a very soft mud bottom into which the whole potato bait persistently sank. He pre-baited and hook-baited with flat slices of potato, and these planed to the bottom and there rested on top of the mud.

Margin fishing is also a Walker-devised method, and a very deadly and desperately exciting one it is. Carp, on warm summer evenings, as the light is going, and during the earlier and warmer hours of dark, often come cruising slowly round the margins of lakes. They come just under the surface, sucking vastly and resoundingly at what they find on the surface. These are the fish that margin fishing catches. The angler comes to the water utterly silently, often creeping on all fours. He crouches behind any cover that marginal growth gives. He has two rod rests, his Mark IV Carp Rod, a big-eyed hook tied to the line on which there is no other addition. His bait is a piece of crust as big as a matchbox, and he has a number of other pieces of crust as big. As he lies in his ambush, he tosses one or two of his great crust pieces on to the water as attractors, and he has the rod, in the rests, with the bait hanging just above the surface. Probably the small fish will come gobbling and nibbling at his attractor pieces, and as they disintegrate he replaces them.

Then a sudden pause will come upon the little fish; there will be a sense of hush. He will hear the slow approach of a great carp, and he will lower the hook bait so that it just floats on the surface. This is a moment of the most desperate excitement. He will hear the carp suck in one of his attractor crusts, and then it is the one on the hook which is taken. He strikes. It can be imagined what a nerve-strung tense delight there is in this fishing—hearing, perhaps seeing, this great fish, possibly near enough to be touched, waiting for the large mouth to open and engulf the bait so closely; and with the knowledge that the least betraying sound or movement will send the fish away in panic.

Fig. 87. Method of baiting crust

There is a best way of putting the crust upon the hook. The hook should be passed into the bread from the crumb side, and then passed back through from the crust side. The illustration shows the way.

Carp that cruise slowly during the warm hours of day or lie among the lily pads, may sometimes be caught. The bait may be a worm and the tackle is, of necessity, strong; the line should not be less than fourteen pounds breaking strain because it will have to cope with the fight of big carp in the lily pad jungle. The carp will have been seen to be moving among the lilies, and where they move the bait is cast so that it falls across the lily leaves. Then it is just drawn till it slips over the edge of a leaf to hang in the cool twilight under the leaves while the line lies across the leaves. Now the angler waits till the line slides away.

Floating crust is often to be used successfully apart from margin
fishing. In the early hours of sun carp are active near the surface, and
then a big piece of crust can be cast to float on the surface where carp
are known to be. A highly tense business it can be when a carp is seen
to drift slowly up to the crust, swim round it inspecting it, nudging it
with its snout. It may do this cautiously for a short or long time; then,
if it is satisfied, it may suck it in.

## The Crucian Carp

A small modest inconspicuous relative of the great carp itself is the
crucian carp. It lives mostly in ponds and lakes and gravel pits and such
places, and may, on occasions, be found in slow rivers. There are far

Fig. 88. Crucian carp

more crucian carp under a pound than over, and one of, say, two and a
half pounds may be considered a very worthy specimen. The British
record stands so far, and has for long stood, at four pounds eleven
ounces.

It is a short, deep, very solid-looking fish, rather handsome in its stout
fashion—large-scaled, with the characteristic dark centre to the scales.
It has the long dorsal fin as the carp itself has, but not as long, and
it lacks the barbules of its great relative. Its diet is much the same as
the carp's. A peaceful browser through the weed jungles this small
carp is.

Most bottom fishing methods will catch it—float fishing on the
bottom, legering; it is thus that most crucian carp are caught. But it is
seldom fished for with any specialized zeal, perhaps because it lives
rather under the shadow of its formidable cousin. But if specimen
crucians were to be pursued with determination, the methods that take
big carp would probably take them too—scaled down of course.

## The Pike

If we were on ground from which legend springs when talking of the carp, so indeed we are when it is of the pike we talk. There is that about the pike, in the sullen ferocity of its look, in its nature, that breeds legend and drags from buried primitive depths of instinct all sorts of hardly understood responses. The pike, and only the pike in our fresh-waters, is a reminder of the beast that lurked beyond the cave entrance when humankind was new upon the earth. So, in anglers, the pike draws up a kind of atavistic fear, a primitive dread. Some anglers thrill to this, are drawn by it to a life-long joy in pike fishing; others, moved by they know not what, find a goose-pimpled hatred of the pike and are im-pelled to persecute it. Though it must be admitted that there are circum-stances in which pike must be kept down, or even eliminated, as in

Fig. 89. Pike

closely preserved trout streams, the hatred of some anglers for the pike goes far beyond what is justified by such necessities.

The pike is, almost entirely, a preyer upon other fish; that is the central thing about it. For that it was designed by Nature, and every-thing about it expresses that purpose. It is wolfishly ferocious in appear-ance and habit, and this forbidding form and nature are highly efficient for what it must do. It lies in wait for its prey, then seizes it with a sudden, short, projectile-like rush. As it waits, its greenish flanks flecked with pale yellow, it melts into the dapple of light in weed and water; and, in its rush, it is made more lethal by that shape which is so well designed for a brief fast rush from a standing start.

The snout of the pike is flat and shovel-like, two great lean jaws which are lined with teeth on every inner surface. There are big dog teeth round the edges of the jaws; teeth cover the palate and the tongue. It is a formidable mouth, bony, hard, excellent for the grabbing and holding of fish, but a hard mouth in which to set a hook securely. In that lies the cause of many a loss of a pike that is hooked but kicks free in the subsequent fight. It also imposes the need for wire, not nylon, in the terminal tackle.

It is a big fish, this pike—or it becomes so in favourable circumstances. There are a great many waters, overcrowded ones, partially polluted ones, ones deficient in nourishment, in which the average pike will be from about a pound to three pounds—jack, such little pike are called. But if a water is healthy, big enough, rich enough in life, pike may grow to very great sizes—and it is from that, and the morose fury that such big pike can show, that the legends spring. But wild as some of the legends are, plain fact has often been as extraordinary. The pike that holds the record for England and Wales weighed thirty-seven and a half pounds (or so it is at the time of writing); the record holder for Scotland weighed forty-seven pounds eleven ounces. Great fish these, but, undoubtedly, far smaller than pike do grow in, for example, some of the great lakes of Scotland and Ireland. However, as pike fishing stands in the majority of British waters, a water that can show an average of from five to eight pounds can be considered a good one. Such a water is always likely to produce a much bigger pike from time to time. A reasonable standard is that a pike becomes a specimen, something memorable, when it overtops twenty pounds.

Spinning is one of the main methods of fishing for pike. In those waters where it is reasonably certain that big fish will not be taken, where the sport is likely to be with fish from a couple of pounds or so up to, once in a while, a fish of seven or eight pounds, a fixed-spool reel with a six-pound line and a seven-foot rod is rational tackle to use. But where big pike are likely to be found, such tackle is not really apt for the need. For one thing, these bigger fish need bigger baits, heavier baits, and such tackle is not strong enough to cast them; nor has it the substance or the reach for the proper playing of big pike. A fixed-spool reel can still be used, with a line of, say, ten or twelve pounds breaking strain, but it should be used with a rod of ten feet—salmon spinning rods are suitable. There is no doubt though that the best outfit is a multiplying reel with a braided line, with the same rod. This is much more accurate, and in pike fishing that is often important when a bait has to be cast into those close and tucked away corners in which pike are prone to lie. It is also more capable for the casting of heavy baits and for the striking home of big treble hooks which are used in fishing for big pike. The trace should be wire.

Natural baits—small dace or roach, big gudgeon, sprats—are the best of all baits; but spoons and plugs can do very well. On the big Irish lakes the local anglers swear by big copper and silver spoons, not less than three inches long, and, generally, in big and deep waters, a spoon can hardly be too big. The author has found very successful some tandem spoons he had made up—two spoons mounted, one in front of the other on a leaded bar articulated in the middle, the whole being about seven or more inches long. Plugs do specially well in shallow water, and particularly in those open areas of water between weed clumps.

River spinning for pike is not a matter of indiscriminate progress down the river casting at random. Pike lie in clearly definable places. They like to lurk in close corners, out of the current's force, close to water in which smaller fish live. Holes under tree roots, quiet eddies in bends of the river, protected bays in the rushes, easy water downstream of weed beds, under willows that trail their boughs into the water, the entrances of small sluggish sidestreams. Through all such places the bait should be brought, slowly, deeply, wavering and faltering.

In lakes, bays in the reeds usually hold pike, and pike often lie just off points of reeds that project into the lake, though indeed, big pike will often be found, apparently at random, in the open water. In the big lakes, Irish and Scottish, big fairly shallow bays will hold pike, particularly if a rushy shore suggests a silty bottom. Where a deepish channel, say up to about thirty feet deep, comes under a rocky shore, there often big pike are to be found. In any pike water, lake or river, pike will often advertise themselves by the eruptions at the surface of small fish flying in panic from the pike's onslaught, and, on these occasions, the swirl of the pike itself will often be seen. That area of water should be spun through at once.

When a pike seizes the bait a strike must be made, and it should be a strong firm one if it is to secure a good hold in the craggy jaw. It should be made not in a vertical plane, but nearer the horizontal, thus avoiding bringing the hooks against the bony roof of the mouth, but, rather, against the softer margins of the jaws or the lower jaw in which there are large areas of soft tissue.

In the great lakes, though spinning tackle *is* used, spinning is not usually the method. With such great areas of water to cover, spinning is inadequate; trolling is the way of fishing. The boat is taken very slowly over the likely water, either by rowing or by outboard engine throttled right down. If the angler is by himself, he props the rod against a wooden pin set in the gunwales, with the bottom of the butt wedged down on the floor boards or held there by the foot. Usually a big stone holds the line down on one of the thwarts or on the floor boards, to provide a resistance against a striking fish. If there is a boatman the angler can hold the rod, and this is much more sensitive. He can respond to differing depths, letting out line or taking it in as necessary, causing the bait to come swimming up slopes or diving down into depths. Similarly variation can be induced by the action of the boat. In

places where a slope is known to fall away, the boat can be turned so
that the bait swerves and tumbles; such a manœuvre often produces
takes. There is no need for too long a line to be out—from thirty to fifty
yards is enough. The bait should work deeply.

Live baiting is a method which, though more practised than any
other, has come in recent years to be increasingly deplored as being
cruel. It is often pointed out that other methods, which will be described, serve the same purpose without the use of a living bait. However, it cannot be denied that there is great fascination in the method.
The usual tackle is a strong rod—strong because it has to cast heavy
baits—a line of, say, twelve pounds breaking strain, a big float, a wire
trace, a live bait mounting tackle—the most commonly used is the
Jardine snap tackle. How this terminal tackle is used is shown in the
illustration.

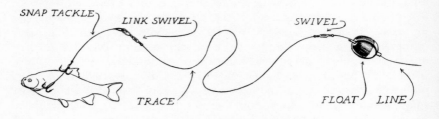

### Fig. 90. Terminal tackle for live baiting
### for pike

As live baiting is usually done a swim is chosen, the tackle is cast,
and there left until a strike does or does not come. How deeply the bait
is set to work depends on the depth of the water. It is obviously not
much use setting the bait at three feet in water twelve feet deep; the
bait should be at about nine feet deep in twelve feet of water. Such fishing as this does produce many pike, but there are many pike that live
baiting could catch that are not caught thus. Assuming that this is lake
fishing, the boat can be taken to the first likely place, the bait cast—
against the reeds perhaps, in an open patch among weed beds—and
there left for ten minutes or so. If no run from a pike comes, then the
bait should be cast into the next likely place, and so on, going from
place to place prospecting.

On rivers also it is usually more profitable to move down, from place
to place, using the current to trot the baited tackle into good pike lies,
not stopping too long in one place. It may sometimes be, on river or
lake, that it is a particular known big pike which is being fished for, and
in that case, obviously, the angler should wait patiently—all the more

so because the bigger a pike is the less constantly it feeds. To move might be to move just before the moment when the fish *did* feed. Pike are, anyway, erratic and rather unpredictable feeders. While it may be said, and, broadly, rightly said, that the best conditions for pike fishing are soft mild days of autumn and winter, perhaps with a slight drizzle, perhaps with occasional small gleams of sun, there are the most confounding exceptions to this. It is true of all the coarse fish that they tend to become torpid and disinclined to feed in very cold water; but there are plenty of exceptions. Pike fishing is usually regarded as essentially a sport of autumn and winter, starting in October—many River Boards indeed have a byelaw to that effect.

When a run does come in live baiting, let the pike run with the bait, feeding line to it. Soon it will stop, and then, soon, a jerk will be felt as the pike turns the bait preparatory to swallowing it. This is the time to strike, not before. A certain number of pike will always be lost through the hooks failing to secure a hold.

The ways of fishing that, it is claimed, make live baiting unnecessary are based upon the use of a dead bait. One such method, a very simple one and a very deadly one for big pike, uses a fresh herring as bait. Two big treble hooks are used on a wire mount, one at the end of the wire and one about three inches higher up. These are stuck into one side of the herring, the end one nearer the head of the bait, and the wire secured with two turns of thread or fuse wire round bait and wire. The bait is cast and left to lie on the bottom where a big pike might be expected to live. Because one side of the bait is weighted by the hooks, that side will be downward, thus giving less chance of the hooks warning the pike. The rod is put in a rest and the angler waits. Sooner or later, if all goes well, movements of the rod top will be seen, the line will start to move away, and line should be fed so that the pike feels no resistance. As with live baiting, the strike should not be made until the pike has been given time to turn the bait. For whatever reason, this mode of fishing tends to produce big pike rather than small ones.

Sink-and-draw is another and often deadly way of using dead bait for pike. A sprat, a dace, a small roach, are all good baits. The bait should be mounted on a flight of two treble hooks so arranged that the head of the bait is pointing up the trace. On the line, just above the top swivel of the trace a lead is put—a spiral lead does well. Now, when the cast is made, the bait will make its movements, down to the bottom, towards the surface, with the head going first—and that is more natural than the opposite way.

To land a pike, if it is of any size, it must be gaffed. Small pike can be lifted straight out or netted. But for big or biggish pike a gaff must be used, and there is only one proper place to use it—under the chin.

That gives a very secure hold, it is an easy place to put the gaff in, it does the fish no injury so that it can be returned unharmed to the water.

## The Grayling

It is true, but odd, that in many of the waters in which the grayling thrives best it is despised and persecuted. It is all the more odd, so you might think, because the grayling is most elegantly beautiful, it rises well to fly, it gives delicately delightful sport on bottom fishing methods, and, if it is big, fights well. And, if that were not enough, it makes better eating, properly cooked, than the trout itself. The fishing for it, at its best time, is as subtly delightful as anything in fishing.

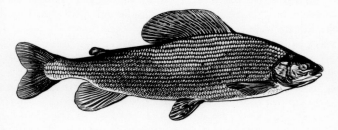

**Fig. 91. Grayling**

The oddity arises from the grayling's highly developed capacity to compete successfully with the trout for living space, for food. The grayling, a member of the salmon family, a relative of the trout, will, if allowed to, increase so much in numbers, and thus eat so much of the food it shares with trout, that the trout lose ground. Where grayling become established, they become very well established indeed.

But they are fussy in their needs. They must have only the purest water; it must be lively and well oxygenated and it must be cold. It is indeed that water which suits the trout best, though the trout will live in waters that would be unacceptable to the grayling.

The grayling is long and fine in shape, small of head. Just before its tail fin it has that small fleshy rayless fin, the adipose fin, which shows it to be a member of the salmon family. But its dorsal fin is what distinguishes it most. It is like a banner, this great silken-looking fin, softly and beautifully coloured. Grayling vary in colour in different rivers (and the grayling is essentially a river fish), but the dorsal fin will usually have some blend of green and puce and iridescent gleams of blue. The general effect of the body is grey, pale grey with grey lines running lengthways along the body; but within that there is a subtle play of all kinds of violet and amethyst and metallic green. Its eye, often, is violet. It is called, not surprisingly, 'lady of the river'.

It eats caddis, shrimps, insect larvae, snails, all such small animals as are to be found on the bottom and in the weeds, and it is a free taker of flies from the surface. In its northern rivers a grayling of a pound is quite a good one, but in the southern chalk streams, into which it was introduced and has there thrived so well, it is reckoned a good fish at a pound and a half upwards. The British record stands now at seven pounds two ounces, but that is wildly beyond the ordinary expectations of the grayling fisher.

Dry fly fishing for grayling is delightful sport and, on most rivers, productive. On some rivers grayling are exceedingly difficult to catch, whether by fly fishing or by bait fishing. But, generally, dry fly works well; and grayling have a special taste for bright tinselly flies. Treacle Parkin, John Storey, Red Tag, Bradshaw's Fancy, Grayling Witch, Green Insect, are good flies; but grayling will also take the flies used for trout, especially those imitating the natural flies which may be hatching. Trout, as we know, lie close to the surface when taking fly; but not grayling. They lie against the bottom, coming up from there in a spiral to take the fly, then going down again. Because this gives them the capacity to see the fly farther off, to see the trail of cast attached to the fly, casting from upstream and drifting down usually works better than upstream casting.

Wet fly fishing also takes grayling, though the sport is less enchanting. Nymph fishing, as it is practised for trout on chalk streams, is a highly effective method for grayling, particularly when the advance of autumn cools the water and makes the fish less ready to respond to a dry fly.

Bait fishing for grayling is a thing of delicacy and neatness. It is more done in winter than at other times, after fly fishing has passed its best— and indeed all the best of grayling fishing comes in autumn and winter, and not even the coldest iciest day of winter will make it impossible to catch grayling. In winter they will be found in the long smooth glides and in the streamy water below rapids, and to them there goes the bait fisher with a long rod, usually twelve feet and rather quick in action. From his neck hangs a linen bag, and in it, in moss, he has his gilt tails. A gilt tail is a little worm described earlier in this book. The line is fine, a pound and a half breaking strain perhaps, the float small and the hook too. The reel is a very smoothly running centre-pin.

With this tackle the bait is run down long distances, fifty yards, seventy yards, and it *must* be so done that there is no check to the float. The best depth for the bait is usually two or three inches off the bottom. That is trotting for grayling as it is done on its native waters, those

northern rivers such as the Wharfe in Yorkshire. Maggots can be used,
and often are; but the classic fishing is that with gilt tails. On its day it
can produce big bags.

There is another traditional mode of fishing for grayling, and this one
is native to the Herefordshire Wye, and its tributaries; grasshopper
fishing it is called. The grasshopper is big, on a No. 5 or 6 hook perhaps;
it has a big fat leaded body covered with green wool and a slip of straw
is held along the side with a ribbing of straw-coloured silk. Maggots
are added to the point of the hook, and the whole is fished sink-and-
draw. Tradition says that this is a good means of taking very big
grayling.

The grayling, when hooked, has an odd and unmistakable way of
fighting. It backs away, turning its body broadside to the current and
offering the great expanse of its dorsal fin to the current. A big grayling
fights very well, but it is a fight different from that of the trout, not so
brilliant, more dour and nagging.


## The Trout

Let it be admitted that the aristocracy of the trout has been too well
acclaimed in the past, so that the pleasures of the coarse fish have been
less recognized than is their due; but, still, it is hard to overpraise the
trout. It is, at its best, very beautiful, with a fierce purity of shape and
lovely colour. It is strong-looking but classically fine of shape, small
headed but, within its streamlined flow of form, deep bodied—or so it
is in some waters. There must always be this qualification as to the
water in which it is found, when describing the trout, because it varies
so very greatly in differing waters. It varies in colour, in shape, in size.
A Highland burn has its swarming little fish, greedy and rather big-
headed, brilliantly coloured and spotted, a few inches long. Chalk
streams have short thick small-headed fish, more silvery sometimes,
with a fine show of buttercup gold often about the lower part of the
head, and usually with more widely spaced spots. Loch Leven trout,
though still this same brown trout, are silvery and black spotted, without the red spots that are mixed with the black or dark brown on many
other trout. A trout of so fine a Welsh river as the Usk is good at a
pound and very good at a pound and a half; but on the Kennet a trout
of two pounds is thought a very ordinary fish. The great lakes of Ireland
and Scotland have much bigger trout—ten pounds, fourteen pounds,
and there are bigger ones by far as yet uncaught. The new reservoirs
that have been coming into being in recent years make big trout, and
on these fish of three and four pounds are ordinary occurrences.

But whatever the variations of trout, they have in common in almost all their waters their beauty, whatever its variety, their fire and speed and leaping fury when hooked. In all fishing there is no more intense delight than in fly fishing for trout on a fine day of May or early June.

As to the methods of fishing for trout, that has been largely covered in the chapters on fly fishing. Spinning with a dead minnow is sometimes done for trout—sadly it is much more done than formerly because of the ease with which it may be done with the fixed-spool reel. There are cases, perhaps, in which spinning may be justified. Very big trout that have ceased to rise to fly, and which get their living largely by eating smaller trout, offer an unquestionable reason for the use of the minnow—as long as that is not made a pretext for fishing at large with

Fig. 92. Trout

the minnow. Some very big lake trout are only to be caught thus; on the great Irish lakes the very big trout are trolled for with minnow or spoon, and, but for that, would be unlikely to be caught at all.

But on too many rivers now, rivers which have provided good sport for fly fishers, minnow spinners now come combing through the water. Many of the fish they hook are smaller than should be taken from the water, but, having been hooked on the treble hooks of a spinning flight, they have to be killed or put back so injured that they are a prey to fungus disease. For this spinning it is claimed that on rivers of the rocky kind July and August bring periods when trout will no longer take a fly, and, so, spinning is justified.

But, before the fixed-spool reel was invented, these were the times when the high skills of the low-water upstream worm fisher were used, and so they can be still. On Yorkshire streams, fortunately, some anglers still do so fish. They use a long rod, as much as fourteen feet, not less than twelve feet,* and to the end of the line is tied a Stewart

* It is perfectly practical to use a shorter rod. Some anglers use that same fly rod that they use while fly fishing, thus making it possible to interchange fly and worm fishing.

or Pennel worm tackle. A Stewart tackle has three hooks, facing alternate ways, a Pennel tackle has two hooks facing opposite ways. On these the worm is mounted, being passed round the nylon between the hooks. A little lead may be used just above the tackles or not according to the depth and strength of the water.

The worm fisher finds his trout in the shrunken broken water to which the fish go for its higher oxygen content when the river is low. He works upstream slowly, crouching, even sometimes going on to all fours, so that he may approach the trout from behind without detection. He does not have out much line—as much as the length of his rod it may be. He swings the baited tackle ahead of him and then lets it work back rolling and trundling through the shallow runs between the stones. As it comes he raises the rod at the same pace, keeping in touch with the bait. He may see the line tighten, he may see it stop; he may see the golden flash of a turning trout. Whatever the sign is he pauses to let the trout take the bait well into its mouth; then he tightens to set the hooks. This is a delicate and accomplished way of fishing.

Another method of taking trout, almost entirely a North Country one, is Stonefly fishing. The Stonefly, known in the North as the Mayfly, is easily the biggest of water flies; the female, which is bigger than the male, is about an inch and a quarter long. It is dull, brownish, touched with yellow on the body, and its long wings, which project beyond the end of the body, fold flat along the back; it has two stubby tails. The smaller male has only rudimentary wings, much shorter than the body, and useless for flight. This male, after hatching from the nymph, shelters under stones at the river's margin—the nymph itself is known as the creeper. For this fishing, so traditionally a part of North Country angling, both the creeper and the mature fly are used, in their natural state. The creeper is to be found among the stones in the shallow water at the river's edge from some time in April till it hatches during May. It provides a deadly form of fishing, as much looked forward to, with the fishing of the mature fly which follows, as is that other Mayfly fishing so loved on southern rivers.

A two-hook tackle is used, both for the creeper and the mature fly, rather like a Pennel tackle, but with the lower hook, which points downwards, larger than the upper hook. The bigger lower hook goes downward through the abdomen of the creeper, the smaller upper hook goes upward through the head. A fly fishing cast is as much used as anything, sometimes with a longish fly rod, sometimes with the rod that is used for upstream worming. The bait is smoothly cast ahead of the angler as he creeps and crawls up the thin and shallow margin of the river, and allowed to drift back with the current. When the creeper disappears in a boil or a ring, there is a brief pause before striking.

When the mature flies hatch, they are fished in the same way, more particularly the female. Epic sport is sometimes had with stonefly fishing. The mature fly is also used for dapping under the trees that overhang the river, in the manner described in dapping for chub.

Bustard fishing is equally something of northern trout rivers, and could loosely be compared to the late evening sedge fishing of the South. But it is not the great sedges that the bustard imitates, but the great downy moths that come about the water as the light goes. Some of the biggest trout, inviolate at other times, come greedily out then. The artificial Bustard is tied in three broad kinds of pattern—brown, white, yellow, big flies that do look quite like moths, and are fished wet. At twilight the angler comes, and it is to the broad easy tails of pools that he comes, to gliding quite shallow flats, quiet water. He uses two Bustards on a cast, one at the point and one as a dropper, and he casts them across and rather down to swing round to the dangle below him. Though it is at twilight that he comes, it is not till the light dark of these July and August nights has fallen that he fishes. Magical fishing it can be, in the soft summer night; and desperately exciting when the unseen trout wrenches the fly with that boldness that trout in darkness have.

The fishing for Thames trout is specialized, as specialized as is the trout for which the fishing is done. Thames trout are not, as other trout are, widely about all over the river. They are few and solitary, big fish that have their lairs and live entirely by preying upon small fish. They may be four pounds, five pounds, or up into the teens of pounds, great fierce fish. Those who pursue them with specialization first locate a particular fish, come to know the time in each day when it emerges to make its lethal raids upon the small fish. Then they live bait for it with a bleak, that little silvery fish, or they spin for it with a dead bleak. The most constantly fished places for Thames trout are the weir pools; but they are to be found in the open river too. Apart from the closely watching specialists, many more casual anglers fish for these great trout, doing it mostly in the weir pools, standing on the apron of the weir and running the bleak live bait on float tackle down the runs of white water, or spinning across them. It is a long-term game, with much time of fishing for no result. But, from time to time, a trout is taken.

In some trout rivers and lakes there are rainbow trout, a species introduced here from America, fast growing and a most spectacular fighter. Their spots are small and black, and along their flanks is a brilliant smear of carmine. Methods that take brown trout will take them too, though they are inclined to need a quicker strike than do brown trout.

## The Sea Trout

The sea trout is the same species as the brown trout; but, instead of remaining in freshwater, it goes to sea, there to do the bulk of its feeding and growing. Its ultimate size, as a result, tends to be much greater than that of brown trout (excluding, though, the great lake trout). To the less perceptive eye it looks as much like a small salmon as a trout; it is silvery all over like the salmon, and may sometimes be as big. But the mouth of the salmon goes back only as far as the centre of the eye; the mouth of the sea trout, like that of the brown trout, goes back to the rear edge of the eye or past it.

In some rivers you may catch sea trout during the day; but on far more than not, fishing must be done at twilight and after the fall of dark. It is only then that the highly sensitive timidity of the sea trout can be overcome. Then the fish come up on to the shallow tails of pools,

Fig. 93. Sea trout

and there the angler casts his wet fly downstream and across; a thrilling form of fishing this is. The angler comes as the light begins to go to find his position and prepare his tackle. The owls come out, and, as the light dies, he steps gently, quietly, into the river and starts to fish. He casts, lets the fly, or flies, swing round till it or they are below him, then casts again, edging down stealthily and slowly as he casts—or so it is on big rivers. On small rivers, such as those, for example, of Cornwall, he may take his place on a pool and there stay. Then, suddenly, out of the darkness comes a fierce wrench and the line is screaming from his reel— or so it is sometimes. Quite often he will feel just a gentle pluck to which he must respond instantly. He can see little, for it is the dark nights which are best, but he may see the momentary flash as the fish jumps. Jump it will, repeatedly, making wild runs between. About this fishing there is a not-quite-earthly magic that can become as obsessional as a drug. The fisherman edges down, silently foot by foot, and has no sense of time, hardly of place. When he reaches the bottom of the pool he returns, still in his dream, to the top to fish down again.

On some rivers—the Towy in South Wales is one—day fishing is done and is successful, the cast being made a little upstream and across and allowed to come round till it is downstream a little. Then it is picked off and cast again. Spinning with the minnow is also done, though that cannot compare in delight with the taking of fish on fly. It is indeed true that sea trout could be taken by day, particularly evening, far more than they commonly are; there are many occasions when they are to be seen rising persistently to surface fly, and then a small dry fly sensitively presented to them can take fish well.

On lakes that have a connexion with the sea by spate water burns and small rivers, as is often the case in the west of Scotland and the west of Ireland, boat fishing is done as it is done for brown trout. On some rivers of Norway dry fly fishing with very big bushy flies catches huge sea trout.

# CHAPTER FOURTEEN

# The Salmon

THE salmon has been called the King of Fishes; it has been called many other fine things. It has been written of with every sort of ecstatic phrase, and an atmosphere of almost mystical wonder has been woven about it. Because of this, and because salmon fishing has been expensive and a privilege of the more fortunate—except in some remoter places—coarse fishermen have tended to depreciate it, to suggest that its glory is something far less than has been claimed.

This is unfair to the salmon and unfair to salmon fishing which is, at its best, magnificent sport. It must be admitted that there are many

**Fig. 94. Salmon**

times in salmon fishing, when the river is not in the best condition, when the angler may fish for hour after hour for no result whatever. But, sooner or later, his reward comes and he will be an unusual fisherman if he does not feel that all his waiting and trying have been worth while.

In contrast is a charge against salmon fishing that at those times when all is exactly right with water and conditions, any fool can catch salmon. At such fortunate times it is true that the novice or the bungler may catch salmon with relative ease; but a good angler will catch more, will lose fewer after hooking. And these times are far from being all the times that salmon are to be caught if the angler has the skill, knowledge, experience to do it. Sometimes, too, a newcomer to salmon fishing may hook, play, and land a salmon and then say that the power and the glory of the salmon's fight is a myth. This fish, he may say, put up only the dullest and unexciting fight. So it may sometimes be; but to understand the significance of that you must know something of the salmon's life history. This fish will be a tired fish, one that has just arrived at the place at which it was hooked after a long journey up the river against the current. If that same fish were to be hooked the following day, when it had rested, it would show a different fight, more true to its reputation. The fight of a rested salmon can be magnificent.

Let us go briefly over the story of this fish before this moment. Its life began on what is called a redd, and a redd is a bed of large gravel over which flows a quick shallow current. There a cock salmon and a hen salmon had mated and the hen had deposited her eggs, covering them with gravel dislodged by her tail. That had been in winter, and by spring a tiny fish had come from the egg, wearing under its throat a yolk sac, and on the contents of that sac it had lived at first. When that had been absorbed it had started to feed on tiny animals of the water. Now, in spring, it was growing fast and soon became a parr—a rather trout-like little fish with a series of dusky mauvish thumb marks along its sides. As a parr it remained in the river probably for two years, though it *may* be one year and is sometimes more. Then, about six inches long, it had become silver in colour, had become a smolt and had gone down to the sea, because it is in the sea that the major part of its feeding and growing must be done. It could have returned to the river after only one winter in the sea, and if so, it would have been a grilse.

But this one stayed another winter in the sea, growing fast. If it had returned as a grilse it could have weighed anything from about four pounds to eight or nine pounds. The later in the year the return was made the greater its weight would have been. Now, returning after two winters in the sea, it weighs fifteen pounds. How much it might weigh at this time is something which varies in different rivers—some rivers have bigger salmon than others for the same stage of life; and, the longer a salmon stays in the sea without returning, the bigger it will be. On rivers famous for their big fish, such a river as the Wye, a salmon returning for the first time after four sea years may be fifty pounds or even much bigger than that.

That this salmon *has* returned is because it too must now spawn on the redds high up the river. That all salmon must do, and, with a few exceptions, they return to the river in which they were themselves born. Once this return is made the salmon eats no more for all the time it is in the river. It may come up from the sea in spring, but, though it will not spawn till winter, it will fast, live only on the fat accumulated in its tissues. If it is a cock fish, as the months of river life pass, as it makes its way by stages up the river to where it will spawn, its lower jaw will develop a great hook, a kype as it is called, and red patches will come upon its body. If it is a hen fish it will become dark and leaden. Some salmon come later in the year, and for them the bodily toll is less. Some come actually in the winter, when they are out of season for fishing. They come straight up, spawn, and go down again. When a salmon has spawned it is a poor, sick, debilitated creature, what is called a kelt. A great many kelts die before they can return to the sea; but some do succeed in getting back and subsequently make one or more returns to the river to spawn. To fish for and take kelts is illegal; a kelt accidentally caught must be returned immediately and carefully to the river. The taking of parr is also illegal.

But our fish is typical of those with which the angler is concerned. When there is enough water coming down the river it will run, leaping such obstacles as weirs. When the water level falls it will cease to run and will wait in a pool until a spate shall come again and it can run again. It is during these pauses between running that the angler has his chance to fish for the salmon. It is a broad truth that when a salmon is running it will not take a bait or a fly, though there are to be found places on the river which seem to contradict this. If the angler stands at such a place, continually casting when the water is high and the salmon are running, sometimes he will catch a salmon. But these places usually have one thing in common. They are preceded, coming upstream, by an ascent of fast water that pours down an incline in the river bed. Salmon that have made such an ascent are tired; they pause to rest at this place.*

Salmon do not lie anywhere in a pool. If the angler casts at random all over the pool most of the time he will not be casting over salmon. The places in which salmon lie come to be known, and in those places, those same places, each new arrival of salmon dispose themselves. Sometimes it can be seen very well why the fish lie where they do, sometimes it cannot. Sometimes you may say, there is a place where a salmon is certain to lie, but no salmon has ever been found there. A salmon chooses its resting place where it can have well-oxygenated water but some feature, a rock, a declivity in the bottom, something, gives it comfort and it is able to hold its place without effort. In this context it is again necessary to refer to Righyni's *Salmon Taking Times*; in the book there is a completely rational analysis of the behaviour of water and its relationship to the resting places of salmon which, if intelligently applied, does make it possible to detect salmon lies on unfamiliar water with fair certainty.

The main methods of salmon fishing are fly fishing, spinning, bait

---

* For a penetrative examination of why and where and when a salmon will take, read *Salmon Taking Times* by R. V. Righyni, published by Macdonald.

fishing. There are two forms of fly fishing. One is sunk fly fishing; the other is floating line fishing. Till recently the latter method was called greased line fishing, because the line was greased to make it float. Now self-buoyant lines have made this unnecessary.

Sunk fly fishing used to be much more widely practised than it is now; it is a method of using the fly for that early part of the season when the water is cold and the fish lie low and dour; nowadays spinning is more often used in these conditions. The essence of the sunk fly is that the fly, a big one, shall be fished deeply, close to the bottom, and that it shall come round and by the fish as slowly as possible. For this end there is an established technique which has the object of combing the pool completely, close to the bottom and as slowly as possible. It is a technique not so much for fishing each known lie as for leaving no inch of the likely water of the pool uncovered by the fly. Unless that golden moment is chanced upon when the salmon are taking freely, it may be a rather dull and mechanical business—though indeed, expectancy in the angler is hard to defeat.

The angler starts at the top of the pool, and casts as long a line as will cover the whole width of the likely water, downstream and across; if the cast is made at an angle of about thirty degrees to the current, it is about right. This acute angle reduces as far as possible the chance of the current forming a belly in the line and thus dragging the fly round quickly. It is a further aid to the same purpose to make a mend of line upstream as soon as the cast has been made, before the line has sunk. When the line has swung round to the dangle, the angler takes two paces downstream and recovers some line by drawing it with the left hand. A salmon that has been following the fly may take it at this time. If it does there should be no haste in striking—as often as not the fish will have taken the fly securely before the angler is aware of it, and then he need only raise the rod firmly to pull the hook home. But if he should see the fish swirl at the fly he should wait until he feels its weight before pulling the hook in.

But, assuming there is no such event, he makes another cast, at the same angle and with the same length of line. Thus he goes down the pool, two paces at a time; and thus he will cover all the water. On the way a salmon may be seen to come at the fly but not take it, or it may be felt to pluck at the fly without taking it firmly. In such a case the fish should not be hammered with a series of further casts. The place should be marked, perhaps by a heel hole in the bank, or a stick, and a change made to a smaller fly*—or, it may be, a darker or lighter fly. Then the angler can go back several yards and fish down again till he comes to

* *Salmon Taking Times*, by R. V. Righyni, is again illuminating on the choice of fly. The book throws a clear light on the subject.

that place again, or he may fish down again from the top of the pool. If
that does not work a cast from a different angle can be tried, even from
rather downstream, or square across, thus giving the fish a more broadside view of the fly. Sometimes, if that is possible, a cast from directly
upstream can be made and the fly plucked slowly up by the left hand so
that it comes past the fish.

If fishing the pool down in this fashion produces no result, what is
called 'backing up' may work. The angler starts again, but from the
bottom of the pool, taking his two paces upstream between casts, and
taking them as the fly fishes round.

That is the old and strictly conventional mode of fishing the sunk
fly; but there are ways of more virtuosity, and, naturally, of more
interest, and they can be applied to known lies. The object, remember,
is to bring the fly slowly and deeply past the fish. So let us suppose a
salmon is known to be lying on the farther side of the main current;
perhaps the boil at the surface of a stone can be seen, a stone which
gives shelter to the fish. Whatever the indication or lack of it, cast only
a little downstream or even square across, and, at the moment the line
drops on the water, mend a belly of it upstream, rolling it up with a
rolling action of the rod. If this were not done, the current would make
and rapidly increase a belly of line downstream and that would make
the fly skate high in the water and drag it quickly over the fish. But,
with the mend upstream, the drag is delayed so that the fly can sink and
come more slowly past the fish, showing its broadside view. Once this
principle for fishing a particular lie has been used, other ways of using it
will come naturally—providing that it is always in mind that salmon
lying deeply in cold water are unwilling to move far, and it is remembered that the object is to present the fly to them as slowly as possible,
and, preferably, broadside-on. The properly presented fly will appear
to the salmon to be a small fish—the action of the current on the
dressing will suggest a swimming movement. This should affect the way
the fly is worked—it should always move in such a way that the current
is sleaking it back into a fishlike form, not ruffling up the dressing.

In this cold-water fishing of the early part of the season, in January,
February, March, and it may be in a very cold year, April, the fast
streamy top of the pool is unlikely to hold fish. More probably they
will be in the 'dub'—the lower, deeper, smoother part of the pool. What
size of fly is used is partly a matter of the particular river; smaller
shallow rivers *usually* demand smaller flies than bigger deeper rivers;
but on any river the size of cold spring flies should be larger than would
be used in warmer later water. In big fly rivers the earliest fishing may
be done with flies as big as 5/0. Colour of the fly is a matter of weather
and light. Broadly dark overcast days need a dully coloured fly, bright

days a brightly coloured fly—but here again there must be reference to that brilliant book, *Salmon Taking Times*. The author gives a lucid and revealing examination of how a salmon sees a fly and how this should be translated into choice of pattern.

Fly fishing with the floating line becomes necessary and rewarding when the water has warmed with the warming of the season. When the water temperature reaches forty-eight degrees Fahrenheit it becomes practical to use the floating line, and that increases not only the chance of taking salmon, but, as much, the absorbing pleasure of the fishing. The object now is not to fish the fly deeply, but to fish it just under the surface. A pool that may hold fish all the way down can be fished right down with the floating line; but even if there are known spaced-out lies, it is still better to fish the pool right down—thus avoiding showing the fly to the fish so often that it becomes familiar and therefore not likely to stimulate the fish into taking.

The thermometer shows the water temperature to be forty-eight degrees, and the river is fairly high. This is the bottom range of conditions for the floating line, and will probably demand a fly that, by floating line standards, is a big one. A fly about size 4 to 6 can be tried, and, because it is a rather overcast day a dullish naturally coloured fly, not black, not too bright—say March Brown or Logie.

The cast is made downstream at an angle of about forty-five degrees to the current. At once it is apparent that the strongest water of the main current is pressing on the line between the rod and the fly, and that this, if allowed, will bring the fly skating round quickly instead of coming slowly and dragging as little as possible. So a belly of line is mended upstream; before the main current can take that out the fly will have had the chance to move some way slowly and at the dictation of the angler rather than of the current. If the intervening current is very heavy it may be necessary to make another mend before the fly has come round to being right below the angler. As the fly works round, the angler may take in a little line with his left hand to keep in touch with the fly and to keep it moving with a sense of life—broadly, the slower the water the more the need for this arises because the less the current is giving life to the fly.

When the fly has come round to the dangle, a few feet are taken in by the left hand and the angler moves down two paces. Now he casts again and so continues down the pool. His object all the time is to achieve this slow travel of the fly, under his own direction, not that of the stream. Sometimes the water through which the fly is moving is faster than that between it and the rod, and then it may be necessary to make a mend downstream to prevent the nearer slower water dragging the fly. In fishing known lies any tactics of casting that study of the water suggests to bring the fly nicely over the lie can be used. Occasionally repeated mending may be necessary—but mending can easily become a fetish, and sometimes, particularly on smaller rivers, no mending at all may be necessary. The fly can be led by dropping the rod point downstream, or indeed in any direction that helps the fly to work at the dictated pace through the relevant area.

While the fly is fished the rod point is best held high, so giving a sagging belly of line out of the water; and, in the left hand, two or three yards of loose line are held. When a fish comes to the fly it may be seen by the hanging line tightening or, sometimes, a boil in the vicinity of the fly—and it may be only a very minor boil. Anyway, the angler does not strike. He drops the rod point and lets slip through the rings the loose line he holds. The object is to allow a belly of line to form below the fish which pulls the fly back into the angle of the jaws, where the hook finds a hold. Then, when the tightening and moving off of the line signals the moving off of the fish, he can raise the rod firmly. That is, as it were, the standard way of doing it—but the set of the current may not be such as to make it work, and quite often after the earlier part of the season the salmon do not retain the fly long enough. Then, and it may be at all times, a better average of successful hooking will be had by holding the rod high, quite near the vertical, and letting the fish hook itself.

And now another fishing day, with the water temperature higher, say fifty-three degrees. If the day is dull then again the fly should be a sober naturally coloured one but smaller, perhaps a Logie size 6 or 7—in such conditions the fish can see well and precisely. But perhaps the sun is high and strong and, to the upward-looking fish, dazzling. So a dark fly is needed, say Thunder and Lightning or Blue Charm, and it should be bigger than for a dull day; it must be easy for the fish to see in the prismatic dazzle above. But this is a very generalized guide, and the reader must again be urged to read the masterly analysis in *Salmon Taking Times*. For times when the sun comes slanting at a sharp angle Righyni gives what he calls the Translucent Illusion, a fly dressed bright and light so that the slanting sun suffuses it, shines through it.

As water temperatures go higher fly sizes must become progressively smaller, in times of low and warm water as small as size 10. In these conditions, a quickly moving fly is often more likely to induce a take than a slowly moving one, and then all the devices of line management and leading should be used to that end—a reversal of the slow fishing of the bigger cooler water. There is then more need of the left hand to draw and coil line, particularly in the slower pools.

What might be called normal spinning can be used for salmon in the earlier part of the season, when water temperature and height of water make floating line fishing useless; its use in those conditions has largely displaced the use of the sunk fly on many rivers. Some anglers use both fly and spinning, trying fly first and then spinning over the same water. Probably the most used reel today is the fixed-spool, and its use is often abused by too-light lines and rods which are not adequate for the stresses of big spring salmon in high water. Too often the result is fish lost with a minnow in their jaws and a trail of nylon behind.

If a fixed-spool reel is used it should be with a line of suitable strength, not less than twelve pounds breaking strain. A multiplying reel with a ten-foot salmon spinning rod is more suitable tackle, with a line of from twelve to fifteen or sixteen pounds breaking strain.

Size of minnow may be variable on different rivers, but for most, with big cold waters, one of three inches will be right. On some rivers gillies will swear that only a dead bait—a natural minnow, a loach, a gudgeon—is any good; on others they will be as certain that you must use a particular colour of artificial minnow—blue and silver, brown and gold—but it is doubtful if there is any better basis for this than established custom. Generally salmon do seem to show a preference for that range of colour from red to yellow, including those with some brown. Buoyant minnows are preferable to heavy ones; extra weight should be in the lead rather than the minnow. A heavy minnow is dead, unresponsive to the current—unless the current is very heavy, as it often is in Norwegian rivers.

It is important that the right weight of lead shall be used—one that will keep the bait close to the bottom but not to become snagged there; changing the lead on the way down one pool is often necessary. At the top of the pool, where the current is heavy, an ounce of lead or even an ounce and a quarter may be needed; but lower down, where the current slackens, half an ounce may be enough. Sometimes a plug bait, with or without lead, will do very well, though they may at other times be relatively ineffective.

The best way to cover a pool is not dissimilar to that used with the fly, though as often as not the cast needs to be made at a less acute angle downstream, even sometimes being made nearly square. Then, in most cases, the bait is allowed to swing round with no winding on the reel until it has come to the dangle downstream. From there it may be wound very slowly for two or three yards to give a chance to a salmon that may be following or to one under the bank; then it can be wound back quickly for the next cast two paces down. That is the basic way of doing it, and circumstances may suggest their own variants on it. Water that is less activated by current will give less life to the bait, and slow winding as the bait comes round will help. In the fishing of fast heavy water, to let a little line slip away as the bait comes round will suggest a small fish trying but partly failing to hold against the current. It is to this same end, making the illusion of a small fish in the current, that a cast more square than downstream is usually better. Small fish in the strong waters of salmon rivers are unlikely to swim steadily upstream against the current. They are more likely to move across the current just holding against it, or not quite doing so, according to its strength. As with fly fishing, it is a mistake to linger over a fish. If it has too many chances at one time to see the bait, it will become stale to it, it will see through the falsity; it should be surprised into taking at the first sight. If a fish offers but does not take, fish down to it again from above, perhaps with a smaller bait.

As the season grows from the first early cold and the water warms and shrinks, a change must come upon spinning similar to that which comes to fly fishing. The minnow becomes progressively smaller till, in the low bright water of summer, it may be only half an inch long. The fishing of such baits does demand the fixed-spool reel; no other reel could cast them. In this low thin water, with the pools deficient in oxygen, salmon often lie in streamy broken water for its better oxygenation. To fish for them then upstream casting is often better, bringing the bait down over them at a speed related to the speed of the current. In very fast broken water the retrieve may have to be as fast as the reel can be wound, and a salmon may come half out of the water as it takes. This fishing demands that the line shall be lighter if so small a minnow is to be cast, not more than eight pounds breaking strain, but not less than six pounds. These summer fish are invariably smaller than those that run up in spring; springers, on the majority of rivers, are the big fish, and summer fish are consistently smaller, thus making more practical the use of finer lines. A river that, in spring, shows many fish of twenty to thirty pounds with some much bigger, will give summer fish of eight to twelve pounds. In autumn, on some rivers, there is again a run of big fish.

For the salmon at its various stages in freshwater there are different names—one newly up from the sea is a 'fresh-run fish', and on it there may often be the so-called sea lice, rather flattened looking creatures; a common place is close to the tail of the fish. A fish which has been in the river for some time, and has lost condition, is called a 'potted fish'. A cock fish ripe for spawning, with a big kype and red blotches, is called a 'red fish'. In the spring kelts are sometimes caught which, untypically, are bright silver, with a spurious look of well-being; they are 'well-mended kelts'. Such a fish may be so silver, and just active enough, to persuade a beginner that it is a 'clean fish', that is a fish which has not spawned and is in good condition, and may therefore be taken. But it will have a flat lean belly, back and belly almost parallel, and its gill filaments, under the gill covers, will be eroded and pallid and infested with gill maggots. Usually its vent will be enlarged. And, whatever the show it makes, its fight does not compare with that of a clean fish.

Salmon which have been some time in the river become increasingly difficult to take, and all the more so if the river runs low. It is for them that bait fishing is used—or so it is by some anglers; the most common form of bait fishing is with the prawn. On some rivers the use of prawn is not allowed; on others it is allowed only after a certain date, and then it may be used whatever the conditions. This is a pity; prawn fishing has disadvantages. Sometimes it is deadly, sometimes it frightens the fish so much that they will take nothing; anyway, once prawning starts the chance of taking salmon by the prettier means of fly or light spinning are greatly lessened. Prawn fishing is a cruder method, one of expediency; it puts before all else the gaining of the valuable fish rather than the finer pleasures of angling. The too-ready use of prawn is an outcome of what has done so much to spoil salmon fishing—the high commercial value of the salmon. Too many people are too anxious to catch too many salmon for the price they will fetch.

But the prawn may have its justification; if your fishing opportunity is rare and short, and if the conditions are adverse, it may give you sport when there would be none otherwise. There are two main ways of fishing it—as a spinning bait or as one worked round close to the bottom by the action of the current. Various flights for mounting the prawn are to be had, but the best is a treble hook attached to a wire trace. On the trace is a prawn-length pin with an eye at its upper end which is threaded on the trace, and the pin is pushed through the length of the prawn from tail to head. There the treble is arranged to lie among the feelers that project and the legs are arranged to lie on either side of the trace. Then trace and prawn are secured together with a spiral of fine copper wire, with care not to tie in the legs.

To induce the bait to spin the best means is what is called an uptrace spinner, and it is so that its spin may be passed down to the prawn that wire is used for the trace, not nylon. The uptrace spinner is a pair of vanes of colourless plastic which is threaded on the trace near its top, and about an inch below it a piece of matchstick is twisted into the wire so as to make a stop across the trace. As the bait is retrieved water pressure sends the vanes on to the matchstick, which engages into a slot in the vanes. When a fish is played water pressure in reverse sends the vanes free of the matchstick so that they no longer impart spin. As in other spinning, there is an anti-kink lead above the swivel of the trace.

The lead also, of course, helps the prawn to get down, and a prawn should be fished as close to the bottom as possible and as slowly as possible. The non-spinning prawn should also be fished thus, and it can be fished on the same mount. The cast for both spinning and non-spinning prawn should be only a little downstream, nearly square, so that the bait may go deep. The latter, when cast, should be allowed to work round with the current, and as it does so the rod should be raised and lowered, slowly and smoothly. This, with the action of the current, induces in the bait a wavering shivering action, as if it were trying not very successfully to swim against the current.

Prawns most suitable for salmon fishing are not easily to be had; they should be fresh and deeply coloured, and are the more attractive if they have the cluster of eggs on the underside of the body. The best source of supply, if it can be had, is a professional prawn catcher. Bottled prawns may fail on some rivers, and deep-frozen ones are undoubtedly better. The lower and clearer the water, the smaller should be the prawn; in very low clear water a shrimp may work when a prawn will not.

On a low river, a long time without a spate and with the fish held in the pools, they are often exceedingly difficult to stir with fly or spinning. It is then that worming is a last resort method. Big lobworms are used, and the hook is also big, say size 1/0 or 2/0 attached to a not-too-frail length of nylon. A ten-foot spinning rod serves as well as any. Lead can be used a foot or so from the bait, but if it can be avoided the action of the bait is the better for it. To bait the hook a worm is threaded over the point and worked round the bend and up the shank to the top with the two ends left to hang free there, the hook having been passed through only a section of the worm. The first worm is followed by more, with the object of making a big gobbet of worms with a loose and copious hang of free ends.

The salmon to which this bait is to be offered will probably be lying in quite shallow activated water, perhaps at a place where a boil shows on the surface declaring a rock beneath, or where knowledge of the water tells that there is a declivity in the bottom. The angler swings out the bait across the current, farther out than the lie, and upstream of it. Using the current, and coaxing with the rod, he works and rolls the bait along the bottom so that it comes, stopping and starting as if only the current were working it, into the lie of the fish. There he tries to hang it, letting it wash about with the play of water just where the salmon is known to be or thought to be.

The first sign of the salmon's interest in the bait is likely to be a series of short plucks—an electrifying thing—and presently this changes to a steady pull, and at that he strikes.

Something should be said about the playing of a salmon. The principle of it is to induce the salmon to tire itself, not to subdue it by sheer strength of pulling, matching pull of rod against pull of fish. At the first moment that a salmon is hooked there is, almost invariably, a pause, as if the salmon does not at once realize that something has happened to it. In this pause the spinner can slip on the check of his multiplying reel. Then, as often as not, the salmon will begin to run downstream—though a fish may sometimes remain more or less where it is and thrash and bore in that small area. If it does go downstream, running hard or boring and jagging, the angler should follow. If he is wading he must back to the shallows or the bank to give himself freedom of movement, and then go down with the fish. As long as the fish is below the fisherman it has the advantage of him; it is hanging on the line, and no leverage can be exerted on it. So the angler should go down till he is, if allowed the chance, rather downstream of the fish. There he should turn his rod over towards the bank and in a downstream direction, and pull on the fish. Now he will have leverage; the pull will put the fish off-balance, and, anyway, a salmon tends to run in the direction opposite to that in which it is pulled. So now it will turn and run upstream, no longer with the current, but against it and fighting it and the pull of the rod. The principle of playing the fish is to keep it on the move, tiring itself and, as much as possible, running against the current, not with it. Too light and timid playing of a salmon is mistaken; it should be hustled, kept moving. The longer it is allowed to prolong the fight, the greater the chance of the hook-hold wearing and giving way.

A fish that is given the chance (or cannot be prevented from taking it) will try to run down through the broken water of stickles into the pool below, and every tactic should be used to keep it in the deeper quieter water of the pool in which it is hooked; the most essential part of this is keeping constantly abreast of the fish's movements and using sidestrain. A big strong salmon may override the best that you may do and rush down the white water into the pool below, and then you must hope and follow and renew the tactics in the new environment.

Sometimes a salmon that has not been hustled enough, or in spite of hustling, will go to the bottom and sulk, pushing its head into the bottom. Sidestrain from all available angles can be tried and will sometimes work. If it fails lower the rod to point it directly at the salmon and give long jarring pulls on the line by hand. If that too fails, stones thrown in the vicinity of the fish may move it. One other device is to take off all strain, peeling off loose line, so giving the fish the illusion of freedom so that, presently, it moves.

A salmon can be taken from dangerous situations by leading—or, as anglers say, walking it up. Perhaps the fish is hooked close to trees or bushes downstream which prevent following, so as soon as it is hooked, the angler holds the reel to stop the turning of the spool, keeps the rod up, and walks steadily and slowly upstream to a safer distance. Mostly the salmon will come like a led dog. It can be so led when it pauses dangerously near the bottom of a pool, and so it may be when, more or less played out, it can be led to a second party who waits with the gaff. In the same way it may be beached on a shingly margin.

The techniques of playing a salmon so far described have assumed at least a partially open bank, but such is not always the case. Trees and bushes both upstream and downstream may allow only the smallest movement either way, and then the playing must be done from that nearly fixed position. In most cases that can be done successfully, if with difficulty, and in spite of the often severe handicap of having to bring the fish up against the current. But it may happen that a very strong and lively fish will set off downstream in a run that shows no sign of stopping. To put on more pressure will urge it on—it is the very pressure which actuates it. The only chance there may be of stopping it is the cessation of the pressure. To do so drop the rod point and strip line from the reel as fast as it may be done; then, as the current carries the line away, the pressure on the fish from upstream will cease and, even better, a belly of line will be formed downstream of the fish, so setting up pressure from below. There is at least a fair chance of success for this manœuvre.

However wisely and well the angler plays his fish it will sometimes be lost; it may not be well hooked, trace or cast may be cut on a sharp-edged rock, in a long fight the hook-hold may work loose. But, all being well, a salmon will be tired at last and must be landed. The normal means is the gaff, and if the angler is gaffing his own fish he must play it till it is quiet and no longer thrashes. Then, in quiet shallow water if possible, he must draw it up to him from downstream, holding the rod in the upstream hand and using the gaff in the downstream hand. When the fish is opposite him he reaches out till the gaff is over the back of the fish immediately in front of the dorsal fin. Now, with one continuous strong movement, not a snatching swiping one, he pulls in the point of the gaff and continues the movement so as to lift the fish from the water with the gaff held vertically. He takes it well back to the edge of the bank—many a salmon has thrashed its way back into the river—and there delivers the heavy rap on the rear part of the head to kill it. The priest sold by tackle dealers is much the most effective instrument for this.

On some rivers the gaff is not allowed in the early part of the season (usually till the end of April) because there are still many kelts that have not returned to the sea, and a gaffed kelt would have its chances of survival greatly reduced. At the end of the season when the river is full of potted fish ripe for spawning the same ban is often imposed. So

instead of a gaff a tailer is used, and then it is even more important that
the fish shall be completely played out and quiet. The open noose is
passed over the tail of the fish, given a jerk, and it snaps tight round the
wrist of the tail. The fish can be taken out with a vertical lift.

At times when the gaff is banned—or any other time—a salmon may
be beached if there is a suitable place for doing it. In such a place
shallow quiet water laps on to a shingle beach without an acute upward slope. The angler holds the reel so that it cannot revolve, and
walks slowly and steadily back, leading the fish. When the salmon is
brought to the shingle it will often help itself out and on to the shingle
by its thrashing. Now the angler walks quietly and gently round the
fish, reeling up the line, till he is between it and the water, and then
grasps the wrist of the tail with thumb and forefinger towards the tail.
Thus tailed it can be carried well back from the water.

In places where beaching is not possible a fish may be landed by tail-
ing if there is not a high bank to be reached over—and again and
obviously, the fish must be thoroughly quiet before it is attempted.

# CHAPTER FIFTEEN

# Final matters

THERE are just a few things more that the reader should know for his peaceful pursuit of angling. He should know about fishing seasons. They are established by statute, and worked with some local variations by byelaw.

The statutory season for coarse fishing (or, as the law calls it, fishing for freshwater fish) is from the sixteenth of June to the fourteenth of March inclusive. Thus, from the fifteenth of March to the fifteenth of June, inclusive, it is illegal to fish for coarse fish. There are some exceptions. In the area of the Yorkshire River Board the coarse fish close season is from the twenty-eighth of February to the thirty-first of May. In the area of the East Suffolk and Norfolk River Board fishing is allowed at Easter and Whitsun. On Slapton Ley, which is a splendid coarse-fishing lake in South Devon, there is no close season; and in some places where the main concern of Authority is the preservation of salmon and trout, there is no coarse fish close season.

The statutory close season for trout is from the first of October to the last day of February; but this is liberally varied locally. On some trout waters, for example, chalk streams mostly, the season does not start till the first of May. Local enquiry should be made as to when the season does start; and it is anyway stated on the fishing licence.

The statutory close season for salmon is from the first of November to the thirty-first of January; but this too is varied locally by byelaw.

In the majority of places no fishing may be done until a River Board Rod licence has been bought; and they are to be bought from the Fisheries Officer of the River Board, and usually from tackle dealers, hotels, and post offices. A licence for coarse fishing may vary from one River Board to another, but is in any case a matter of a few shillings. A trout licence may have different costs too, but is likely to vary from a few shillings up to about thirty shillings. Salmon licences may vary, but a typical price is £3–£5—though it may be more. All these are licences for the whole season, but it is also possible to buy shorter term licences—usually weekly and monthly ones—for smaller prices.

The possession of a licence does not, by itself, permit the bearer to fish anywhere he likes within the area covered by the licence. He must also have the permission of the owner or lessee of the water, and this permission may be freely given or had by the buying of a fishing permit. Alternatively an individual or a group of individuals such as a club or syndicate may acquire fishing rights on a water from the owner by permission or by buying them on a rental which may or may not be under lease. Permits for fishing apart from such leases or rentals may be had by the individual angler by season ticket, monthly ticket, weekly ticket, or day ticket—or, at least, that is the case where such tickets are issued. Fishing permits and licences must be produced on the demand of an accredited bailiff or keeper. One large and important area in which licences are not issued is the Thames and its tributaries; on most of this water however, a fishing permit is needed, the only considerable exception being that part of the Thames between Richmond and the London Stone at Staines.

It is often supposed that if a public road or footpath runs beside private water, or if a public road bridge crosses it, it is permissible to fish from those places. This is not so; private fishing is private whatever public access is by or over it.

It is essential that the angler recognizes and supports the generally accepted code of behaviour by the water. The essence of it is that he shall in no way behave to spoil or limit the enjoyment of other anglers' fishing or in any way behave to spoil the peace and beauty of the waters which he has the privilege of fishing.

This means in practice that he shall not use methods of fishing which may spoil the fishing of others, that he shall not in any way interfere with other fishermen—as by, for example, casting his bait or fly into water which another angler is fishing, or fishing unnecessarily close to another angler. It also means—and means with the greatest possible emphasis—that he shall not leave litter on the bank, but will seek to leave no sign of his having been there but the inescapable trampling of the growth of the bank; even this he should limit as far as he may. Such are the horrors that recent times have brought upon us that it is even necessary to point out that to bring transistor radios to the waterside is exceedingly offensive to all true anglers to whom a river bank is a place of undisturbed Nature.

If it should seem that this book is finishing on an admonitory note, it is so because, as was said at its beginning, it has the object of leading the reader to the greatest possible enjoyment of fishing. Failure to observe these things must, in the end, spoil the pleasure of him who offends. Now the author wishes his readers the great happiness, excitement, and contentment that fishing can bring. He wishes them many years of good fishing days, with many soft mild-weathered days when fish move well, with here and there a red-letter day, and with some poor days to give the greater delight to the red-letter days.

# Index